PREACHING

REDEEMER

PREACHING

Communicating Faith
in an Age of Skepticism

TIMOTHY KELLER

VIKING

3507680

VIKING
An imprint of Penguin Random House LLC
375 Hudson Street
New York, New York 10014
penguin.com

All Bible references are from the New International Version (NIV),
unless otherwise noted.

ISBN: 978-0-525-95303-6

Printed in the United States of America
1   3   5   7   9   10   8   6   4   2

Set in ITC Galliard Std
Designed by Leonard Telesca

*To the members of West Hopewell Presbyterian Church
(1975–1984) who called me "Preacher" even as I was
stumbling to learn how to be one*

CONTENTS

PREACHING

INTRODUCTION: THREE LEVELS
OF THE MINISTRY OF THE WORD

Australian theologian Peter Adam argues that what we call preaching, the formal public address to the gathered congregation on a Sunday, is only one form of what the Bible describes as the "ministry of the Word" (Acts 6:2, 6:4).[1]

On the day of Pentecost Peter cited the words of the prophet Joel, who said that God would pour out his Spirit on all his people, and as a result "your sons and daughters will prophesy" (Acts 2:17). Gerhard Friedrich, in the *Theological Dictionary of the New Testament,* says that there are at least thirty-three Greek words in the New Testament usually translated as "preaching" or "proclaiming." Adam observes that these words describe activities that could not all be public speaking.[2] For example, Acts 8:4 says that all the Christians except the apostles went from place to place "proclaiming the Messiah." This cannot mean that every believer was standing up and preaching sermons to audiences. Priscilla and Aquila, for example, explained the Word of Christ to Apollos in their home (Acts 18:26).

We can discern at least three levels of "Word ministry" in the Bible. Paul calls all believers to "let the message

of Christ dwell among you richly" and to "teach and
admonish one another with all wisdom" (Colossians
3:16). Every Christian should be able to give both teaching (*didaskalia,* the ordinary word for instruction) and
admonition (*noutheo*—a common word for strong, life-
changing counsel) that convey to others the teachings of
the Bible. This must be done carefully, though infor-
mally, in conversations that are usually one on one. That
is the most fundamental form of the ministry of the
Word. Let's call it level 1.

At the more formal end of the spectrum are sermons:
the public preaching and exposition of the Bible to assembled gatherings, which we could call level 3. The book
of Acts gives us many examples, mainly drawn from the
ministry of Peter and Paul, though also including an address by Stephen that probably summarizes his path-
breaking teaching. Acts gives us so many of these public
addresses that we could almost say that, from the point
of view of Luke (the author), the development of the
early Christian church and the development of its preaching were one and the same.

There is, however, a "level 2" form of the ministry of
the Word between informal, every-Christian conversation and formal sermons. In an overlooked passage the
apostle Peter describes the spiritual gift of "speaking":

> Each of you should use whatever gift you have
> received to serve others, as faithful stewards of
> God's grace in its various forms. If anyone
> speaks, they should do so as one who speaks the
> very words of God. If anyone serves, they should

do so with the strength God provides, so that
in all things God may be praised through Jesus
Christ (1 Peter 4:10–11).

When Peter speaks of spiritual gifts he uses two very
general terms.[3] The first is the word for speaking: *lalein.* In
the rest of the New Testament this word can denote simple
daily speech between anyone (Matthew 12:36; Ephesians
4:25; James 1:19). It can also refer to a preaching ministry,
as with Jesus (Matthew 12:46 and 13:10) or Paul (2 Corinthians 12:19). What is Peter talking about here?

When we map this passage over Paul's gift lists in Romans 12, Ephesians 4, and 1 Corinthians 12 and 14, we
see that there is a whole category of Word-ministry gifts
that function in ways beside public preaching to the assembled Sunday congregation. It includes personal exhortation or counseling, evangelism, and teaching individuals
and groups. Biblical scholar Peter Davids concludes that
when Peter writes of the spiritual gift of "speaking" he is
"not referring to casual talk among Christians, nor . . . referring only to the actions of [pastors] or other church officials" but rather to Christians with "one of these verbal
gifts" of counseling, instructing, teaching, or evangelizing.
In this category of ministry, Christian men and women
aren't preaching *per se;* they prepare and present lessons
and talks; they lead discussions in which they are presenting the Word of Christ.[4]

Even though Peter is not only talking to public speakers he warns those who present the Word to others in
any form to take their task seriously. He adds that when
Christians teach the Bible their speech should be "as . . .

the very words of God" (1 Peter 4:11). Davids notes that the little word "'as' allows a slight distancing between their speaking and God's words." No Christian should ever claim that his or her teaching is to be treated with the same authority as biblical revelation; nevertheless, Peter makes the powerful, eye-opening claim that Christians who are presenting biblical teaching are not to be simply expressing their own opinion but giving others "the very words of God." Just as in public preaching, Christians are to convey the truth as they understand it to be revealed in the Scriptures.[5] And if they explain the meaning of the Bible faithfully, listeners will be able to hear God speaking to them in the exposition. They are listening not merely to an artifact of human ingenuity but, as it were, to the very words of God.

Every Christian needs to understand the message of the Bible well enough to explain and apply it to other Christians and to his neighbors in informal and personal settings (level 1). But there are many ways to do the ministry of the Word at level 2 that take more preparation and presentation skills yet do not consist of delivering sermons (level 3). Level 2 today may include writing, blogging, teaching classes and small groups, mentoring, moderating open discussion forums on issues of faith, and so on.

This book aims to be a resource for all those who communicate their Christian faith in any way, particularly at levels 2 and 3.

The Irreplaceability of Preaching

It is dangerous, then, to fall into the unbiblical belief that the ministry of the Word is simply preaching sermons. As Adam says, that will "make preaching carry a load which it cannot bear; that is, the burden of doing all the Bible expects of every form of ministry of the Word."[6] No church should expect that all the life transformation that comes from the Word of God (John 17:17; cf. Colossians 3:16–17 and Ephesians 5:18–20) comes strictly through preaching. I shouldn't expect to be shaped into Christlikeness even by listening to the best sermons. I also need other Christians around me who are "handl[ing] the word of truth" (2 Timothy 2:15) by encouraging me, instructing me, and counseling me. I also need the books of Christian authors whose writings build me up. Nor is it right to expect that those outside the church who need to hear and understand the gospel will be reached only through preaching. I myself found faith not through listening to preaching and speaking but through books. (Is anyone surprised by that?) We must beware of thinking the Sunday sermon can carry all the freight of any church's ministry of the Word.

Yet despite Adam's rightful warning against overemphasizing preaching in a church's ministry, this may not be the church's greatest danger today. We live in a time when many are resistant to any hint of authority in pronouncements; so the culture's allergy to truth and the great skill that is required mean the church loses its grasp on the crucial nature of preaching for the ministry of the gospel.

Edmund Clowney, in his commentary on 1 Peter 4:10, writes:

> It is true that every Christian must handle the word of God with reverence, and seek the help of the Spirit to make it known to others. Yet there are also those with special gifts of the Spirit for the preaching . . . of the word of God . . . [with] a special charge to tend and feed the flock of God ([1 Peter] 5:2). There is some danger that, in reacting against clerical-ism, the church may forget the importance of the ministry of the word of God by those called to be under-shepherds of the flock.[7]

Clowney warns us against seeing *no* qualitative differ-ence between proclaiming the Word in the gathered as-sembly and leading a small-group Bible study. The difference between the two goes beyond ceremonial and logistical matters—it is not just a matter of the number of people present, or the space to fill, or voice projection and pace. Those who have preached to a congregation know that there is a qualitative difference as well between the sermon and a study, or even a sermon and a lecture. A quick survey of the addresses by Peter, Stephen, and Paul in the book of Acts shows the extraordinary power of preaching when undertaken "as . . . the very words of God" and through the unique authority that the Spirit of God can bring in a public worshipping assembly.

While we will always require a host of varied forms of Word ministry, the specific public ministry of preaching is irreplaceable. Adam strikes the balance nicely when he says a church's gospel ministry should be "pulpit-centered, but not pulpit-restricted."[8]

So there are three levels of Word ministry, and they are all crucial and support one another. The public preaching of Christ in the Christian assembly (level 3) is a unique way that God speaks to and builds up people, and it sets up the more organic forms of Word ministry at levels 1 and 2. Likewise, the skilled and faithful communication at levels 1 and 2 prepares people to be receptive to preaching. This volume will speak to all those who are wrestling with how to communicate life-changing biblical truth to people at any level in an increasingly skeptical age. It will also serve as an introduction and foundation for working preachers and teachers in particular.[9]

PROLOGUE: WHAT IS GOOD PREACHING?

One of those listening was a woman from the city of Thyatira named Lydia, a dealer in purple cloth. She was a worshiper of God. The Lord opened her heart to respond to Paul's message.

—Acts 16:14

The Secret of Great Preaching

Not long after I began my preaching ministry I noticed a puzzling inconsistency in the response of my listeners. Sometimes I would get gratifying feedback in the week after a particular sermon. "That sermon changed my life." "I felt you were speaking directly to me. I wondered how you knew." "I'll never forget it—it felt like it was coming right from God!" When I heard such comments I assumed that I had preached a *great* sermon—something to which every young minister aspires.

It wasn't long before I realized that others would be saying—about the same message—something like "meh." My wife, Kathy, often would say, "It was okay, but not one of your best ones," while someone else would be telling me in tears the next day that they would never be the

same after hearing it. How was I to read this? At first I
began to wonder if a sermon's beauty was only in the eye
of the beholder, but that was surely too subjective an explanation. I trusted Kathy's judgment and my own that
some of my sermons were simply better crafted and delivered than others. Yet some of those I considered medio-
cre changed lives—while others I felt pretty good about
seemed to have little impact.

One day I was reading Acts 16, the account of Paul's
planting of the church in Philippi. On this occasion Paul
presented the gospel to a group of women and one, Lydia,
put her faith in Christ because "the Lord opened her heart
to respond to Paul's message" (Acts 16:14). While all the
listeners heard the same address, only Lydia seems to have
been permanently changed by it. We should not overread
this to imply that God works only through a message at
the moment of delivery or that he did not also help Paul as
he formulated the message earlier. Nevertheless, it was
clear to me from the text that the sermon's differing impact on individuals was due to the work of God's Spirit.
Maybe Paul had Lydia in mind when he described the act
of preaching as the gospel coming to listeners "not simply
with words but also with power, with the Holy Spirit and
deep conviction" (1 Thessalonians 1:5).

I concluded that the difference between a bad sermon
and a good sermon is largely located in the preachers—in
their gifts and skills and in their preparation for any particular message. Understanding the biblical text, distilling
a clear outline and theme, developing a persuasive argument, enriching it with poignant illustrations, metaphors,
and practical examples, incisively analyzing heart motives

and cultural assumptions, making specific application to real life—all of this takes extensive labor. To prepare a sermon like this requires hours of work, and to be able to craft and present it skillfully takes years of practice.

However, while the difference between a bad sermon and a good sermon is mainly the responsibility of the preacher, the difference between good preaching and *great* preaching lies mainly in the work of the Holy Spirit in the heart of the listener as well as the preacher. The message in Philippi came from Paul, but the effect of the sermon on hearts came from the Spirit.

This means God can use an indifferently crafted message as great preaching, which explains the answer one older Christian minister gave when he was asked to compare the great eighteenth-century preachers Daniel Rowland and George Whitefield. He responded that you always got great preaching from both men, but with Rowland you also always got a good sermon, which was not always the case with Whitefield.[1] Regardless of how any particular sermon was crafted, the sense of God's presence and power always seemed to accompany Whitefield's preaching.

You may be eager to learn "the secret to great preaching" as a set of instructions for the formation of a discipline. That way you could nearly always accomplish great preaching if you followed the directions to the letter. However, I cannot give you such a formula—and no one can—because that secret lies in the depths of God's wise plans and the power of God's Spirit. I'm talking about what many have referred to as "unction" or "anointing." I will discuss your role in this dynamic in the final chapter of this book, but there are no how-tos that guarantee it. Some will point rightly to the minister's prayer life. "Isn't that the secret to great preaching?" they will ask. The answer is yes and no—while a deep and rich prayer life is a requirement for great and even good preaching, it by no means secures greatness on its own. We should do the work it takes to make our communication of God's truth *good* and leave it up to God how and how often he makes it great for the listener. "Should you then seek great things for thyself? Do not seek them" (Jeremiah 45:5).

The "Absolutely Perfect" Preacher

This distinction may lead you to assume that Christian communicators need to do nothing but explain the biblical text and that it is "up to God to do the rest." That is a dangerous misunderstanding and reduction of the preaching task.

Theodore Beza was a younger colleague and successor of John Calvin, the founder of the Reformed branch of Protestantism during the Reformation. In his biography of Calvin, Beza recalled the three great preachers in Geneva during those years—Calvin himself, Guillaume Farel, and Pierre Viret. Farel, said Beza, was the most fiery, passionate, and forceful in his sermonic delivery. Viret was the most eloquent, and audiences hung on his skillful and beautiful words. The time flew by fastest when sitting under his preaching. Calvin was the most profound, his sermons packed full of "the weightiest of insights." Calvin had the most substance, Viret the most eloquence, and Farel the most vehemence. Beza concluded "that a preacher who was a composite of these three men would have been absolutely perfect."[2] Beza is acknowledging here that his great mentor, John Calvin, was not the perfect preacher. He majored in great content, but he was not as skillful as others in commanding attention, in persuasion, and in the engagement of heart motives. Viret and Farel were more engaging and moving.

In the first Christian preaching manual St. Augustine wrote that the duties of preachers included not only *probare,* to instruct and prove, but also *delectare,* to rivet and delight, and *flectere,* to stir and move people to action.[3] Although Augustine condemned the bankruptcy of pagan philosophies, he believed Christian preachers could learn from their works on rhetoric. The Greek word *rhetorike* first appears in Plato's dialogue *Gorgias,* meaning "the work of persuasion."[4] Classics scholar George Kennedy writes that in one sense rhetoric "is a phenomenon of all human cultures" because most acts of communication have the goal of not merely expressing information but affecting the beliefs, actions, or emotions of the one(s) receiving them.[5] Everyone uses rhetoric to some degree, even if it means altering the volume, pitch, or pace to be emphatic. Everyone must choose vocabulary and metaphors that illuminate and compel, as well as find other verbal and nonverbal ways to gain and keep attention and emphasize certain points over others.

John Calvin himself agrees. When commenting on 1 Corinthians 1:17, where Paul eschews using "wisdom and eloquence," Calvin asks "whether he means . . . that the preaching of the gospel is vitiated if the slightest tincture of eloquence and rhetoric is made use of for adorning it." Calvin responds that "what Paul says here, therefore, ought not to be taken as throwing any disparagement upon the [rhetorical] arts, as if they were unfavorable to piety."[6] Paul is warning against their abuse. Rhetoric can become an end in itself, its entertaining and pleasing forms obscuring the simplicity of the biblical message with a "silly fondness for high sounding style."[7] Long stories, florid language, and dramatic gestures can captivate attention while the actual message of the text is ignored.

Calvin goes on to say that we should despise neither simple expressions of the truth nor skilled oratory, provided they are in service of the text. "Eloquence is not at all at variance with the simplicity of the gospel, when it does not disdain to give way to it, and be in subjection to it, but also yields service to it, as a handmaid to her mistress."[8] Preaching should not be a human performance that merely entertains nor a dry recitation of principles. Spiritual eloquence should arise out of the preacher's almost desperate love for the gospel truth itself and the people for whom accepting the truth is a matter of life and death.

In the end, preaching has two basic objects in view: the Word and the human listener. It is not enough to just harvest the wheat; it must be prepared in some edible form or it can't nourish and delight. Sound preaching arises out of two loves—love of the Word of God and love of people—and from them both a desire to show people God's glorious grace. And so, while only God can open hearts, the communicator must give great time and thought both to presenting the truth accurately and to bringing it home to the hearts and lives of the hearers.

Preaching Christ

There may be no more important Bible passage on preaching than 1 Corinthians 1:18–2:5.[9]

> When I came to you, I did not come with eloquence or human wisdom as I proclaimed to you the testimony about God. For I resolved to know nothing while I was with you except Jesus Christ and him crucified. I came to you in weakness with great fear and trembling. My message and my preaching were not with wise and persuasive words, but with a demonstration of the Spirit's power, so that your faith might not rest on human wisdom, but on God's power (1 Corinthians 2:1–5).

Paul says, "As I proclaimed to you the testimony about God . . . I resolved to know nothing while I was with you except Jesus Christ and him crucified" (1 Corinthians 2:1–2). At the time Paul was writing, the only Scripture to preach from was what we now call the Old Testament. Yet even when preaching from these texts Paul "knew nothing" but Jesus—who did not appear by name in any of those texts. How could this be? Paul understood that all Scripture ultimately pointed to Jesus and his salvation; that every prophet, priest, and king was shedding light on the ultimate Prophet, Priest, and King. To present the Bible "in its fullness" was to preach Christ as the main theme and substance of the Bible's message.

Classical rhetoric allowed the speaker *inventio*—the choice of a topic and the division of the topic into constituent parts, along with elaborate arguments and devices to support the speaker's thesis. For Paul, however, there is always one topic: Jesus. Wherever we go in the Bible, Jesus is the main subject. And even the breakdown of our topic is not completely left up to us—we are to lay out the topics and points about Jesus that the biblical text itself gives us. We must "confine ourselves" to Jesus. Yet I can speak from forty years of experience as a preacher to tell you that the story of this one individual never needs to become repetitious—it contains the whole history of the universe and of humankind alike and is the only resolution of the plotlines of every one of our lives.[10]

So Paul hasn't preached a text unless he has preached about Jesus, not merely as an example to follow but as a savior: "Christ Jesus, who has become for us . . . our righteousness, holiness and redemption" (1 Corinthians 1:30).

Paul sees Christ as the key to understanding each biblical text (the first aspect of good preaching) and also as the key to bringing the Word home persuasively to the heart and life of the listener (the second aspect). He writes: "I did not come with eloquence or human wisdom as I proclaimed to you the testimony about God." At first glance this seems to argue against using any craft at all in preaching, but the rest of the New Testament (as Calvin indicates) makes it impossible to hold that Paul never used logic, argument, rhetoric, or learning as he preached. In the book of Acts, as we will see, Paul skillfully uses different arguments for different audiences; and in 2 Corinthians 5:11 he "persuade[s]" listeners, so it cannot be that he has no strategies for changing people's minds.[11] New Testament scholar Anthony Thiselton draws on recent scholarship on classical rhetoric to help us understand what Paul means in 1 Corinthians by "eloquence" and "wise and persuasive words." Paul is rejecting verbal bullying (using the force of one's personality or witty and cutting disdain); applause-generating statements that play to a crowd's prejudices, pride, and fears; and manipulative stories or techniques that overwhelm the audience with shows of verbal dexterity, wit, or erudition.[12]

Against all these rhetorical abuses Paul puts the message of "Christ and him crucified," but consider the meaning of this contrast. Paul indeed wants to reshape the foundations of listeners' hearts—he wants to change what they most fundamentally love, hope, and put their faith in. Yet he insists that this change must *not* come about through human ingenuity but *only* through a "demonstration of the Spirit's power" (1 Corinthians 2:4)—which can be translated "through transparent proof brought home powerfully by the Holy Spirit."[13] What does that mean? Thiselton looks forward in the text and writes, "as becomes clear from 1 Corinthians 2:16–3:4, '*Spirit*' is defined Christologically." In this passage Paul speaks of the "self-effacing Spirit who points beyond himself to God's work in Christ."[14] Paul is likening himself to the Holy Spirit, whose job is, like a floodlight, not to point to himself but rather to show us the glory and beauty of Christ (cf. John 16:12–15).

So this is the Christian preacher's power. This is how to deliver not just an informative lecture but a life-changing sermon. It is not merely to talk about Christ but to *show*

him, to "demonstrate" his greatness and to reveal him as
worthy of praise and adoration. If we do that, the Spirit
will help us, because that is his great mission in the world.

Preaching to the Cultural Heart

We have not exhausted this passage's rich theology of
preaching. When Paul speaks of life-changing preaching
he is not limiting himself to the listeners' inner world.
He is also looking at the culture in which they live.

> For since in the wisdom of God the world
> through its wisdom did not know him, God was
> pleased through the foolishness of what was
> preached to save those who believe. Jews de-
> mand signs and Greeks look for wisdom, but we
> preach Christ crucified: a stumbling block to
> Jews and foolishness to Gentiles, but to those
> whom God has called, both Jews and Greeks,
> Christ the power of God and the wisdom of
> God (1 Corinthians 1:21–24).

Theologian Don Carson calls this a description of the
"fundamental idolatries of [Paul's] age."[15] Paul here deftly
summarizes the differences between Greek and Jewish
cultural narratives. Each society has a worldview or "world
story" or "cultural narrative" that shapes the identities
and assumptions of those in that society. In general, the
Greeks valued philosophy, the arts, and intellectual attain-

ments, while the Jews valued power and practical skill over discursive thought. Paul challenges both cultural narratives with the cross of Jesus. To the Greeks, a salvation that came not through elevated thought and philosophy but through a crucified Savior was the opposite of wisdom—it was foolishness. To the Jews, a salvation that came not through power, through a deliverer who overthrew the Romans, but through a crucified Savior was the opposite of strength—it was weakness. Paul uses the gospel to confront each culture with the idolatrous nature of its trusts and values.

And yet after challenging each culture, he also discerns and affirms its core aspiration. You want wisdom, says Paul to Greek listeners, but look at the cross. Didn't it make it possible for God to be both just *and* justifier of those who believe? Isn't this the ultimate wisdom? You want power, says Paul to his Jewish listeners, but look at the cross. Doesn't it make it possible for God to defeat our most powerful enemies—sin, guilt, and death itself—without destroying us? Isn't this the ultimate strength?

So Paul clarifies each cultural narrative, then confronts each of its idolatries—the intellectual hubris of the Greeks and the works-righteousness of the Jews—showing them that the way they have been pursuing their greatest and proper goods is sinful and self-defeating. Yet this is no mere intellectual exercise or clever rhetorical strategy—it is an act of love and care. We are social-cultural beings, and our inner-heart motivations are profoundly shaped by the human communities in which we are embedded. In the course of expounding a biblical text the Christian preacher should compare and contrast the Scripture's message with the foundational beliefs of the culture, which are usually invisible to people inside it, in order to help people understand themselves more fully. If done rightly it can lead people to say to themselves, *Oh, so that's why I tend to think and feel that way.* This can be one of the most liberating and catalytic steps in a person's journey to faith in Christ.

To reach people gospel preachers must challenge the culture's story at points of confrontation and finally retell the culture's story, as it were, revealing how its deepest aspirations for good can be fulfilled only in Christ. Like Paul, we must invite and attract people through their culture's aspirations—calling them to come to Christ, the true wisdom and the true righteousness, the true power, the true beauty.

The Tasks of Preaching

What, then, is good preaching? Let me pull all these ideas together into a single description.

It is "proclaim[ing]. . . . the testimony of God" (1 Corinthians 2:1)—preaching biblically, engaging with the authoritative text. This means preaching the Word and not your opinion. When we preach the Scriptures we are speaking "the very words of God" (1 Peter 4:11). You need to make clear the meaning of the text in its context—both in its historical time and within the whole of Scripture. This task of serving the Word is *exposition*, which is to draw out the message of the passage with faithfulness and insight and with a view to the rest of biblical teaching, so as not to "expound one place of Scripture, that it be repugnant to another."[16]

It is also proclaiming to *"both Jews and Greeks"* (1 Corinthians 1:24)—preaching compellingly, engaging the culture, and touching hearts. This means not merely informing the mind but also capturing the hearer's interest and imagination and persuading her toward repentance and action. A good sermon is not like a club that beats upon the will but like a sword that cuts to the heart (Acts 2:37). At its best it pierces to our very foundations, analyzing and revealing us to ourselves (Hebrews 4:12). It must build on Bible exposition, for people have not understood a text unless they see how it bears on their lives. Helping people see this is the task of *application,* and it is much more complicated than is usually recognized. As we have said, preaching to the heart and to the culture are linked, because cultural narratives profoundly affect each individual's sense of identity, conscience, and understanding of reality. Cultural engagement in preaching must never be for the sake of appearing "relevant" but rather must be for the purpose of laying bare the listener's life foundations.

Expository preacher Alec Motyer sums it up this way. He says that we have not one but two responsibilities when we preach. "First to the truth, and secondly to this particular group of people. How will they best hear the truth? How are we to shape and phrase it so that it comes home to them in a way that is palatable, that gains the most receptive hearing, and . . . avoids needless hurt?"[17]

These are the two tasks of preaching, and there is one key to both of them—preaching Christ. This is not a discrete task to add to the other two but is rather the essence of how you do each of them. Remember that biblical accuracy and Christocentricity are the same thing to Paul. You can't properly preach any text—putting it into its rightful place in the whole Bible—unless you show how its themes find their fulfillment in the person of Christ. Likewise, you can't really reach and restructure the affections of the heart unless you point through the biblical principles to the beauty of Jesus himself, showing clearly how the particular truth in your text can be practiced only through faith in the work of Christ.

Kathy once pointed out to me that the earlier parts of my talk might be a good Sunday-school lecture, but the moment I would "get to Christ" the lecture turned into a sermon. You may want your listeners to take notes on much of the sermon, but when you get to Christ, you want them to *experience* what they were taking notes about.

The famous nineteenth-century British preacher Charles Spurgeon was bold in his insistence that every sermon lift up Jesus for all listeners to behold. He complained that he often heard sermons that were "very learned . . . fine and magnificent," yet all about moral truth and ethical practice and inspiring concepts and "not a word about Christ." Here is what he says about such preaching, evoking the words of Mary Magdalene: "They have taken away my Lord, and I know not where they have laid him. I heard nothing about Christ!"[18] He is right. Unless we preach Jesus rather than a set of "morals of the story" or timeless principles or good advice, people will never truly understand, love, or obey the Word of God. What Spurgeon calls for is harder than it sounds and rarer than you would think.

So there are two things we must do. As we preach, we are to serve and love the truth of God's Word and also to serve and love the people before us. We serve the Word by preaching the text clearly and preaching the gospel every time. We reach the people by preaching to the culture and to the heart.

Then there is what God must do. He brings the Word home to our hearers through the "demonstration of the Spirit and of power" (1 Corinthians 2:4). According to Paul you can preach with genuine spiritual power only if you offer Christ as a living reality to be encountered and embraced by those who listen. This means to preach with awe and wonder at the greatness of what we have in Christ. It means to exhibit an uncontrived transparency, showing evidence of a heart that is being mended by the very truth you are presenting. It entails a kind of poise and authority rather than an insecure desire to please or perform. So your love, joy, peace, and wisdom must be evident as you speak. You should be something like a clear glass through which people can see a gospel-changed soul in such a way that they want it too, and so that they get a sense of God's presence as well.

How do all these things happen? They all happen as we preach Christ. To preach the text truly and the gospel every time, to engage the culture and reach the heart, to cooperate with the Spirit's mission in the world—we much preach Christ from all of Scripture.

PART ONE

Serving the Word

PREACHING THE WORD

If anyone speaks, they should do so as one who speaks the very words of God.

—1 Peter 4:11

The unfolding of your words gives light.

—Psalm 119:130

God's Word and Human Skill

In the first Protestant preaching manual, *The Art of Prophesying* (1592), William Perkins wrote, "The Word of God alone is to be preached, in its perfection and inner consistency."[1] This may seem to many today to be an obvious point. Of course a Christian preacher or teacher should be communicating the Bible, they say. In Perkins's cultural moment, however, this was not obvious. For many preachers of his day, "[God's] grace was not irresistible. It needed to be supported by eloquence. . . . The faithful needed the miraculous power of preaching to buttress the Scripture."[2]

Preaching in England at that time had become filled with verbal pyrotechnics, thick with ornate language, classical allusions and quotations, poetic images, and soaring rhetoric. Of course, preachers were still beginning with Bible passages—but very little time was given to actually unfolding the texts. They seemed to think the Bible needed a lot of help. A baseline confidence in the power and authority of the Scripture itself had been lost.

William Perkins and his contemporaries reacted against "the cultivated oratory" of their time. They believed that the main aim in preaching had been lost: that we let the Bible itself speak, so it can pour forth its own power. The early part of Perkins's brief volume spends substantial time establishing that the Bible is God's perfect, pure, and eternal wisdom and that it has the power to convict the conscience and penetrate the heart.[3] Perkins knew that communicators' beliefs about the character of the Bible had a major effect on how they actually handled it. Do we, as communicators of the Bible, truly know that it carries God's own authority and power? If we do, we will be more focused on unfolding *its* insights than on using it merely to support our own. "The preaching of the Word is the testimony of God and the profession of the knowledge of Christ, not of human skill," argues Perkins. He quickly adds, however, "but this does not mean that pulpits will be marked by a lack of knowledge and education. . . . The minister may, and in fact must, privately make free use of the general arts and of philosophy as well as employ a wide variety of reading while he is preparing his sermon." These things should "not [be] ostentatiously paraded" before the congregation.[4]

Perkins means that the purpose of preaching is not to present the results of your empirical investigation or philosophical reasoning or scholarly research. Nor is it to sense an insight or burden—one that you believe has been put on your heart by God—and then hunt for a biblical text that gives you an occasion for telling people what you want to tell them anyway. The purpose of preaching is to preach the Scripture with its own insights, directives, and teachings. Along the way, as Perkins says, we can and must use all the "arts" to help our hearers understand the biblical author's meaning. All of this is done in subservience to the first great task of preaching: to preach God's Word, and to let listeners sense its very authority.

Expository and Topical Preaching

What is the best way to do that?

Hughes Oliphant Old has written a magisterial seven-volume series on the history of preaching.[5] Old looks at Christian preaching in every century and in every branch of the church—Eastern Orthodox, Catholic, mainline Protestant, evangelical Protestant, and Pentecostal—and, by the end of the survey, at churches on virtually every continent. The scope and variety of his research are breathtaking. In his introduction to the series he names five basic types of sermons that he discerns over the centuries, which he calls expository, evangelistic, catechetical, festal, and prophetic.

He defines expository preaching as "the systematic explanation of Scripture done on a week-by-week . . . basis at the regular meeting of the congregation."[6] The other four types of preaching may at first glance seem quite different from one another, but in one key respect they are the same. Unlike exposition, these other four forms of preaching are not necessarily organized around a single passage of Scripture. That is because the main purpose of each is not the unfolding of the ideas within a single biblical text but rather the communication of a biblical idea from a number of texts. Old calls this broad approach "thematic" or "topical" preaching. The topical sermon may have any one of several aims. It may be to convey truth to nonbelievers (*evangelistic* preaching) or to instruct believers in a particular aspect of their church's confession and theology (*catechetical* preaching). *Festal* preaching helps listeners celebrate observances in the church year such as Christmas, Easter, or Pentecost, while *prophetic* preaching speaks to a particular historical or cultural moment.

There are, then, in the end, two basic forms of preaching: expository and topical. Throughout the centuries both have been widely used—and, as Old demonstrates, they *must* both be used. For example, in the book of Acts Paul did Bible exposition in a synagogue but employed topical oratory, using no Scripture at all, in the public square of Mars Hill. His points were all truths taken from the Bible, but the method of presentation was more like classical oratory in which he set forth theses and made arguments in their favor. In Paul's judgment, it was not appropriate to offer a careful Bible exposition to an audience who not only disbelieved in the Bible but also was profoundly ignorant of even its most basic assumptions. Evangelistic occasions are, then, one place where more topical Christian messages may be appropriate.

There are other occasions when the basic message you want to share is a biblical one, but it may not be possible to say enough of what the Bible has to say on your subject from one passage alone. Imagine you want to teach college students what the Bible says about the Trinity—that God is one and three. There is virtually no single biblical text that would enable you to expound this profoundly biblical doctrine. Instead you will need to quote and cite several texts to support the teaching. In expository preaching, by contrast, your job is to go wherever the single text takes you. The points of the message emerge as the text is explained, as its meaning is drawn out.

It is also worth noting that the two types of preaching are not mutually exclusive, and absolutely pure forms of either are rare. They are actually overlapping categories or two poles on a spectrum. Even the most careful verse-by-verse exposition will usually refer to other places in the Bible that treat the same topic. For example, if the Holy Spirit appears in your text, you may need to explain that the Holy Spirit is an equal divine person with the Father and the Son. The Holy Spirit is a "he," not an "it." It is likely that in your text there is nothing said directly about the personality of the Holy Spirit, but unless you give a brief topical overview of the biblical doctrine of the Spirit, the message of your passage will be misunderstood. So all expository preaching is partially topical. Then again, any topical sermon that is faithful to the Scripture will have to consist of several "mini expositions" of various texts. That is, passages of Scripture used to fill in the topic must be explained within their own context.

Expository preaching grounds the message in the text so that all the sermon's points are points in the text, and it majors in the text's major ideas. It aligns the interpretation of the text with the doctrinal truths of the rest of the Bible (being sensitive to systematic theology). And it always situates the passage within the Bible's narrative, showing how Christ is the final fulfillment of the text's theme (being sensitive to biblical theology).

The Case for (Usually) Doing Expository Preaching

Just as throughout church history both kinds of preaching have been necessary, so Christian teachers and preachers today need to see both as legitimate forms they can skillfully use. Nevertheless, I would say that expository preaching should provide the main diet of preaching for a Christian community. Why? I can think of at least six reasons, though I will dwell on the first one at greater length.

Expository preaching is the best method for displaying and conveying your conviction that the whole Bible is true. This approach testifies that you believe every part of the Bible to be God's Word, not just particular themes and not just the parts you feel comfortable agreeing with. A full confidence and rich grasp of the authority and inspiration of the Bible is absolutely crucial for a sustained, life-changing ministry of Bible teaching and preaching. When you have settled that, a sustained expository approach over time—in which you take care to draw out the meaning of each text, to ground all your assertions in the text, and to move through large chunks of the Bible systematically—will best pass your confidence in the Scripture along to your listeners.

It is not enough for you to just have a general respect for the Bible that you may have inherited from your up-bringing. As a preacher or teacher you will come upon many difficulties in the Bible; and inevitably the biblical authors say things that not only contradict the spirit of the age but also your own convictions and intuitions. Unless your understanding of the Bible—and your confidence in its inspiration and authority—are deep and comprehensive, you will not be able to do the hard work necessary to understand and present it convincingly. Your lack of conviction will also show up in your public teaching, blunting its impact. Instead of proclaiming, warning, and inviting, you will be sharing, musing, and conjecturing.

Of course, there is also a danger that a preacher of the gospel of grace will be overbearing and unnecessarily dogmatic at places where faithful believers differ. We will address that issue later. Here I want to stress the danger of making the opposite mistake. It is no more effective to be apologetic and unassertive than to be too confrontational and harsh. The balance is important. As Timothy Ward writes, "[If] the preacher exercises too much power he can be fought. If he is too weak he can be ignored."[7]

One way to develop an appropriate confidence in the Scripture is by seeing what the Bible says about itself. Start with a thorough study and analysis of Psalm 119, and distill all it says about the character of the Scripture and its role and use in our lives. Then there are several volumes and essays about the authority of the Scripture that are crucial for you to read carefully and know well, if your communication is going to bear fruit.[8] It is important to know not only in general that the Bible is true but also that in the Bible God's words are identical to his actions. When he says, "Let there be light," there is light (Genesis 1:3). When God renames someone, it automatically remakes him (Genesis 17:5). The Bible does not say that God speaks and then proceeds to act, that he names and then proceeds to shape—but that God's speaking and acting are the same thing. His word *is* his action, his divine power.[9]

So how do we hear God's active Word today if we are not prophets or apostles who actually sat at Jesus' feet? God's words in the mouths of the prophets (Jeremiah 1:9–10), written down, are *still* God's words to us when we read them today (Jeremiah 36:1–32). Ward says that it is crucial for the preacher to recognize this. "God's ongoing dynamic action through the Spirit" is "supremely related to the language and meanings of Scripture."[10] In other words, as we unfold the meaning of the language of Scripture, God becomes powerfully active in our lives. The Bible is not merely information, not even just completely true information. It is "alive and active" (Hebrews 4:12)—God's power in verbal form. It is only as we understand the meaning of the words that God names us and shapes us and recreates us.

If you, the Christian communicator, know and believe this doctrine of the Bible, it will have a profound influence on how you preach. If you believe only that the

Spirit may, in some general way, attend to the preaching of the Bible under some circumstances, then you are likely to undermine its power and authority as you preach by overemphasizing your own experiences or by locating the authority in your church's tradition and beliefs rather than in the Bible itself. Or you may use the Bible as a set of assorted wise remedies for contemporary social and personal problems. If, however, you believe that the preaching of the Word is one of the main channels for God's action in the world, then with great care and confidence you will uncover the meaning of the text, fully expecting that God's Spirit will act in listeners' lives.[11]

Therefore famous verses about God's Word being "like fire . . . and like a hammer that breaks a rock in pieces" (Jeremiah 23:29) are not mere rhetoric. I have seen hundreds of specific cases in which the Bible itself contained a power to penetrate people's spiritual indifference and defenses in a way that went far beyond my powers of public speaking. A handful of times I have even had conversations with angry people who were sure that one of their friends had told me about them and that I had singled them out in the sermon. I was able to swear honestly that I had had no idea at all about their issue—that it was the Bible itself exercising its power to lay bare the "secrets of their hearts" (1 Corinthians 14:25). I don't enjoy angry listeners, but I must say I love those conversations.

So the primary reason we should normally do expository preaching is that it expresses and unleashes our belief in the whole Bible as God's authoritative, living, and active Word.

The other reasons to make expository preaching a

church's main diet are more practical but no less important. One is that a careful expository sermon makes it
easier for the hearers to recognize that the authority rests
not in the speaker's opinions or reasoning but in God, in
his revelation through the text itself. This is unclear in
sermons that touch lightly on Scripture and spend most
of the time in stories, lengthy arguments, or thoughtful
musings. The listener might easily wiggle out from under
the uncomfortable message by thinking, *Well, that's just
your interpretation.* Clear and solid exposition, however,
takes pains to show what the passage means—and better
attests that what is being said is not the product of the
speaker's views or prejudices but has come from this authoritative text.

Expository preaching enables God to set the agenda
for your Christian community. Exposition is something of
an adventure for the preacher. You set out into a book or a
passage intent on submitting to its authority yourself and
following where it may lead. Of course, you still have to
choose which books and passages of the Bible to preach,
and any experienced student of the Bible will know basically what is within particular parts of the Bible. However,
expository preaching means you can't completely prede-
termine what your people will be hearing over the next
few weeks or months. As the texts are opened, questions
and answers emerge that no one might have seen coming.
We tend to think of the Bible as a book of answers to our
questions, and it is that. However, if we really let the text
speak, we may find that God will show us that we are not
even asking the right questions.

Modern people, for example, may come to the Bible looking for answers to the question "How do I build up my self-esteem and feel better about myself?" Yet in the biblical passages on sin and repentance, they will discover that the more basic human problem is too *high* a view of ourselves. We are blind to the depths of our own self-centeredness and overconfident that we have the wisdom to manage our own lives. Then in passages on adoption and justification they will learn that by asking to "feel better about themselves" they were asking for too little—too little in comparison with what our new identity in Christ can be. In the end, unfolding God's Word carefully will so transform our thinking that we will see the inadequacy of the original line of questions we brought to it.

A related reason is that expository preaching lets the text set the agenda for the preacher as well. It helps preachers resist the pressure to adapt messages too much to the culture's preferences. It brings you to subjects that you would rather not touch on and that you might not have chosen to address, since some of the Bible's positions—on subjects like sexuality—are so unpopular right now. Expository preaching only encourages you to declare God's will on such matters and also forces you to find ways of addressing and handling tough issues publicly.

In this way exposition can prevent us from riding our personal hobbyhorses and pet issues. It has been said that even the best preachers have only a dozen or so sermons that they repreach, simply using the biblical passages as starting points. It is then added that the worst preachers have only one, repeated until it drives everyone crazy. That criticism is closer to the truth than we preachers would like to admit, but only the discipline of expository preaching will give us a fighting chance of escaping that trap.

A steady diet of expository sermons also teaches your audience how to read their own Bibles, how to think through a passage and figure it out. Exposition helps them pay more attention to the specifics of the text and helps them understand why different phrases mean what they do within the story line of the Bible. They become savvier and more sensitive readers in their own study.

I'd like to give one last reason to rely on expository preaching, and in light of what we just observed, it may seem counterintuitive. As we saw, sustained expository preaching keeps you away from pet themes and gets you into a greater range of passages and subjects. Yet it also should lead you to see even more clearly the one main biblical theme. Twice in my life I have spoken to men who explained to me that they came to vital faith in Christ only after they had become preachers and, in fact, had been converted by their own sermons. I also know of a minister who came to vital faith listening to his associate pastor's expositions. How did that happen?

In expository preaching the meaning is discovered by looking at context, context, context. To understand a meaning of a sentence, we must ask, "How does this verse fit in with the rest of the passage?" To understand the meaning of the passage, we must ask, "How does this fit in with the rest of the book?" To understand the message of the book, we must ask, "How does this fit in with the rest of the Bible?" If you do this week after week you will discover the main story line of the Bible—the gospel of Jesus itself. Because the gospel is the resolution of every plotline and narrative and the fulfillment of every concept and image in the Bible, then week after week the listeners—and the preacher—will become ever clearer about the character of Christ's gracious salvation. And yet no one will be bored because you will see the gospel in all its endlessly variegated, multidimensional glory. Expository preaching can imprint that reality on people better than its alternatives.

Dangers to Avoid

Exposition should be the main diet of preaching for every congregation. Nevertheless, there are dangers attending this approach as well.

One is that some exposition enthusiasts are unwilling to take the mobility of our society into account. Hughes Old shows us that the original preaching of the church in its first five centuries used the *lectio continua* method—consecutive, verse-by-verse exposition through whole books of the Bible, taking years to bring the congregation through great swaths of biblical material. As time went on the number of feast days and holy days multiplied in the church calendar until, in the medieval church, the *lectio selecta* method ruled. It meant that people got short devotionals on various subjects rather than robust systematic teaching through the Bible.[12] In the twentieth century prominent preachers D. M. Lloyd-Jones, James M. Boice, and John MacArthur made it a hallmark of their ministries to take months or years to work through entire books of the Bible, leaving no stone unturned. This has led to a welcome revival of old-school expository preaching.

Many today believe this is the best and purest form of expository preaching. Yet most people in ancient times, and even in more recent times, lived all their lives near where they grew up. A preacher knew he would be preaching to the same basic group of people for years with little change in the membership. Today the population is far more mobile and church attenders much more transient. In the *lectio continua* method it is easy to spend a year or more on a single book of the Bible. However, if a family is going to be at your church for two years, do you really want them to learn only from 1 Samuel? Or even just from the Gospel of John with no time in the Old Testament? One of the strengths of exposition, as we have seen, is that it exposes the congregation to the full range of biblical teachings and subjects. Yet a strict, consecutive, whole-Bible-book approach will guarantee that most of your people will actually be exposed to less of the Bible's variety.

Even D. M. Lloyd-Jones did not use this approach for his Sunday-evening congregation. That audience was full of non-Christians and other inquirers brought by Christian friends from all over the city. And Lloyd-Jones did his most deliberate, years-long exposition of Bible books on Friday nights for Christians who wanted more extensive and advanced teaching.

Those speaking to congregations filled with many people at different stages of belief, and with highly mobile people, would do better following the lead of the British Anglican evangelicals like John Stott and Dick Lucas.

They are excellent models of preaching by the expository method. Their sermon outlines follow the main ideas of the passage and they are careful, crisp, and clear teachers of the text. Yet as pastors of congregations in highly mobile center-city settings they knew that they had many listeners for a couple of years at most. Their response was to modify the *lectio continua*. Rather than tackling whole long books of the Bible they offered expository series of consecutive passages through short books of the Bible, or they worked through longer books without covering every chapter, or they worked verse by verse through a couple of longer significant chapters in one book.[13]

If you are going to cover all the various parts and genres of the Bible—Old and New Testaments, narrative and didactic literature, prophets and poets—in a reasonable amount of time, you will have to move around in the Bible and do expository mini series.[14]

This isn't the only danger that comes with a commitment to exposition. While most topical preaching puts more emphasis on rhetorical devices such as image and illustrations, eloquent and skillful language, and use of story, expository preachers rightly put greater energy into the exegesis of the passage. However, preaching is not only explaining the text but also using it to engage the heart. I often see preachers giving so much time to the first task that they put little thought and ingenuity into the second. Indeed, some schools of expository preaching actively discourage preachers from doing much more than presenting the data from their biblical research. Anything beyond that is seen to be entertainment and showmanship. As we saw in the prologue this attitude comes, ironically, from an inaccurate reading of Paul's warnings in 1 Corinthians 1 and 2 against using "human wisdom" in preaching. Neglecting persuasion, illustration, and other ways to affect the heart undermines the effectiveness of preaching—first because it's boring and second because it's unfaithful to the very purpose of preaching.

On a related point, there is a danger in overdefining expository preaching. Enthusiasts of expository preaching (and I am one of them!) are eager to guard its quality, and for good reason, as a great deal of it is woeful. But this desire can lead some to define exposition too narrowly.

Some say exposition must be a verse-by-verse running commentary without sermon outlines and headings. Though that was the main approach to preaching in the earliest centuries, over the last few centuries most expository preachers have moved to using sermon outlines to good effect. On the other hand, if we are tempted to insist (as many preaching professors do today) that verse-by-verse commentary is absolutely wrong, we must remember that both John Calvin and John Chrysostom, two of the greatest preachers in history, did it that way. We must not try to define expository preaching too strictly in either direction. Some expositors move through the text consecutively, covering almost every verse, while others use outlines that extract the main ideas of the passage and treat it more selectively.

It is also customary today to define an expository sermon as one in which "the main point of the text is the main point of the sermon." This assumes that every biblical text has only one big idea or main point to it.[15] Then, it is said, the preacher must structure the sermon outline and points around this main theme, passing by any other matters in the text. Certainly in the majority of cases, the message will be clearer if the speaker is ruthless in pruning tangents out of the presentation, but this rule can be applied too rigidly.

In some Bible passages it is not easy to discern one clear central idea.[16] This is especially true in narratives. What is the one main point of Jacob's wrestling with the Lord in Genesis 32? What is the one reason the genealogies of Jesus were included at the beginning of Jesus' life in Matthew 1? What is the one point of the account of the dead man who came to life when his corpse came into contact with the bones of the prophet Elisha in 2 Kings 13? Then there is the strange account of the seven sons of Sceva (Acts 19:11–20) who tried to cast a demon out of a man "in the name of Jesus whom Paul preaches." In the comical result, the demon talked back through the man to the would-be exorcisers: "Jesus I know, and Paul I know about, but who are you?" before leaping upon and beating all seven of the sons. What was Luke trying to get across to us by including this incident in his book of Acts? I've heard a number of great expositions of this passage, and all of them were well grounded in the text and not contradictory of one another. Nevertheless, they were not the same. Multiple valid inferences can be drawn from such narratives, from which a wise preacher can select one or two to fit the capacities and needs of the listeners.[17]

The Bible is particularly rich, and this is why nearly always when you return to a text several years after having studied it or preached on it you see new ideas and meanings that you hadn't seen before. That doesn't mean that you should throw out the notes or the recording of the earlier sermon! Your new study and treatment will supplement and sharpen what you understood about the passage before. The richness of Scripture means that there are always new things to see and find.

This is why Alan M. Stibbs, in his forgotten classic *Expounding God's Word*, defines expository preaching as presenting the *ideas* (plural) and even the *implications* of the text, what the *Westminster Confession of Faith* calls "good and necessary inference."[18] He writes that expository preaching is

> to stick to the passage chosen and to set forth *exclusively what it has to say or to suggest*, so that the ideas and the principles enunciated during the course of the sermon plainly come out of the written Word of God, and have its authority for their support rather than just the opinion . . . of their human expositor.[19]

Having said this, often the biblical author *does* have one main theme that becomes evident with careful study.[20] Expository preachers must major in the text's major ideas and not get lost in the details and tangents that misrepresent the biblical author.[21]

Defending the Lion

It would be natural at this point to ask how effective the careful exposition of the Bible could possibly be in a culture that is becoming more and more averse to authority, particularly religious authority. Recently Fred Craddock died. He was a great United Methodist preacher whose book *As One Without Authority* moved mainline Protestant preaching decisively away from the expository method. He sensed that people did not accept the authority of either the Bible or the preacher to tell them how to live. Instead he called for preaching consisting of "open-ended stories" that allow listeners to "draw their own conclusions."[22]

This differs sharply from the advice of the nineteenth-century Baptist preacher Charles Spurgeon, who famously said:

> There seems to me to have been twice as much done in some ages in defending the Bible as in expounding it, but if the whole of our strength shall henceforth go to the exposition and spreading of it, we may leave it pretty much to defend itself. I do not know whether you see that lion—it is very distinctly before my eyes; a number of persons advance to attack him, while a host of us would defend [him]. . . . Pardon me if I offer a quiet suggestion. Open the door and let the lion out; he will take care of himself. Why, they are gone! He no sooner

goes forth in his strength than his assailants flee. The way to meet infidelity is to spread the Bible. The answer to every objection against the Bible is the Bible.[23]

The Bible is like a lion, Spurgeon claims, so you must not spend too much of your breath describing it, defending it, or arguing about why it should be believed. Instead, he urges you to put your energy into simply preaching it—into actually exposing people to it in its clearest and most vivid form. Then the extraordinary power and authority of the Word will become self-evident—even in the most antiauthoritarian settings, among the most skeptical people. I know this to be true.

TWO

PREACHING THE GOSPEL EVERY TIME[1]

When a man is driven to acts of obedience by the dread of God's wrath revealed in the law and not drawn to them by the belief of his love revealed in the gospel; when he fears God because of his power and justice, and not because of his goodness; when he regards God more as an avenging Judge, than as a compassionate Friend and Father; and when he contemplates God rather as terrible in majesty than as infinite in grace and mercy; he shews that he is under the dominion, or at least under the prevalence, of a legal spirit.

—John Colquhoun[2]

The Message of the Bible

In order to understand and explain any text of the Bible, you must put it into its context, which includes fitting it into the *canonical context:* the message of the Bible as a whole.

What is that message? From the perspective of the Old Testament, it is that "salvation comes from the Lord" and only from the Lord (Jonah 2:9). We are too fallen to save ourselves, too flawed to keep our covenant with God. There will have to be an intervention of radical grace, and it can come only from God himself. In the New Testament, we see *how* salvation comes from the Lord. It is only through Jesus. "'This is what I told you while I was still with you: Everything must be fulfilled that is written about me in the Law of Moses, the Prophets and the Psalms.' Then he opened their minds so they could understand the Scriptures" (Luke 24:44–45). Jesus told his disciples that unless you understand who he is and what he came to do, you can't understand either God's salvation or the Bible itself.[3]

To show how a text fits into its whole canonical context, then, is to show how it points to Christ and gospel salvation, the big idea of the whole Bible. Every time you expound a Bible text, you are not finished unless you demonstrate how it shows us that we cannot save ourselves and that only Jesus can. That means we must preach Christ from every text, which is the same as saying we must preach the gospel every time and not just settle for general inspiration or moralizing.

It is much more difficult to avoid this in Bible teaching and preaching than you may think.

The Two Enemies of the Gospel

A classic formulation of the gospel and its relationship with life is this: that we are saved through Christ alone, by faith alone, but not by a faith which remains alone. True salvation always results in good works and a changed life.

This formulation of the gospel focuses on the role of our ethical "good works" and our moral character. It first makes clear that such things play no role at all in our acceptance before God. Romans 4:5 says that we are "ungodly" when God justifies and accepts us through faith. It is not our moral behavior or even the quality of our faith that is the basis for the acceptance. None of those things are taken into account at all—God does not look at them. Rather, faith unites us to Christ, so that his righteousness and record are now legally ours. God sees us as "in Christ" (Philippians 3:9). As a result of this saving faith, the Holy Spirit always proceeds to work an inner-heart transformation, so that we want to and do begin to obey God out of gratitude and love (James 2:14–19).

Since the Protestant Reformation, it has been understood that there are two apparently opposite mistakes or errors into which you can fall so as to lose your grasp on this biblical gospel and its power. They are called "legalism," the view that we can put God in our debt and procure his blessing with our goodness, and "antinomianism," the idea that we can relate to God without obeying his Word and commands. Both words, derived from the Latin and Greek words for "law," miss a crucial aspect of how the gospel functions.

Legalism is far more than the conscious belief that "I can be saved by my good works." It is a web of attitudes of heart and character. It is the thought that God's love for us is conditioned on something we can be or do. It is the attitude that I offer certain things—my ethical goodness, my relative avoidance of deliberate sin, my faithfulness to the Bible and the church—that support Christ's work and contribute to God's goodwill toward me. A legalistic spirit leads to being ungenerous, harsh, overly sensitive to criticism, deeply insecure, and jealous of others, because our "sense of personal identity and worth has become entwined with performance and its recognition rather than being rooted and grounded in Christ and his [un]merited grace."[4]

Antinomianism too is more than just the formal belief that "I don't have to obey God's law." It is the thought that since God loves me regardless of my record, he doesn't mind how morally or immorally I live. It's the attitude that "God so accepts me as I am; he only wants me to be myself." Often it can metastasize into the belief that the only way to be a free person is to jettison belief in God altogether.

The most famous place where these two mind-sets are laid out is in Romans. In Romans 1:18–32, Paul shows that because the pagan Gentiles disregard God's law—and so are anti-law—they have lost any connection to him. Then in Romans 2:1–3:20 Paul proceeds to argue that law-abiding, Bible-believing Jews are alienated from God too. Why? Because they rely on their law keeping rather than on God's grace for their relationship with God and therefore they are legalists. They seek a "righteousness of [their] own" that comes from obeying the law (Philippians 3:9 cf. 3:3–6). Externally they are righteous but internally they are self-righteous and so do not depend on God for salvation as they should. So both reject God's grace and salvation in different ways, resulting in Paul's stark assessment that "'there is no one righteous, not even one; there is no one . . . who seeks God'" (Romans 3:10–11).

There are massive external differences between irreligious people, who may loudly denounce and subvert traditional moral norms, and very moral, religious, Bible-believing people who rely on their ethical goodness for their standing with God. Yet Paul says both are functioning as their own spiritual saviors, revealing that the internal differences are slight.

Biblical communicators must always have these two views of life in mind as we preach and teach. Individual texts usually contain exhortations on how believers should live that, expounded in isolation from the rest of the Bible, could support the legalistic view. Other passages will depict God's gracious provision of salvation and unconditional love—which in isolation could give the impression that free grace does not lead to life change. In *The Art of Prophesying* William Perkins writes that "preachers need to know the true relationship of law to gospel."[5] The law can show us our need for the gospel and then, once we embrace God's salvation by faith, the law becomes the way to know, serve, and grow into the likeness of the one who saved us. It is crucial in our preaching that we do not simply tell people all the ways they must be moral and good without relating such exhortation to the gospel. Nor should we simply tell them over and over that they can be saved only by free grace without showing how salvation changes our lives.

Perkins does not mean that we can simply assign every single Bible verse to one category or another—those that tell you what to do and those that tell you we are saved regardless of our record. He gives an example of two texts that, you could say, "put it all together": John 14:21

and 14:23.[6] There Jesus tells his disciples, "Anyone who loves me will obey my teaching. My Father will love them, and we will come to them and make our home with them." These texts make it clear that the gospel transforms obedience to God's commands from a legalistic means of acquiring salvation to a loving response to a received salvation. Obedience to God's law, flowing out of gospel grace, becomes a way to know, resemble, delight, and love the one who saved us at infinite cost to himself. John 14, then, is neither a simple "law" passage nor a "gospel rather than law" passage.

Seldom does a single passage so perfectly show the relationship of law to gospel as John 14. Usually the text you are preaching on majors in law or in gospel grace, and therefore you must always, always put the text in the context of the whole Bible, namely, the message of the gospel.

"Non-Identical Twins from the Same Womb"

One of the keys to doing this is to understand the underlying root of both the legalistic and the antinomian mindsets. Because of the massive external differences between them, we are prone to think of these two as opposites. If we do, we will instinctively and unwittingly try to heal one with a dose of the other, and that can be lethal.

Theologian Sinclair Ferguson analyzes the dialogue between the serpent and the first human beings in the story of the fall in Genesis 3. He points out that in God's original command, "Do not eat the fruit of this tree," he did not tell them why. He did not forbid them to eat of the tree because it would be bad for them in a particular way. His lack of an explanation was a call to obey out of love and trust in God for who he was in himself. So the command sought not merely behavioral compliance but also a particular attitude and relationship to God. That relationship was what the serpent immediately attacked.

In Genesis 3:1 the serpent said that God had forbidden them from eating the fruit of any of the trees of the garden—which he had not. Then in Genesis 3:5 the serpent argued that disobedience to God would be liberating—which it was not. Nevertheless, humanity believed the serpent and this spiritual poison, this "lie of the serpent," passed deeply into us with its assertion that God "was in fact restrictive, self-absorbed and selfish"[7] and that he could not be trusted to have our best interest at heart. If we obeyed him fully, the serpent implied, we would be miserable. Ferguson writes: "The lie was an assault on both God's generosity and his integrity. Neither his character nor his words were to be trusted. This, in fact, is the lie which sinners have believed ever since—the lie of the Not-to-be-Trusted-because-he-does-not-love-me-False-Father."[8] This lie has "entered the bloodstream of the human race" as the default heart condition, "deep in the human psyche."[9] Now at the bottom of our souls, whether we follow God's laws or not—human beings do not trust God's goodwill toward us.

On the basis of this insight, Ferguson then makes a remarkable claim. This lie of the serpent—that we can't trust God's goodness or his commitment to our happiness—is the single root of both legalism and antinomianism. They are "in fact non-identical twins that emerge from the same

toward morality and law, you will assume the remedy is to talk less about mercy and acceptance and more about God's righteousness and holy commands. In short, you will try to cure one with a dose of the other. That will be a disaster, because both of them have the same root cause. Both come from the belief that God does not really love us or will our joy, and from a failure to see that "both the law and the gospel are expressions of God's grace."[13] For both the legalist and the antinomian, obedience to the law is simply the way to get things from God, not a way to get God, not a way to resemble, know, delight, and love him for his sake.

Because legalism does not grasp God's grace, it distorts the law from its proper function as a guide for our lives, a way to become our true selves and to please God—and instead turns it into a burdensome system of salvation through which we obligate God to bless us. The only thing that will demolish legalism is not just the abstract principle that "you are accepted and forgiven" but a new understanding of God's goodness and his costly love in Jesus Christ.

Because antinomianism does not grasp God's loving grace, it also sees the law as an obstacle to freedom and personal growth rather than as the great means by which God grows us into both. It is a mistake, then, to pound only on antinomianism with statements of God's unyielding righteousness and holiness. Our hearts will only use this to fuel the serpent's lie about the severity of the divine character. Instead God's costly love in Jesus Christ—who fulfilled God's righteous law in his life and death—must be lifted up and grasped in order to combat the toxic untruths in our souls. Ferguson concludes that both legalism and antinomianism essentially require the same treatment: a new vision of the beauty of God himself and his glorious, free, and costly grace. Both legalism and antinomianism are healed only by the gospel.

> The gospel is designed to deliver us from this lie [of the serpent], for it reveals that behind and manifested in the coming of Christ and his death for us is the love of a Father who gives us everything he has: first his Son to die for us, and then his Spirit to live within us. . . . There is only one genuine cure for legalism. It is the same medicine the gospel prescribes for antinomianism: understanding and tasting union with Jesus Christ himself. This leads to a new love for and obedience to the law of God.[14]

An understanding of the kinship of these "twins" could not have greater practical implications for preachers. If you think the *real* problem out there in the world is legalism, you probably have one foot in antinomianism, and if you think the *real* problem with people is antinomianism, you probably have one foot in legalism.

Two Reasons Why We Should Preach Christ Every Time

To preach the gospel in a penetrating way, then, you do not merely want to talk about an abstract concept of forgiveness and acceptance. You want to show listeners Jesus himself and all that he came to do for us. To preach the gospel every time is to preach Christ every time, from every passage.

Only if we preach Christ every time can we show how the whole Bible fits together.

When Jesus met the two disciples on the road to Emmaus, he discovered that they were in despair because their Messiah had been crucified. He responded, "'How slow [you are] to believe all that the prophets have spoken!' . . . and beginning with Moses and all the Prophets, he explained to them what was said in all the Scriptures concerning himself" (Luke 24:25–27). Later he appeared to the apostles and other disciples in the upper room and explained the same thing to them, namely, that he is the key to understanding "the Law of Moses, the Prophets and the Psalms" (Luke 24:44). Jesus blamed the confusion of the disciples on their inability to see that the Old Testament is all about him and his salvation.

The apostolic writers are famously "Christ centered" in their interpretation of the Hebrew Scriptures. They often quote psalms as the words of Christ—and not just "messianic" or "royal" psalms where the speaker is clearly a messianic figure. For example, Hebrews 10:5–6 quotes Psalm 40:6–8 as something Christ said when "he came into the world."

> Sacrifice and offering you did not desire, but my ears you have opened—burnt offerings and sin offerings you did not require. Then I said, "Here I am, I have come—it is written about me in the scroll—I desire to do your will, my God. . . ."

But when we look at Psalm 40, we see absolutely nothing to indicate that the speaker is Jesus or some messianic figure. Why would the Hebrews author assume that Psalm 40 was about Jesus? He does so because he knows what Jesus told his disciples in Luke 24, that all the Scripture is really about him. The Bible is in the end a single, great story that comes to a climax in Jesus Christ.

God created the world and created us to serve and enjoy him and the world he had made. But human beings turned away from serving him; they sinned and marred themselves and the creation. Nevertheless, God promised to not abandon them (though it was his perfect right) but to rescue them, despite the guilt and condemnation they were under and despite their inveterately flawed hearts and character. To do this, first God called out one family in the world to know him and serve him. Then he grew that family into a nation; entered into a binding, personal covenant relationship with them; and gave them his law to guide their lives, the promise of blessing if they obeyed it, and a system of offerings and sacrifices to deal with their sins and failures. However, human nature is so disordered and sinful that, despite all these privileges and centuries of God's patience, even his covenant people—who had received the law, promises, and sacrifices—turned away from him. It looked hopeless for the human race. But God became flesh and entered the world of time, space, and history. He lived a perfect life, but then he went to the cross to die. When he was raised from the dead, it was revealed that he had come to fulfill the law with his perfect life, to offer the final sacrifice, taking the curse that we deserved and thereby securing the promised blessings for us by free grace. Now those who believe in him are united with God despite our sin, and this changes the people of God from a single nation-state into a new international, multiethnic fellowship of believers in every nation and culture. We now serve him and our neighbor as we wait in hope for Jesus to return and renew all creation, sweeping away death and all suffering.

What is all that? That is a story—a unified narrative plotline, resolving and climaxing in Jesus. The disciples knew the stories of each prophet, each priest, each king, each deliverer from Gideon to David. They knew about the temple and the sacrifices. But while they knew all the substories, they couldn't—until he showed them—see *the* story, about the ultimate prophet, priest, king, deliverer, the final temple and sacrifice. They couldn't see what the Bible was all about.

Try reading only one chapter out of a Charles Dickens or Victor Hugo novel without reading anything before or afterward in the book. Would you be able to understand and appreciate the chapter? Certainly you would learn about the characters, and some relatively complete narrative action or subplot could take place within the portion of the book you have read. But much would be inexplicable, because you wouldn't know what came before, and many things that the author was doing in the chapter would be invisible if you didn't see how the story played out. That is what it is like to read and preach a text of the Bible and not show how it points to Christ. If you don't see how the chapter fits into the whole story, you don't understand the chapter.

So preaching Christ every time is the way to show people how the Bible fits together. As we have seen, however, the preacher has two responsibilities, not only to the truth of the Bible but also to the spiritual needs of the listeners. And indeed, preaching Christ every time is also the only way to truly help people change from the inside out.

Any sermon that tells listeners only how they should live without putting that standard into the context of the gospel gives them the impression that they might be complete enough to pull themselves together if they really try hard. Ed Clowney points out that if we ever tell a *particular* Bible story without putting it into *the* Bible story (about Christ), we actually change its meaning for *us*. It becomes a moralistic exhortation to "try harder" rather than a call to live by faith in the work of Christ. There are, in the end, only two ways to read the Bible: *Is it basically about me or basically about Jesus?* In other words, is it basically about what I must do or basically about what he has done?

If on any level I believe that through moral efforts—living a chaste life, surrendering my will to him, helping the poor, converting others to faith—I can secure God's favor for my prayers or earn his blessing, then my motivation for doing all these things is some mixture of fear and pride. The fear is the desire to avoid punishment and get some defense and leverage over God and others. The pride is the sense that, because I am so decent and accomplished, I am "not like other people" (Luke 18:11) but a cut above. In the final analysis all the good I am doing I am doing for myself. My deeds of service to God and to my neighbor are ways of using God and my neighbor to build up my self-image, to secure respect and admiration from others, and to gain leverage over God so that he owes me something. Ironically and tragically, all my goodness is for me, so I am nurturing sinful self-centeredness, the ultimate idolatry, in the very midst of my efforts to lead a moral and good life.

This moralistic way of living feels like being on the end of a yo-yo. If I feel I am reaching my goals and meeting my standards, I become self-righteous, entitled, less patient and gracious with others. If I am failing in any way, I fall into self-loathing, because my very identity is based on my image of myself as a better person than others. This yo-yo moralistic existence is transcultural, by the way. People in traditional cultures get their identity and self-worth from living up to family expectations and making their family proud. People in individualistic Western societies get their identity and self-worth through self-expression, through identifying and fulfilling their dreams and desires. As radically different as these two cultural mind-sets seem to be, they are both self-salvation strategies, and the gospel challenges them both.

What if you are preaching a text on Joseph resisting the temptation of Potiphar's wife, or of Josiah reading the forgotten law of God to the assembled nation, or of David bravely facing Goliath, and you distill the lesson for life—such as fleeing temptation, loving the Scripture, and trusting God in danger—but you end the sermon there? Then you are only reinforcing the self-salvation default mode of the human heart. Your sermon will be heard as encouraging the listeners to procure God's blessing through right living. If you don't *every time* emphatically and clearly fit that text into Christ's salvation and show how he saved us through resisting temptation, fulfilling the law perfectly, and taking on the ultimate giants of sin and death—all for us, as our substitute—then you are only confirming moralists in their moralism.

Only if we hammer home the gospel, that we are loved sinners in Christ—so loved that we don't have to despair when we do wrong, so sinful that we have no right to be puffed up when we do right—can we help our listeners escape the spiritually bipolar world of moralism. And secular people, even if they are inclined against moralism, will need to hear it critiqued in our preaching for two reasons. One is that they won't even consider real Christianity unless they see it is not identical to moralism. Second, any person who is beginning to be drawn to God will automatically move toward him expecting to have a moralistic relationship. The eighteenth-century evangelist George Whitefield preached this warning in one of his sermons. We may choose less theological and archaic language, but we must convey this basic understanding of things.

> When a poor soul is somewhat awakened . . . then the poor creature, being born under a covenant of works, flies directly to a covenant of works again. And as Adam and Eve hid themselves among the trees of the garden, and sewed fig leaves together to cover their nakedness, so the poor sinner, when awakened, flies to his duties and to his performances, to hide himself from God, and goes to patch up a righteousness of his own. Says he, "I will be mighty good now—I will reform—I will do all I can; and then certainly Jesus Christ will have mercy on me." But . . . our best duties are as so many

splendid sins. . . . There must be a deep conviction before you can be brought out of your self-righteousness. It is the last idol taken out of the heart. . . . Can you say, "Lord, thou mayst justly damn me for the best duties that I ever did perform?" . . . If you are not thus brought out of self, you may speak peace to yourselves, but yet there is no peace. . . . You must lay hold by faith of the all-sufficient righteousness of Jesus Christ, and then you shall have peace.[15]

The only way to avoid what Whitefield is describing—the person spiritually searching for a relationship with God falling into the universal trap of moralistic religion—is to preach Christ from every text of the Bible, to preach the gospel every time.

Two Dangers to Avoid

1. Preaching a Text, Even About Jesus, Without Really Preaching the Gospel

If you come upon an essay on "preaching Jesus from every part of the Bible," you will expect it to address how to see Christ in the Old Testament. But it's possible to preach the New Testament—even passages in the Gospels about Jesus—without preaching the gospel.

Some years ago I read two sermons on Mark 5 by two different preachers on Jesus' healing of the demoniac. Of course both of the sermons are about Jesus, because the

text is an account of an episode in Jesus' life. The first sermon was great in many ways. It spoke of Jesus as Christ the
liberator. This tortured man is naked; he is in chains. He is
isolated from all other human community, crying out
in his agony. And Christ takes that chained man and liberates him; he takes that isolated man and makes him fit
again for human community. He stops his cries of agony
and fills him with quietness. Now the man is in his right
mind. And so the message of the sermon was, basically,
that you come to Jesus and whatever your problem is, he
can come into your life and make it right. He can heal you
of whatever ails you. If you have low self-esteem, he'll show
you how much he loves you. If you have addictions, he will
release you from bondage. Now, all this is absolutely right
(as long as you don't raise false expectations of instant and
easy sanctification). And I would never want to preach that
text without talking about Christ as a liberator.

But I read the second sermon not long afterward, and
in that one, near the end, the preacher asked an important question. The preacher said: This man's nakedness
and chains and isolation and his raving and crying out
are a picture of us all. We are sinners, and the Bible says
we are all spiritually enslaved to sin, to idols, and to the
"prince and power of the air." We need to be transferred
from the kingdom of darkness into the kingdom of light.
We're all in this condition—his case is just more poignant and obvious. He and we are in this condition as
sinners. Then Jesus liberates him. Here's the question:
Why can Jesus forgive and restore him?

The preacher answered that the reason he could forgive
this man and us comes at the end of Jesus' life. There we

see Jesus stripped naked, Jesus a prisoner, Jesus isolated and crucified outside the gate, Jesus crying out, "My God, my God, why hast thou forsaken me?" That's the answer. Jesus was able to heal the demoniac even though he was a sinner because eventually he exchanged places with him. Jesus is our substitute. Jesus could come into this man's life and heal him because Jesus died for him and paid the penalty and essentially bore all those things himself. He was stripped so we could be clothed. He was thrown into the deepest despair and agony so we could know God's love and forgiveness and have inner quietness.

The contrast between the two sermons was striking. Both were about Jesus, but only one sermon laid out the gospel clearly. The first sermon could give the impression that salvation was about healing your hurts and that the way to get that healing was to simply ask Jesus to come in and meet your needs. The issues of sin and grace were not clearly laid out. There was no need for the cross—it didn't make the gospel very clear. The second sermon did. The misery of the demoniac was used to vividly picture the pain and agony that fell on Jesus on the cross. A central teaching of the Gospel of Mark is that Jesus is our substitute. He gave his life as a ransom in our place (Mark 10:45).[16] That sermon read the individual episode in light of the great gospel theme of the whole book.

Having done that, it is not difficult to make the practical application to the listeners. It is only the recognition of his sacrificial death that can break the power of sin in our own lives. That is what reveals to us the wrongness of our efforts at self-salvation, and that is what makes them unnecessary. And when we stop trying to save ourselves, then the things that drive us and enslave us can do so no longer. Satan loses his power over us.

It's possible to preach the New Testament and not really preach Christ and his saving work. We think our problem is how to get to Jesus out of a particular psalm or out of 2 Kings. No, the problem is bigger than that. Preaching Christ means preaching the gospel. Preaching the gospel means preaching Christ and his saving work and his grace, and we can fail to do that in any part of the Bible.

2. Preaching "Christ" Without Really Preaching the Text

There is another mistake into which we can fall. It is possible to "get to Christ" so quickly in preaching a text that we fail to be sensitive to the particularities of the text's message. We leapfrog over historical realities to Jesus as though the Old Testament Scriptures had little significance to their original readers. Ferguson writes that this mistake "is likely to produce preaching that is wooden and insensitive to the rich contours of biblical theology."[17]

The result will be this: Because we have not spent time in the text itself, the way that Jesus is described will sound the same from week to week. Jesus will not be truly the resolution or climax of the particular theological theme and the answer to the specific practical problem. But if you do go deeply enough into the original historical context, there will be as many different ways to preach Christ as there are themes and genres and messages in the Bible.

There are many passages in the prophets, for example, where God speaks about how he will send a king to bring about complete, unprejudiced justice. In Isaiah 11:3 it says this king "will not judge by what he sees with his eyes, or decide by what he hears with his ears." He will redress wrongs and render justice to the oppressed and weak. Isaiah 11:1–16 is about the righteous "branch" (Jeremiah 23:5) who will do all this, and this person is commonly seen to be the Messiah. Isaiah's original readers probably understood him to be talking of a great, future king. Preachers of this chapter will tend to quickly begin showing all the ways Isaiah 11's descriptions fit Jesus and his salvation. However, the original hearers would have first heard a ringing affirmation of the importance of social justice, of not oppressing the poor, of living generously. By moving to the future too quickly and not staying long enough in the author's (and his hearers') time, the preacher can miss much of the meaning of the passage.

So we have a balance to strike—not to preach Christ without preaching the text, and not to preach the text without preaching Christ. Charles Spurgeon tells of a Welsh minister who spoke to a younger minister about his sermon after hearing it. "It was a very poor sermon," he told the young man. "Will you tell me why you think it a poor sermon?" came the response. "Because," said the Welsh minister, "there was no Christ in it." "Well," said the young man, "Christ was not in the text; we are not to be preaching Christ always, we must preach what is in the text." The exchange continued:

"Don't you know young man that from every town, and every village, and every little hamlet in England, wherever it may be, there is a road to London?" "Yes," said the young man. "Ah!" said the old divine, "and so from every text in Scripture, there is a road to the metropolis of the Scriptures, that is Christ. And my dear brother, your business is when you get to a text, to say, 'Now what is the road to Christ?' and then preach a sermon, running along the road towards the great metropolis— Christ. And," said he, "I have never yet found a text that had not got a road to Christ in it, and if I ever do find one that has not a road to Christ in it, I will make one; I will go over hedge and ditch but I would get at my Master, for the sermon cannot do any good unless there is a savor of Christ in it."[18]

This illustration is quite helpful. Let's draw it out a bit and apply it to our preaching:

Know the main point of the author and spend time there. *First (to extend our metaphor) we must identify the "high street" or the "main street" of the town.* That means we should be sure to identify the main thrust and message of the text for the original hearers, the "town residents." Some texts have a simple, single point, while others are a bit more complex, just as some towns have one broad main street and others have a couple of main arteries that weave their way through. Know them; travel on them; don't leave the town too soon. Go down deep into the text and be sure you know the author's meaning to his listeners. That's how you are sure to be true to what God is saying. If there is time, even glance down some side streets. Interesting shops are there sometimes. But never go too far from the main street, lest you not be able to find your way back in time.

Second, as Spurgeon suggests, there is some way that every main street connects to a road that goes out of town to London. Find how the main road connects to the road to London. Not every road out of town actually goes toward London, of course. If you take the wrong road out, you may end up having to cut across someone's land or fields to get to London. That's laborious and maybe illegal! In the same way, you should not think that anything in the text that vaguely reminds you of Jesus is a way to get to Jesus. If the Old Testament text is about the temple, then you may preach Christ as the Final Temple (John 2). That is how the main street of that text connects to Jesus. However, you can't just throw in anything you think of. Perhaps the scarlet cord that Rahab hangs from her window (Judges 2:18) reminds you of the blood of Christ, but that does not mean that is what it represents. From the main point in every text, there is *some* way to preach Christ with integrity. Point to that road and travel down it before ending your sermon.

THREE

PREACHING CHRIST FROM ALL OF SCRIPTURE

When they had lifted up their eyes, they saw no man, save Jesus only.
—Matthew 17:8, King James Version

The key to preaching the gospel every time is to preach Christ every time, and the key to that is to find how your particular text fits into the full canonical context and participates as a chapter in the great narrative arc of the Bible, which is how God saves us and renews the world through the salvation by free grace in his Son, Jesus Christ.

To help us discern ways to always preach Christ, we have many good authors and books to help us.[1] They each have their own list of categories for discerning and preaching Jesus from texts.[2] There are also more dimensions and ways to do this than we can cover in one chapter.[3] Speaking as a practitioner more than as a theorist, here are six basic ways to do so.

Preach Christ from Every Genre
or Section of the Bible

If you read Alec Motyer's *Look to the Rock* or Ray Dillard and Tremper Longman's *An Introduction to the Old Testament* or Ed Clowney's *The Unfolding Mystery*, you will get a good sense of how each part of the Bible points toward Christ in its particular way. He is the hope of the patriarchs. He's the angel of the Lord.[4] Then go to Exodus through Deuteronomy. He's the rock of Moses. He's the fulfiller of the law—both the ceremonial law, because he makes us clean in him, and the moral law, because he earns the blessing through his perfectly righteous life. He's the final temple. Now go to the history of Israel after Moses. He's the commander of the Lord's host (Joshua 5). He's the true king of Israel—indeed, he's the true Israel. He fulfills everything Israel was supposed to do and be. Now look at the Psalms, the songs of David, in which Jesus is the sweet singer of Israel (Hebrews 2:12). Then go to the prophets, and there he is the promised King (Isaiah 1–39), the suffering servant (Isaiah 40–55), and the world healer (Isaiah 56–66). Go to Proverbs and find that he is the true wisdom of God. To those who are being saved, the cross is the wisdom of God (1 Corinthians 1:22–25).

Each genre and part of the Old Testament looks toward Christ and informs us about who he is in some way that the others do not. For example, Ray Dillard, one of the authors of *An Introduction to the Old Testament*, once told me personally that one of the main questions constantly raised by the historical books, from Judges through 2 Chronicles, has to do with the nature of the covenant. The covenant is "I will take you as my own people, and I will be your God" (Exodus 6:7). The question is this: In light of the constant failures of the people to live up to their covenant promises to serve God, is the covenant conditional or unconditional? Will God say that it is conditional? ("Because you broke the covenant, I will cut you off, curse you, and abandon you forever.") Or will he say it is unconditional? ("Though you have rejected me, I will never wholly abandon you, but I will remain with you.") Which is it? Ray said that anyone reading the Old Testament closely will find that sometimes God seems to be saying it is conditional, while other times he seems to be assuring the people that it is unconditional. This mystery is one of the main tensions that drive the dramatic action. Since his people have forsaken him, will he forsake them?

There seems to be no simple answer that will not compromise something we know of God. Will his holiness give way to his love, so that he overlooks sin? Or will his love be overwhelmed by his holiness and justice, so that the divine hammer falls? Either way it seems he is not as truly loving or as truly holy as he otherwise reveals himself to be. See the plot tension in the story?

And then Jesus comes, and as we see him crying, "My God, my God, why have you forsaken me?" we realize the answer. Is the covenant between God and his people conditional or unconditional? Yes. Yes. Jesus came and fulfilled the conditions so God could love us unconditionally.

We see a similar tension in the book of Isaiah. The first part of the book depicts a kingly figure who is to come and put things right. The last part of the book, however, talks about a perfect, holy, yet suffering servant, who bears the sin of the people. How could both these figures be the Messiah? When Jesus comes, we understand. All the seemingly loose threads and contradictory claims of the rest of the Bible come together in Jesus.

Preach Christ Through Every Theme of the Bible

The Bible is filled with themes that run throughout all or most of its parts and genres. If you find any of the following themes, which thread their way through the entire canon, passing through your particular text, then you can simply "pull on the thread," looking back to where it began and ahead to its fulfillment in Christ now and on the Last Day.

Kingdom. We were made to obey and serve our true King. Sin is rebellion against the true King, but Romans 1 tells us we all must worship and serve *something,* so we will be enslaved by created things until we break their grip on us. What king is powerful enough to liberate us from this bondage and slavery? Only the one who is God himself returning to earth. Jesus is the true King and his death and resurrection broke the power of sin and death over us. Therefore to serve him is perfect freedom.

Covenant. We were made for relationship with God. We were created for covenant relationships, relationships made more intimate because they are more binding. We were made to be his people, he our God. If we keep the covenant, there is the blessing of love and unity and peace. If we break the covenant, there is the curse of separation, aloneness. How can God be holy and still remain faithful to his people? Only through the death of Jesus on the cross—where both love and law are fulfilled, where the Lord became the perfect servant and fulfilled the covenant perfectly and fully on our behalf.

Home and exile. The world was made to be our home, Eden, a place of *shalom* and fulfillment. But because of our sin we are all in exile. The world we live in no longer satisfies. Who can bring us home, bring us peace and fulfillment? Only Christ, who was exiled for us, sent to earth from heaven, sent outside the gate, abandoned by everyone, to die on the cross. Yet because he did all that, the world will become our home again, the new heavens and new earth wherein dwelleth righteousness (Revelation 21–22).

The presence of God and worship. How can sinners cut off from God stand in his life-giving presence and experience joy? We are designed for fellowship with him, to live in his presence—yet he is holy. How can flawed sinners come near God? The flaming sword guarding the way to the presence of God came down on Jesus, and now the way is open (Genesis 3:24; Hebrews 10:19–22).

Rest and Sabbath. We are restless and exhausted because we are doing the "work under our work," the depleting work of trying to get an identity through performance and accomplishment. But in Jesus we rest from that work and know God's unconditional acceptance, because Jesus experienced the cosmic emptiness of God-forsakenness.

Justice and judgment. We need justice in the world, but that presents us with an enormous problem. If there is no judge, what hope is there for the world? But if there *is* a judge, what hope is there for us? O Lord, if you kept a record of sins, who would be left standing? (Psalm 130:3). But here is a wonder: Jesus Christ is the judge of all the earth, who came the first time not with a sword in his hands but with nails through his hands—not to bring judgment but to bear judgment for us. Jesus Christ is the judge who *was* judged, so that all who believe in him can face the future judgment day with confidence. On that day, because we are pardoned, he will be able to end all evil without ending us.

Righteousness and nakedness. Once we had nothing to hide from God's sight or anyone else's. When we lost our original righteousness, we had to cover ourselves and hide from the eyes of others (Genesis 2:24–3:24). Now our shame and guilt need to be covered with God's grace. Because Jesus was stripped naked on the cross, we can be clothed in a robe of righteousness (Isaiah 61:10).

Preach Christ in Every Major Figure of the Bible

All the major figures and leaders of the Scriptures point us to Christ, the ultimate leader who calls out and forms a people for God. All anointed leaders in the Bible—every prophet, priest, king, and judge who brings about "salvation" or deliverance or redemption of any kind or level—are pointers to Christ, in their strengths and even in their flaws. Even their flaws show that God works by grace and uses what the world sees as marginal and weak. The social and moral "outsiders" whom God uses—such as Rahab, Ruth, Tamar, and Bathsheba (Matthew 1:1–11), especially those in the line of the promised "seed"—point to him. He is the fulfillment of the history of the judges who show that God can save not only by many (Othniel) or by few (Gideon) but also by one (Samson). Jesus is the judge all the judges point to (since he truly administers justice), the prophet all the prophets point to (since he really shows us the truth), the priest all the priests point to (since he truly brings us to God), and the King of kings. John Calvin writes, "Therefore, when you hear the gospel presenting you Jesus Christ in whom all the promises and gifts of God have been accomplished," remember this:

> He [Christ] is Isaac, the beloved Son of the Father who was offered as a sacrifice, but nevertheless did not succumb to the power of death. He is Jacob the watchful shepherd, who has such great care for the sheep which he guards. He is the good and compassionate brother Joseph, who in his glory was not ashamed to acknowledge his brothers, however lowly and abject their condition. He is the great sacrificer and bishop Melchizedek who has offered an eternal sacrifice once for all. He is the sovereign lawgiver Moses, writing his law on the tables of our hearts by his Spirit. He is the faithful captain and guide Joshua, to lead us to the Promised Land. He is the victorious and noble king David, bringing by his hand all rebellious power to subjection. He is the magnificent and triumphant king Solomon governing his kingdom in peace and prosperity. He is the strong and

powerful Samson who by his death has over-whelmed all his enemies.[5]

A more modern inventory is the following:

Jesus is the true and better Adam, who *passed* the test in the garden and whose obedience is imputed to us (1 Corinthians 15).

Jesus is the true and better Abel, who, though in-nocently slain, has blood that cries out for our ac-quittal, not our condemnation (Hebrews 12:24).

Jesus is the true and better Abraham, who answered the call of God to leave the comfortable and famil-iar and go out into the void "not knowing whither he went" to create a new people of God.

Jesus is the true and better Isaac, who was not just offered up by his father on the mount but was truly sacrificed for us all. God said to Abraham, "Now I know you love me, because you did not withhold your son, your only son whom you love, from me." Now we can say to God, "Now *we* know that you love us, because you did not withhold your son, your only son whom you love, from us."

Jesus is the true and better Jacob, who wrestled with God and took the blow of justice we deserved so that we, like Jacob, receive only the wounds of grace to wake us up and discipline us.

Jesus is the true and better Joseph, who at the right hand of the King forgives those who betrayed and sold him and uses his new power to save them.

Jesus is the true and better Moses, who stands in the gap between the people and the Lord and who mediates a new covenant (Hebrews 3).

Jesus is the true and better rock of Moses, who, struck with the rod of God's justice, now gives us water in the desert.

Jesus is the true and better Job—the *truly* innocent sufferer—who then intercedes for and saves his stupid friends (Job 42).

Jesus is the true and better David, whose victory becomes his people's victory, though they never lifted a stone to accomplish it themselves.

Jesus is the true and better Esther, who didn't just risk losing an earthly palace but lost the ultimate heavenly one, who didn't just risk his life but gave his life—to save his people.

Jesus is the true and better Jonah, who was cast out into the storm so we could be brought in.

Let's drill down on just one of these examples, Jesus as the "true Jonah." At the end of Mark 4 we see Jesus stilling the storm, and his rebuke: "Do you still have no faith?" (Mark 4:40). It would be easy to preach this in an inadvertently moralistic way. We could just draw out the lesson that we need to work on our faith and trust God when things get bad. That would ultimately be merely a how-to sermon—how to have faith and hold on in storms. It wouldn't show us the gospel very clearly.

But Mark is intentionally recapping the Jonah episode in Mark 4.[6] He uses nearly identical words and phrases. Both Jesus and Jonah are in a boat. Both are in storms described in similar terms. Both boats are filled with others who are terrified of death. Both groups wake the sleeping prophets angrily, rebuking them. Both storms are miraculously calmed and the companions saved. And both stories conclude with the men in the boats *more* terrified after the storm is stilled than they were before. Every feature is the same—with one rather large apparent exception. Jonah is sacrificed into the storm, thrown into the deep, satisfying the wrath of God so the others will be saved from it—but Jesus is not.

Or are the accounts really different at that point? No, they are not. As Jesus says in Matthew 12:41, he is the ultimate Jonah, who was thrown into the ultimate deep—of eternal justice—for us. How ironic it is that in Mark 4 the disciples ask, "Teacher, don't you care if we drown?" (Mark 4:38). They believe he is going to sleep on them in their hour of greatest need. Actually, it's the other way around. In the garden of Gethsemane, *they* will go to sleep on him. They will truly abandon him. And yet he loves them to the end. See? Jonah was thrown overboard for his own sin, but Jesus is thrown into the ultimate storm for *our* sin. Jesus was able to save the disciples from the storm because he was thrown into the ultimate storm.

Now see: By not defaulting to mere exhortation to trust God more but by penetrating to how the text points us to the saving work of Jesus, not only do we have a great picture of the gospel of salvation, but in the end we also have a more powerful, heart-changing motivation to trust God. We also now have a practical application for listeners, grounded in his saving work, not in our efforts. It goes like this: Are you in something like a storm in your life? Have you prayed and felt like God must be asleep? He is not. How do you know? Because he faced that ultimate storm and endured it for you—so you can know he will not abandon you in your infinitely smaller storms. Why not trust the one who did that for you?

If you don't see the storm in Mark 4 as pointing to his finished work, then you will end up almost scolding, "Have faith in the midst of your storms! Have faith in Jesus! He won't let you down!" But you must go deep enough into the gospel to stir in the heart faith in Christ's work, to show people what he did for us. That will actually *instill* the trust right in the sermon. Otherwise you will just be beating on the will to say, "Be faithful."

Preach Christ from Every Major Image in the Bible

There are many images or "types" pointing to Christ that are not figures or persons but impersonal objects and patterns. Many of these symbols vividly depict salvation by grace that finds fulfillment in Christ. The bronze snake in the wilderness and the water of life from the smitten rock point us to Christ of course (since John and Paul tell us they do!). Also the entire sacrificial and temple system is really pointing to him; we know this because the book of Hebrews tells us so. Absolutely everything about the ceremonial system—from the clean laws to the altar, the sacrifices, and the temple itself—reveal who he is and what he has done. Both the Sabbath and the Jubilee laws point to him. He makes them all obsolete. Jesus is the sacrifice that all the sacrifices point to (Hebrews 10). Jesus is the bread on the altar in the temple (John 6), the light stand in the holy place (John 8), and the temple itself (John 2), for he mediates the presence of God with us. Jesus fulfills all the ceremonial clean laws about foods and ritual purification (Acts 10 and 11). Jesus fulfills circumcision—it represents how he was cut off from God. Now we are clean in him (Colossians 2:10–11). Jesus is the Passover lamb (1 Corinthians 5:7).

Many other images can't really be called symbols, nor are they strictly theological themes, but are concrete ideas or subjects that recur and have connections to Jesus. Let me give you an example—work, or labor. In the beginning God created the world using work. Genesis 3 shows that the cursing of work means difficult toil. When Jesus comes, he says, "I am working and my father's working" (cf. John 5:17). And we are saved through Jesus' work, not ours. This isn't usually classified as an intercanonical theme like kingdom or covenant or exile. It's just a recurrent image of laboring and working, and yet even there Christ is the climax of the image—he is the ultimate worker, as it were.

Here is another example: the tree of life. The Bible begins and ends with the tree of life—in Genesis and Revelation. In the beginning we lost the tree of life; we lost paradise. In the end, through the work of Jesus we regain the tree of life, which now stands prominently in the middle of the city of God. So this tree represents eternal life and vitality, as opposed to decay and death working in us. Now, this tree shows up in only one other place in the Bible, in the book of Proverbs. There, wisdom itself is the tree of life. Growth in wisdom is understood as growth in knowing God, in knowing ourselves, and in godly character and relationships—what we would call spiritual growth or the "fruit" of the Spirit. So Proverbs is saying that it is possible, in a sense, to eat from this tree now in an experience of spiritual growth. The New Testament shows us how. The Spirit unites us with Christ by faith, and now "life works within us" even as we still have death working in our bodies. But how is this all possible? Galatians 3:13 reminds us that when Jesus was crucified, he was cursed because he was "hanged on a tree."[7] George Herbert puts it so vividly in "The Sacrifice" when he depicts Jesus speaking from the cross. He says, "All ye who pass by, behold and see; Man stole the fruit, now I must climb the tree; A tree of life for all, but only me. Was ever grief like mine?" What is Jesus saying? Because Jesus got the tree of death, we can have the tree of life. Herbert is even more poignantly saying that Jesus turned the cross into a tree of life for us, at infinite cost to himself.

Preach Christ from Every
Deliverance Story Line

We must notice the *narrative* pattern of life-through-death or triumph-through-weakness, which is so often how God works in history and in our lives. Notice, for instance, how everyone with power and worldly status in the story of Naaman is clueless about salvation, while all the servants and underlings show wisdom. This is a major pattern in the Bible, a gospel pattern, a grace event or story line. In preaching you can move from the grace event to the work of Christ. For example, few have considered either Esther or Ruth to be a "type" of Christ, and yet, in order to redeem the people they love, they must risk loss and do many things that mirror how Christ brought salvation to us. Another important grace-event pattern is the "order" of the Exodus and the lawgiving. God did not first give the law and then deliver the people. He first delivered the people and then he gave them the law. Thus we are not saved *by* the law but saved *for* the law. The law is how we regulate our love relationship with God, not the way we merit the relationship. All of this points to the ultimate way we are saved not by law, but by faith in Christ.

To take another example, look at the story of David and Goliath. What is the meaning of that narrative for us? Without reference to Christ, the story may be preached as "The bigger they come, the harder they'll fall, if you just go into your battles with faith in the Lord. You may not be really big and powerful in yourself, but with God on your side, you can overcome giants."

If I read the story of David and Goliath as basically giving me an example, then it is really about me. *I* must summon up the faith and courage to fight the giants in my life. But if I think of the Bible as being about the Lord and his salvation, and if I read the David and Goliath text in that light, it throws many things into relief. The very point of the passage was that the Israelites could *not* face the giant themselves. They needed a substitute, who turned out to be not a strong person but a weak one. And God uses the deliverer's weakness as the very means to bring about the destruction of Goliath. David triumphs through weakness and his victory is imputed to his people. In his triumph, they triumphed.

How can one not recognize Jesus in this story? Jesus faced the ultimate giants (sin and death) not at the risk of his life but at the cost of his life. But he triumphed through his weakness and now his triumph is ours—his victory is imputed to us. Until I see that Jesus fought the real giants *for* me, I will never have the courage to be able to fight ordinary giants in life (suffering, disappointment, failure, criticism, hardship). How *can* I ever fight the "giant" of failure, unless I have a deep security that God will not abandon me? If I see David only as my example, the story will never help me fight the failure/giant. But if I see David as pointing to Jesus as my substitute, whose victory is imputed to me, then I can stand before the failure/giant. In Jesus I am already loved and acclaimed by God. No worldly success can approximate that. I am no longer petrified by failure, because I triumph in Jesus, our true David. Unless

I first believe in the one to whom David *points*, I'll never become like David at all.

It is not simply the stories of individuals that point us to Christ. The redemptive purpose of God is to redeem a *people* and renew *creation*. Therefore, all the major events in the history of the formation of the people of God also point us to Christ.

Jesus is the one through whom all people are created (John 1). Thus the creation story itself points forward to the new creation in Christ. Jesus is the one who went through temptation and probation in the wilderness. Thus the story of the fall points forward to the successful probation and active obedience of Christ. The exodus story points forward to the true exodus Jesus led for his people through his death (Luke 9:31).[8] He led them not just out of economic and political bondage but out of bondage to sin and death itself through his death and resurrection. The wandering in the wilderness and the exile to Babylon points forward to Jesus' "homelessness" and wandering and wilderness temptation, culminating in his suffering as the scapegoat outside the gate. He underwent the ultimate exile that fulfilled the righteousness of God fully.

Jesus is very literally the true Israel, the seed (Galatians 3:16–17). He is the only one who is faithful to the covenant. He is a remnant of one. He fulfills all the obligations of the covenant and earns the blessings of the covenant for all who believe. When Hosea talks about the exodus of Israel from Egypt, he says, "Out of Egypt I called my son" (Hosea 11:1). Hosea calls all of Israel "my son." But Matthew quotes this verse referring to Jesus (Matthew 2:15) because Jesus is the true Israel.

Preach Christ Through Instinct

Though you should employ many of these ways to preach Christ from all of Scripture, too rigid a formula (or set of formulas) results in being predictable. Often the line from the text to Christ is best perceived by intuition rather than composed by a defined method. Sinclair Ferguson says:

> [Perhaps most] outstanding preachers of the Bible (and of Christ in all Scripture) are so instinctively. Ask them what their formula is and you will draw a blank expression. The principles they use have been developed unconsciously, through a combination of native ability, gift and experience as listeners and preachers. Some men might struggle to give a series of lectures on how they go about preaching. Why? Because what they have developed is an instinct; preaching biblically has become their native language. They are able to use the grammar of biblical theology, without reflecting on what part of speech they are using.[9]

My friend and Old Testament professor Tremper Longman once told me that reading the Bible is somewhat like watching the movie *The Sixth Sense*. That movie has a startling ending that forces you to go back and reinterpret everything you saw before. The second time through, you can't *not* think of the ending as you watch the beginning and middle of the movie. The ending sheds unignorable light on everything that went before. In the same way, once you know how all the lines of all the stories and all the climaxes of all the themes converge on Christ, you simply can't not see that every text is ultimately about Jesus.

Sometimes, then, you can't help but think about Christ even if the text you are looking at doesn't seem to be specifically a messianic prophecy or a major figure foreshadowing Christ or an intercanonical theme or part of a key biblical image or metaphor. Yet you just can't not see him.

Here's an obscure passage in the Bible where we see this played out. At the end of Judges, in chapters 19 through 21, we read a terrible story of a cowardly Israelite with a concubine, a second-class wife, as it were. He comes into a town where some ruffians from the tribe of Benjamin threaten him, and to save himself he offers this woman to them to have their way with. He goes to bed and all that night the men rape her and abuse her. In the morning the husband comes out of the house and finds her on the doorstep, dead. He is furious, and he takes her body home, cuts it into several pieces, and sends one to each of the other tribes of Israel, to inflame them to go to battle against the tribe of Benjamin over this outrage. The husband conveniently fails to tell everyone of his own cowardice. The resulting civil war is bloody and devastating.

What a bleak and terrible passage! How in the world could you preach Christ here?

Actually, there is more than one way to do it. Put this passage into the context of the whole book's theme. What is the theme of the whole book of Judges? The answer to that question is easier to find than in many other books, because the narrator ends his account of this event, and of the entire book of Judges, with this sentence: "In those days Israel had no king; everyone did as they saw fit" (Judges 21:25). The social disorder and moral degradation revealed the desperate need for good governance. As most biblical scholars point out, the author of Judges is making a case for kingship and, along with the book of Ruth, is pointing to King David. However, we know the story of Israel and humanity beyond David and know that, as great as David was, he couldn't heal the people of their sin and rebellions. It would take the ultimate King to change hearts truly. And so fitting this text into its whole canonical context—particularly the intercanonical theme of the kingdom—shows us Jesus. Is that how you preach Christ from such a terrible text? Yes, but it is not the only way.

How can we not see, even in such a dark pool, a reflection of something beyond it? When we see a man who sacrifices his wife to save his own skin—a bad husband—how can we not think of a man who sacrificed himself to save his spouse—the true husband? Jesus gave himself for us, the church, his bride (Ephesians 5:22–33). Here is a true spouse who will never abuse us. Indeed, he subjected himself to abuse in order to make us whole.[10] All human marriages in the Bible point us to the marriage of God and his people, of Christ and his church, and this means that all bad marriages will make us think of and long for the ultimate spousal love of Jesus.

Here's another example of preaching Christ from a text even when it doesn't fit into a traditional Christ-typological category. Look at the beatitudes (the "Blessed are the . . ." statements) in the Sermon on the Mount (Matthew 5:1–10). Most scholars argue rightly that the beatitudes do not depict different groups of people—the poor in spirit, then the mourners, then the meek, then the hungry after righteousness, then the merciful—but rather list the characteristics of one group of people—Jesus' disciples. If we humble ourselves in spirit, if we mourn over our sins—if we are and do these things—then we are truly his disciples. So if we are preaching just on the beatitudes, it would be easy to fall into mere moral exhortation. "Be like this—try quite hard—and you will be Jesus' disciples."

But if you have the instinct to which we have been referring, you might look at those beatitudes, those descriptors and those rewards, and realize that they also describe Jesus himself. And when we think of that we see how what he did gives us what each beatitude promises.

Why can you and I be as rich as kings? Because *he* became spiritually and utterly poor. Why can you and I be comforted? Only because he mourned; because he wept inconsolably and died in the dark. Why are you and I inheriting the earth? Because he became meek; because he was like a lamb before his shearers. Because he was stripped of everything—they even cast lots for his garment. Why can you and I be filled and satisfied? Because on the cross he said, "I thirst." Why are you and I obtaining mercy? Because he got none: not from Pilate, not from the crowd, not even from his Father. Why will you and I be able to someday see God? Because he was pure. Do you know what the word "pure" means? It means to be single-minded, absolutely undivided, laser focused. So why is it that someday we will see God? Because Jesus Christ set his face like a flint to go up to Jerusalem and die for us (Luke

9:51).[11] You and I can see God because, on the cross, Jesus could not.

When you see Jesus Christ being poor in spirit *for you*, that helps you become poor in spirit before God and say, "I need your grace." And once you get it and you are filled, then you are merciful, you become a peacemaker, you find God in prayer and wait someday for the beatific vision, to see God as he is (1 John 3:1–3). The beatitudes, like nearly everything else in Scripture, point us to Jesus far more than we think.

PART TWO

Reaching the People

FOUR

PREACHING CHRIST TO THE CULTURE

And as he was speaking in this way, Festus said in a loud voice, "Paul, you are out of your mind. Your great learning is driving you mad." But he said, "I am not out of my mind, most excellent Festus, but I am speaking true and rational words."

—Acts 26:24–25[1]

The Madness of Christianity

Terry Eagleton, the British literary theorist and critic, writes that "societies become secular not when they dispense with religion altogether, but when they are no longer especially agitated by it."[2] Eagleton believes Western societies are all headed in this direction at one speed or another. By his definition, a society in which there are still outraged atheists hostile to religion has not yet gone very far along the path toward being secular. Today we are seeing growing numbers of people who do not exhibit hostility to religion as much as indifference. The growth is in the "nones"—those who may not necessarily be atheists but who do not feel part of any particular religious institution or even tradition. They see no need to explore possible religious solutions to any of their problems. They do not believe people need God in order to have a basis for meaning or purpose, to have a strong moral framework, to aspire for and achieve greatness, or to simply have a full and happy life.[3]

This is a new situation. For over one thousand years in Western societies, Christian beliefs have been the "deep background" of almost all listeners to any Christian speaker. Preaching and gospel presentations could build on those concepts and count on getting a hearing with some respect. Since the midtwentieth century that has finally begun to change. Large segments of the population—even in the United States—for the first time began to embrace a secular view of life that for decades had been mainly the province of the European intelligentsia.

When Paul preached the gospel to the imperial elites, he called his message "truthful and rational," yet to the listeners he seemed out of his mind. Today again, what Christians think is true and reasonable now appears to be sheer madness to increasing numbers of the population.

Change or Challenge?

Through centuries of habit most Christian speaking and preaching still assumes that listeners have the fundamental understandings of reality that they had in the past. Even the most outwardly focused, evangelistic churches continue to reach mainly people with traditional mind-sets because their communication expects hearers to carry that historical imprint of Christendom. Yet fewer and fewer find the messages comprehensible, much less persuasive. How do we communicate the Christian faith now, in this increasingly secular age, while honoring all that we explored in Part One of this book?

Many say what is needed is a change in the *mode* of our communication. We should abandon the sermon "monologue" and move into interactive discussions in which all participants mutually discover their respective paths. One problem with this view is that the monologue speech is as popular a medium as it has ever been. TED talks and their many imitators are flourishing, and in 2008 one in every four American adults listened to at least one sermon podcast a week.[4] The sermon form is not dead, and many predictions of preaching's imminent demise now feel dated.[5]

Others who still support the classic mode of public address nonetheless propose that our cultural currents require a change in the realm of *content*. Andy Stanley argues that biblical expository preaching worked in a time when our society agreed on the importance and truth of the Scripture. That does not work now, he believes. Instead of starting with the Bible and ending with practical application—as in the traditional sermon—we should start with a current human need or contemporary question and then bring in the Bible for a response and solution. Stanley asks: "To what extreme are you willing to go to create a delivery system that will connect with the heart of your audience? . . .

Are you willing to abandon a style, an approach, a system that was designed in another era for a culture that no longer exists?"[6]

For a contrary view we can turn to P. T. Forsyth, a Scottish Congregationalist minister and theologian at the turn of the twentieth century. He argues that when in history the church was at its most effective, "she did not lead the world, nor echo it; she confronted it."[7] "The Christian preacher is not the successor to the Greek orator, but of the Hebrew prophet," writes Forsyth. "It is one thing to have to rouse or persuade people to do something. . . . It is another to have to induce them to trust somebody and renounce themselves for him. . . . The orator stirs men to [action], *the preacher invites them to be redeemed*."[8]

This ancient debate will ever be with us: Should Christian preachers or teachers change for the culture or challenge it?

Adapting in Order to Confront

It isn't true that Bible exposition developed only in an age where everyone was Christian. Hughes Old shows that expository preaching was the norm during the first five centuries of the church's life, at a time when the society was not merely non-Christian but often virulently anti-Christian. Preachers did not begin with a contemporary problem and bring in the Bible to address it, though perhaps that would have followed the prevailing rhetorical wisdom of the time. It is therefore wrong to conclude that expository preaching belongs only in a Christianity-affirming society.[9]

It is also wrong to think that Bible exposition can't have a very strong focus on human need. Nearly all Bible texts do address such existential issues directly or indirectly. However, if we start with our questions and only then look to the Bible for answers, we assume that we are asking all the right questions—that we properly understand our need. However, we need not only the Bible's prescription to our problems but also its diagnosis of them. We may even have maladies we are completely unaware of. If we don't begin with the Bible, we will almost certainly come to superficial conclusions, having stacked the deck in favor of our own biases and assumptions.

There is no need, then, to pit the goals of Bible exposition and of life change against each other. Similarly the two positions of "adapt to the culture" and "confront the culture" are not as mutually exclusive as they appear. P. T. Forsyth says that preaching should not "echo" the world but "[confront] it."[10] However, lest we jump in our mind's eye to the stereotype of preaching as harangue, notice that in his lecture "The Preacher and the Age" Forsyth immediately adds nuance. He observes how the Gospel writer John requisitioned the pagan term *logos*—a philosophically and culturally freighted word in that society. Greek philosophers believed it was the cosmic order behind the material world. John used it to declare that Jesus Christ is the power and meaning behind the cosmos. It was a bold rhetorical move that filled an existing cultural concept with new meaning but used its older associations to point people to the gospel.[11]

Would it not have been better for John to stay away from compromised Greek cultural categories, to simply say instead, "Jesus is the Son of God"? The answer is that by taking the Greeks' own terms the Gospel writer was tapping into their deepest aspirations. John was saying of their cultural hopes, "Yes, but no, but yes." Yes, Christians agree that history is not random and the world is not meaningless, that there is a *logos,* a purpose and order, behind it all. Yes, too, if you align yourself with that order, you will live well. However, no—it is not something you can find through philosophical reasoning, because it is not an "it" at all; it is a *him.* Jesus Christ is the creator God, come in the flesh. Finally, yes—ultimate meaning in life is possible. What you passionately seek is there, and your desires can be fulfilled if you enter into a reconciled relationship with the one who created you and who governs the universe.

John did not simply tell the pagan philosophers that they were completely wrong and needed to believe the Bible instead of what they already believed. Rather, he showed them, first, that some of their intuitions about the universe—being not random or self-directed but purposefully guided by a supernatural principle that must be discovered—were right. Second, and this is the "but no, but yes" part of his discourse, he showed them that the reality behind this aspiration is embodied only in Christ.

This is ultimately confrontation—a call to repent and believe. The early Christian communicators did not simply seek to answer the culture's questions, because when that is all you do, those questions set the agenda and define the outer boundaries of what is important and what is not. Yet, while they did not allow their agenda to be co-opted, they did not ignore or condemn the vocabulary and concepts of the culture. They understood and affirmed its people's hopes, fears, and aspirations. The early Christian communicators knew the culture intimately and spoke in terms that were never incomprehensible, no matter how startling. They reframed the culture's questions, reshaped its concerns, and redirected its hopes. As Forsyth says, they "converted" their culture—they brought the gospel to bear on it so that it was radically changed. John did not merely confront the culture, nor did he simply adapt to it. He adapted to it in order to confront it in the most compelling and loving way possible. As Forsyth puts it, speaking of the early church, "Yet . . . if she borrowed the thought, the organization, and the methods of the world, she . . . was but requisitioning the ladders by which she escaped from the world, and rose to its command. She used the alloy . . . to make it workable, to make it a currency."[12]

Contextual Communication

This understanding of preaching is one aspect of what missiologists call "contextualization."[13] It means to resonate with yet defy the culture around you. It means to antagonize a society's idols while showing respect for its people and many of its hopes and aspirations. It means expressing the gospel in a way that is not only comprehensible but also convincing.

New Testament scholar Eckhard Schnabel shows that Paul very deliberately adapts his gospel preaching to the different cultures of his listeners in order to confront them.[14] In each setting Paul varies not only his vocabulary and vocal style but also how he expresses emotion and uses reason, how he deploys illustrations and figures of speech, and, most interesting, how he argues. He reasons and seeks to convince his hearers rather than to merely contradict them.[15]

We can discern several things that Paul does in pursuit of persuasion. He uses vocabulary and themes that are familiar, not obscure. In his speech in Athens, for example, Paul describes God in ways that many pagans could accept (Acts 17:22–23, 24–28).[16] He quotes authorities that his listeners respect. Of course he cites the Bible when speaking to Jews or to Gentile "God-fearers" or to converts to Judaism. But when addressing the philosophers on Mars Hill he quotes Aratus, a pagan author (Acts 17:28). Paul always chooses "elements of contact"—points of actual agreement and affirmation of some of the audience's concerns, hopes, and needs.[17] In Athens he chooses five ideas about God from the Bible with which the Stoic philosophers present could agree and proceeds from there.[18]

Finally, Paul also selects what Schnabel calls "elements of contradiction,"[19] which are never incidental to the elements of contact. In fact, he ordinarily uses his point of agreement *as* the point of contradiction. When Paul quotes Aratus, who says of God, "We are his offspring," Schnabel writes that this "can be understood as an accommodation to the philosophical convictions of Paul's audience."[20] However, in the very next sentence Paul argues, "Therefore since we are God's offspring, we should *not* think that the divine being is like gold or silver or stone—an image made by human design and skill" (Acts 17:29, emphasis mine).[21] In short, Paul takes some of his listeners' right beliefs and uses them to criticize their wrong beliefs in light of the Scripture. He shows them that their beliefs fail the test of their own premises.[22] Paul accommodates in order to love and to confront at the same time.[23] By affirming people's better impulses, by granting insights where he finds them, by adopting concepts and ways of reasoning that they can understand, Paul is not merely seeking to refute them, but also to respect them.[24]

Paul contextualizes deliberately and constantly.[25] He does not lay out the good news up front and delay the bad news until some future time but interweaves confirmation and confrontation to prevent listeners from deflecting and resisting the power of the Word's appeal to their minds and hearts. So we see Paul's answer to the question of whether to accommodate the culture or confront it. The answer is not "a little of both" or some other middle-way answer. We adapt and contextualize *in order* to speak the truth in love, to both care and confront.

There are many excellent examples of contextualization in the history of Christian preaching. One instructive example is the American theologian Jonathan Edwards. In 1751 he moved from Northampton to Stockbridge, which was still in Massachusetts but out on the nation's frontier, and there he preached to both Mohican and Mohawk American Indians.[26]

Only a handful of sermons have survived from his Stockbridge years, but all scholars who have studied them note the obvious—that Edwards modified his sermonic approach enormously from his earlier years.[27] He used a whole new set of images and metaphors that better fit his audience. Edwards changed his traditional sermon outline from one that had relied more on classical rhetoric—a more deductive approach that began with a thesis and then analyzed and defended it—to a more inductive approach that began with questions and pulled ideas together into a conclusion. Edwards clearly took into consideration that his listeners had suffered a great deal of oppression and mistreatment, and his messages struck notes of comfort and solace more often than his earlier sermons. Most striking is how he used narrative more extensively than ever before. Edwards was an intentional, masterful contextualizer of the gospel.[28]

Notice I said that he was intentional and skilled at contextualization—not simply that he did it, because contextualization is unavoidable. The moment you open your mouth, many things—your cadence, accent, vocabulary, illustrations and ways of reasoning, and the way you express emotions—make you culturally more accessible to some people and force others to stretch and work harder to understand or even pay attention to you. No one can present a culture-free formulation of biblical truth.[29]

Nevertheless, though inescapable, contextualization is fraught with dangers, and in both directions. If you over-contextualize and compromise the actual content of the gospel, you will draw a crowd but no one will be changed. That is nothing less than a dereliction of the preacher's duty. You will mainly just be confirming people in their present course of life. On the other hand, if you undercontextualize, so that your communication of the gospel is unnecessarily culturally alien and distant from the listeners, you will find that no one will be willing to hear you out. Of course that means that no one is changed by the gospel either, however valiant you are for the truth.

There is no way to avoid this important aspect of gospel communication. Paul and Edwards show us how they contextualized in their times and places. For us the question is how to communicate the Christian faith in a secular age increasingly hostile to belief in God and in Christianity in particular.

Let's lay out six sound practices for preaching to and reaching a culture.

> Use accessible or well-explained vocabulary.
> Employ respected authorities to strengthen your theses.
> Demonstrate an understanding of doubts and objections.
> Affirm in order to challenge baseline cultural narratives.
> Make gospel offers that push on the culture's pressure points.
> Call for gospel motivation.

Use Accessible or Well-Explained Vocabulary

As we have seen, Paul and John were careful to use concepts and themes that were accessible to their listeners. Our evangelical churches once operated in societies in which Christian vocabulary was not wholly alien to any listener. That is changing rapidly. This means that you should not use unexplained theological terms like "hermeneutics," "eschatological," "covenant," "kingdom," or even "theological" repeatedly. If you do, not only will outsiders to the faith be confused, but Christians will intuitively know not to bring their less initiated friends to hear you. If the term is important enough, you should regularly explain it and come up with an accessible definition that you cite often.

A "covenant," for example, could be said to be a stunning blend of both law and love. It is a relationship much more intimate and loving than a mere legal contract could create, yet one more enduring and binding than personal affection alone could make. It is a bond of love made more intimate and solid because it is legal. It is the very opposite of a consumer-vendor relationship, in which the connection is maintained only if it serves both parties' self-interest. A covenant, by contrast, is the solemn, permanent, whole self giving of two parties to each other. This definition appeals to late-modern people who value love, but it challenges them too, by refusing to pit law, authority, and commitment against love, joy, and freedom. Once you have explained this biblical concept of covenant at some length in these culturally accessible terms, you do not have to repeat this in full every time to the congregation. Shorthand expressions such as "more intimate and loving than a mere contract; more binding and accountable than a mere relationship" can stand in and remind listeners who have heard the more comprehensive explanation as well as pique the interest of newcomers.

You should give listeners theological definitions in their own language. Nineteenth-century Scottish preacher Robert Murray M'Cheyne talked about the complex doctrine of double imputation—that our sins are put upon him and his righteousness transferred to us—by saying, "He was a doing as well as a dying Savior. He not only suffered all that we should have suffered, but obeyed all that we should have obeyed."[30] It is possible to take Luther's dictum about justification, that we are *simul justus et peccator,* simultaneously accepted as righteous yet in ourselves sinful, and state it like this: "A Christian is more flawed and sinful than you'd ever dare believe and yet more loved and accepted than you'd ever dare hope—at the same moment."

Avoid evangelical subcultural jargon and terms that are unnecessarily archaic, sentimental, or not readily understandable to the outsider. Some terms, such as "lukewarm," "spiritual warfare," "backsliding," "seeing fruit," "opening doors," "walking with the Lord," and the overused "blessing," do have biblical backgrounds, but can become hackneyed. We have also become accustomed to cloying, stylized prayer language, which overuses phrases such as "just really, Father God," "I just echo that," and "I've been released from that" and which can spill out into public speaking and praying. There is also a younger-generation version of evangelical talk, such as "The preacher really *brought* the word" and "It was a total God thing" and the overuse of the terms "passion" and "passionate" in the same way that older people use the term "blessing."

Please understand that I am not trying to air my personal linguistic pet peeves here. The issue is far more important than generational or regional preferences or some sort of marketing-based concern that such vocabulary doesn't test well with non-Christians. Language like this is used as a boundary marker, a way to tell others that you are in the tribe and they are not. Newcomers certainly get that message, whether you consciously mean to send it. Insider language is frequently also an enabler of hypocrisy, as it offers a shortcut to sounding spiritual without actually having a heart filled with love and delight.

There is one more class of terminology to avoid: the "we-them" language that speaks disdainfully of nonbelievers or of other religions or denominations or simply caricatures or marginalizes the positions of people who do not share your beliefs and views. Again, this is not a matter of message control for greater appeal; it's a matter of gospel integrity and witness. Show yourself to be a member of the whole Body of Christ by speaking generously of those in other branches of the church. And show yourself to be a member of the broader human community in which you reside. Mention in your prayers and speaking the needs and concerns of the neighborhood, city, and region, not just those of the Christian community. Speak often about service to the poor, the marginalized, and outsiders of your community, as well as its leaders. Demonstrate that Christians share a common membership in the earthly city, not just citizenship in heaven.[31]

Employ Respected Authorities to Strengthen Your Theses

If you are preaching or speaking to people who have strong doubts about the Bible, you should reinforce the points you are making from the biblical text with supporting material from sources that your listeners trust. Paul himself most famously does this in Acts 17:28 when he quotes the pagan writer Aratus to an audience of pagan philosophers who would not otherwise grant the Bible any authority.

Many will balk at the idea of supplementing the Bible at all. Shouldn't you simply preach the text itself and allow the Bible's own authority to come through and convince people? The Bible indeed has a unique, divine, living power, a penetrating persuasiveness that issues from God himself (Hebrews 4:12). Yet to quote some other thinker is not fundamentally different from using illustrations out of daily life to reinforce the Bible's teaching. No preacher simply reads the biblical assertions to people; all teachers and communicators deploy anecdotes, examples, stories, and other accounts that convince listeners and drive the biblical truths home.

If you are preaching on the first commandment ("Thou shalt have no other gods before me") or Ephesians 5:5 (which calls greed idolatry) or any of the several hundred other places in the Bible that speak of idols, you could quote David Foster Wallace, the late postmodern novelist. In his Kenyon College commencement speech he argues eloquently and forcefully that "everyone worships. The only choice we get is what to worship."[32] He goes on to say everyone has to "tap real meaning in life," and whatever you use to do that, whether it is money, beauty, power, intellect, or something else, it will drive your life because it is essentially a form of worship. He enumerates why each form of worship does not merely make you fragile and exhausted but can "eat you alive." If you lay out his argument in support of fundamental biblical teaching, even the most secular audience will get quiet and keep listening to what you say next.

If you are teaching on moral absolutes—on any of the hundreds of biblical texts that say God's Word has authority over human opinion and legislation—you could quote Martin Luther King Jr. with great effect.[33] In his "Letter from Birmingham Jail" he cites both Augustine and Thomas Aquinas to argue that human laws are only just when they square with "the moral law . . . the law of God . . . eternal law."[34] King's personal example and argument are very disarming for secular listeners and almost guarantee consideration of your thesis.[35]

When preaching on Psalm 19 or Romans 1 or many other Psalms, of the creation telling of the existence and glory of God, you could quote Leonard Bernstein, who admitted that when he was in the presence of great music and great beauty he sensed "Heaven," an order behind things, "something we can trust, that will never let us down."[36] If you are teaching on virtually any passage on human sin and rebellion—but especially texts, like Romans 8:7, that speak of our heart's natural hostility to God—you would do well to quote a remarkable passage by the atheist philosopher Thomas Nagel, who candidly confessed, "It isn't just that I don't believe in God and, naturally, hope that I'm right in my belief. It's that I hope there is no God! I don't want there to be a God: I don't want the universe to be like that. . . . This cosmic authority problem is not a rare condition."[37]

If you are preaching on Satan, you can be sure your listeners will begin to roll their eyes. You can quote Andrew Delbanco, a secular scholar at Columbia University, whose book *The Death of Satan* argues that "a gulf has opened up in our culture between the visibility of evil and the intellectual resources available for coping with it."[38] He argues that many secular people understandably attribute all human cruelty to psychological deprivation or social conditioning and, in so doing, trivialize the terrible wrongs people are capable of. Delbanco recounts the story of Franklin D. Roosevelt, who along with many of the American elites during the Holocaust gave "no priority to the rescue" of the victims. Late in the war, after the evidence for the atrocities became too great to disbelieve, the president was given Kierkegaard to read and said that, for the first time, the Christian philosopher gave him "an understanding of what it is in man that makes it possible . . . to be so evil."[39] Delbanco avers that secular liberals (a group of which he considers himself a member) had lost any concept of "radical evil." If you speak of the devil to a secular audience, you must use sources such as this to dislodge the posture of ironic incredulity that they would otherwise assume when hearing this biblical teaching.

If you are preaching on original sin, you could cite C. E. M. Joad, a British atheist intellectual who came to belief in God after World War II. "It was because we rejected the doctrine of original sin that we on the Left were always being so disappointed; disappointed by the refusal of people to be reasonable . . . by the behavior of nations and politicians . . . above all, by the recurrent fact of war."[40]

This is a crucial part of preaching to the heart of the culture. It is no guarantee of persuading a skeptical audience, but it will go a long way toward keeping them from tuning you out almost immediately. It often results in their increased respect for the wisdom—and eventually the authority—of the Bible.[41]

Demonstrate an Understanding of Doubts and Objections

The Christian preacher must be a critic of nonbelief. However, there is no virtue in being an unsympathetic one. Do doubters come away feeling you are indifferent, high-handed, or dismissive of their views, or are they surprised, even shocked at how accurately and fairly you represent their own problems with Christianity? Do they think that you can express their skeptical views as well as—or even better than—they can themselves? Christian communicators must show that they remember (or at least understand) very well what it is like not to believe, all the while maintaining that it is possible to come to real assurance of God's reality and love. They must do this by expressing these doubts and objections with appreciation and respect, in a coherent form, showing that they have listened long and hard to them. You cannot fake this; it can come only from spending lots of face time with people who don't believe, as well as from reading the best sources critiquing Christianity.[42]

We must be willing to listen so long and well to their questions, concerns, and hopes that when we do speak, we are so well attuned to their views that they feel the force of our appeals and arguments. When 1 Peter 3:15 says we are to "give the *reason* for the hope that you have" (emphasis added), New Testament scholar Karen

Jobes says Peter is saying "believers must be able to relate the Christian faith to unbelievers by addressing their questions in terms they find meaningful."[43]

How do you demonstrate this posture within your teaching or preaching? The first task is to always be aware of and transparent about your own assumptions. Don't exhort about point D, knowing that it is based on believing A, B, and C, without alluding to them. This might mean saying, "Now, some of you might find *that* implausible, because you don't believe *this*—but I would ask you to bear in mind . . ." Show listeners that you are aware of their problems and queries about what you have just said and have thought through the resolutions and answers.

Another way to directly engage the doubters among your listeners is at the very end of your message. At the conclusion, when you are doing sermon application— urging certain ways of thinking and living in light of the text—you could enter into a brief dialogue with them. Say: "If you are not a believer or not sure what you believe, I'd like you to take this away to think about . . ."

Addressing any group of people directly and invitingly shows people you know they are there. You may even devote one of the points or subpoints of your message to the doubts and concerns of secular people. As you write the sermon, keep in mind the objections that skeptics would have to the teaching of a particular text, then take a moment to address them using agree-to-disagree reasoning. You could say, "I know what I just said may sound outrageous to you, but I'd respectfully ask you to consider this . . ." Unless you are speaking in a setting in which most of the people are skeptical or secular, you should not let these points dominate your messages. You should incorporate these "apologetic sidebars" probably no more than once in a sermon, and not in every sermon.

These apologetic sidebars should address what some have called "defeaters." These are ideas that, if accepted, make one think, *If this is true, then Christianity can't be true.* Common defeaters include "There can't be just one way to God"; "We can't believe in a God who sends people to hell"; "Science has disproven the supernatural"; and "The Bible has many offensive, outdated parts that we can no longer accept." If you ignore the reality of these defeaters, preaching as if people did not hold them, many people will simply find much of what you say unbelievable.[44]

Again, the basic way to handle objections is to sincerely agree with your listeners' beliefs at some point, but then to question a second, mistaken belief on the basis of the first. It is to say: "Since you believe *this,* why not believe *that?*" This forms an alliance between the Bible and one of the listeners' own beliefs, which can powerfully move people to accept other things the Bible says.

If you are trying to convince secular listeners that there is something more than this material world, you could cite Annie Dillard's observation in *Pilgrim at Tinker Creek* that while we are part of nature, in which the strong dominating the weak is absolutely natural, we intuitively refuse to accept this as a pattern for human behavior. "Either this world, my mother, is a monster, or I myself am a freak."[45] Yet how can we consider the natural world abnormal and *un*natural unless there is some standard above nature—a supranatural standard? If you don't think your belief in human rights is an illusion, if you think that the genocide of weak people by stronger people is truly and universally wrong (the point of contact), then why not believe there are moral absolutes in some realm beyond this world (the point of confrontation)?

If you are speaking of the authority of the Bible, you could talk of the importance of having a personal love relationship with God. We know that in mutually loving relationships, both parties must be active agents, able to contradict as well as affirm each other. If person A is never allowed to express a contradictory opinion to person B, then person B has a power relationship with person A, but not a personal one. Now, if you choose to believe only those things in the Bible that you agree with, in what way do you have a God who can contradict you? Only if your God can say things that upset you will you know you have a real God and not just a creation of your imagination. So an authoritative Bible (the point of contradiction) is not the enemy of a personal love relationship with God (the point of contact). It is the precondition.

Here is another way to talk about an authoritative Bible to people who find some of its content offensive. "In every culture there are good and bad elements. Isn't that right? No one culture is perfect or has all truth—agreed?" This is the point of contact—the late-modern belief that no one culture has all truth. Here, then, is how the point of contradiction could be built on the point of contact. "Now, for the sake of argument, imagine that the Bible is not the product of any one human culture or set of authors but is a revelation from God himself. If that were the case, then it would have to offend every person's cultural sensibilities *somewhere*. No matter who you are, you inhabit an imperfect culture that shapes your beliefs, and the Bible—if it were authoritative revelation from God—would then have to be outrageous to you at some place. Since that is the case, it is no argument against the Bible to say, 'It offends me at this point.' That is precisely what you should expect."

The Christian philosopher Miroslav Volf, in *Exclusion & Embrace,* argues that belief in a God of judgment (a point of contradiction) is a crucial resource for nonviolence (a point of contact). Speaking as a Croatian whose people experienced the ethnic cleansings of the 1990s, Volf proposes that "the practice of non-violence *requires* a belief in divine vengeance." If victims of violence believe there is no God, or no God who will bring a final justice on the earth, they will feel justified, or at least provided incentive, to pick up weapons in vengeance. So Volf argues the only way to "prohibit recourse to violence by ourselves" is to fully believe that God alone has that right, and that will square all accounts some day.[46]

If you sprinkle your preaching with these interesting, concise, yet penetrating asides, you will not only encourage secular listeners to return but also motivate Christians to bring their more secular friends to hear you, and you will also be giving believers a set of mini courses in how to handle their own doubts and answer friends' questions about their faith.

Affirm in Order to Challenge Baseline Cultural Narratives

Your preaching must address the common direct objections to Christianity. Yet even more fundamental than addressing these is to engage with the foundational cultural narratives of your time. Unlike with stated objections, people in the culture are barely conscious of these baseline themes. They are things that "everybody knows," premises that seem so self-evident as to be nearly invisible and unquestionable to those who hold them. They are usually expressed in slogans or epigrammatic "truisms" that are spoken to end discussions—they are thought to be beyond argument. "Everyone has the right to their own opinion" or "You have to be yourself" are two of many examples.

These narratives are actually an opportunity for the Christian communicator, since most people, including secular people, have never reflected much on their beliefs, nor sought their justification. When you articulate and set out the deep background beliefs behind the slogans, they almost immediately seem less inevitable. Unless we call these out and contrast them to the great themes and offers of the Bible, both believers and nonbelievers in a culture will be unconsciously influenced by them. We must learn to present the corresponding biblical themes, doctrines, and truths in such a way that the secular culture's narratives are both appreciated and challenged.

We could call this approach "sympathetic accusation" because, particularly in the West, many cultural themes have origins in biblical teaching. This is the case even though each one has become distorted enough through intermarriage with anti-Christian beliefs that it can steer its adherents away—sometimes very far away—from the truth. As Canadian philosopher Charles Taylor says, we need to "criticize these practices from the standpoint of their *own* motivating ideal." Each of the narratives aspires in part to something good, and we must be genuinely appreciative of this. People rightly want to be free; they want justice; they want a truly open and pluralistic society. However, we must show them that only in Christ can these aspirations be rightly fulfilled. "Instead of dismissing this culture altogether, or just endorsing it as it is," Taylor concludes, we ought to show its members "what . . . they subscribe to really involves. This means . . . the work of persuasion."[47]

How do we do this? I will give examples of how to do this in present-day Western secular culture in the next chapter. As a short preview—we must first describe the narratives well, making them "visible" to the listeners. Next we must use the Bible to identify what we can affirm and appreciate about the narrative. Then, using the culture's own respected voices, we must challenge the narrative in several ways. We must show that most of the rest of the world and other cultures do not consider this belief to be self-evident. To act as if "everyone believes this" is therefore ethnocentric. We must also show that the narrative is too simplistic, that it does not account for the complexities of real life, and that it requires leaps of faith as great as or greater than those called for by religion.

Make Gospel Offers That Push on the Culture's Pressure Points

It is not enough only to affirm and then challenge a cultural narrative or belief. "Yes, but no" is only the first two acts of the three-act arc of active contextualization. To complete the process in our preaching we must show at the very point of this particular narrative how Christianity offers far more powerful resources—not only for explaining but also for fulfilling the aspiration or for dealing with the issue. Only in Christ can any cultural plotline have a happy ending; he alone supplies the final "but yes" that consummates the biblical text and reaches people deep in their hearts. For those seeking wisdom, Christ is the true wisdom of God. For those seeking power, he is the true power of God.

The gospel offers many things—forgiveness, community, meaning, contentment, identity, freedom, hope, vocation. Christian communicators must consider how to arrange and articulate these great offers to apply their force frontally at the culture's "pressure points." There are sore spots, as it were, where people who don't believe in Christianity or God feel pinched, like feet in a pair of shoes that are too small, by their view of the world. These are the places where what they profess and say they believe about the world does not fit their intuitions or experiences.[48] Preachers must know those sore spots and press on them with questions, offers, illustrations, and examples that make the tension they feel more acute and the incongruities more troubling.

For example, when preaching on forgiveness, point out the work of sociologists who argue that our modern culture which promotes self-assertion and self-esteem makes forgiveness especially difficult; then show that the gospel gives us the gratitude and humility we need to forgive and be forgiven.[49] When preaching on community turn to research that shows how our contemporary society's commitment to individualism undermines communal ties and social life—then show how the gospel gives us great resources for community.[50] You can pursue similar patterns with many other biblical themes like satisfaction, freedom, hope, and calling.

Call for Gospel Motivation

The question may loom after all of this: How can we spend all this effort engaging with cultural narratives and secular thought and still preach the text and build up the faithful? Aren't we giving too much attention to nonbelievers?

The answer is twofold. It is a mistake to think that faithful believers in our time are not profoundly shaped by the narratives of modernity. We certainly are, and so when you unveil these narratives and interact with them in the ordinary course of preaching the Word, you help them see where they themselves may be more influenced by their society than by the Scripture, and you give them important ways of communicating their faith to others. That is an important way to build up believers.

The key, however, to addressing at the same time both those who believe and those who do not—and even subgroups within cultures—is to go down to the heart level and call for gospel motivation in your preaching. It *is* impossible to address Christians and non-Christians at once if you misunderstand the gospel's versatility and centrality to life. The gospel is not just the means by which people get converted but also the way Christians solve their problems and grow. The typical approach to the gospel is to see it as the "ABCs" of Christian doctrine only, the minimum truth required to be saved, the admissions test, the entry point. Then it is understood that we make progress in the Christian life through the application of other (more advanced) biblical principles. If that were the case, then of course we could not do both evangelism and spiritual formation at the same time. Yet the gospel not only is the way we are saved but also is always the solution to every problem and the way to advance at every stage in the Christian life.

Here's an example from my own ministry. Many Christians in my congregation are Asian and feel quite pressured by parental expectations to achieve and succeed. They often feel they are failing their parents. However, many young Anglo professionals in our church have grown up in a much more individualistic culture and in many ways struggle with anger and bitterness toward parents they feel have let them down and failed them. How might I address this range of motivations in a single sermon? By reminding them that the only parental love you can't lose, and the only parental love you must have, is found in the ultimate, heavenly Father, who secured us through the saving work of Jesus Christ. Even though he was God's Son, he was cast out and lost, so that you could be brought in to the family of God. When you realize that he did that for you, the love of the Father becomes the most precious and real thing to you.

When that happens, if you are bitter because you didn't get your parents' love, you can afford to forgive them, because they haven't impoverished you; you are rich in parental love. And those of you feeling like failures before your parents' expectations can relax, because you have the approval of the only Father whose opinion counts.

When the preacher solves Christians' problems with the gospel—not by calling them to try harder but by pointing them to deeper faith in Christ's salvation—then believers are being edified and nonbelievers are hearing the gospel, all at the same time. This holds true for any subject. If you are calling Christians to be generous with their money, you must address their fears and hard hearts by pointing them to Jesus, who though he was rich became poor, so that through his poverty we might become rich (2 Corinthians 8:9). If you are helping Christians handle unanswered prayer, don't just tell them to "trust the Lord"—which on its own is of limited use to Christians and alien to non-Christians—but also point to the one who had a heartfelt prayer turned down in the garden of Gethsemane, and because he trusted his Father nevertheless, we were saved.

If you solve Christians' problems with the gospel every week, secular people are not only hearing it a little differently each time, and so getting a more comprehensive view of it, but also seeing how faith in Christ actually works and brings about life change. That is crucial for them to see. They are being evangelized very effectively, not superficially, even as Christians are being built up.

FIVE

PREACHING AND THE (LATE) MODERN MIND

The only preaching which is up to date for every time is preaching this eternity, which is opened to us in the Bible alone—the eternal of holy love, grace and redemption, the eternal and immutable morality of saving grace for our indelible sin. . . . Let [the preacher] state the problem . . . power-fully . . . but let him answer it with the final answer Christ left. . . . For He is the answer that they but crave.

—P. T. Forsyth[1]

How can we communicate the gospel of Jesus Christ to our modern culture? One of the first writers to ask that question was P. T. Forsyth, whose classic *Positive Preaching and the Modern Mind* was written in 1907 and yet is remarkably up to date. Forsyth identified a key theme of modernity: that modern people believe "we are our own authority." This is "the popular version [of the

modern mind] with which the preacher has to contend."[2]
By identifying one of the main narratives of modernity
and laying out a way to deconstruct it from within, Forsyth was a pioneer and pathfinder.

As prescient as Forsyth was, things have changed in the
century that has passed since he wrote.[3] Many have labeled
these changes "the postmodern turn." The modern era,
we are told, placed its confidence in reason and science,
while the postmodern age is marked by a loss of the belief
that we can achieve a rational, controllable order or arrive
at certainty of any kind at all. There has been a turn toward experience and openness. This is all true, but it overlooks the fact that underneath the discontinuities with the
modern past there are even stronger continuities.

Perhaps the root idea of modernity, as Forsyth saw, is
the overturning of all authority outside the self. In early
modernity—the seventeenth through the nineteenth
centuries—we were told to lay aside all tradition and religious belief and arrive at truth using our reason alone.
This was an unprecedented move toward individualism,
the idea that each person had within him- or herself the
capability of discovering truth without the aid of ancient
wisdom or divine revelation. In earlier times it had still
been thought that there were moral absolutes and natural laws that had to be followed, but now, it was said, we
could discover them on our own through our individual
powers of exhaustive surveillance.

Since World War II, however, we have moved into a time
in which the whole culture attributes far more importance
and power to the individual self than ever before. No longer
do we think we have the power merely to *discover* moral

reality and truth—we think we have the power to actually *create* it. A famous line in an opinion of the Supreme Court, *Planned Parenthood v. Casey,* captures this principle well: "At the heart of liberty is the right to define one's own concept of existence, of meaning, of the universe, and of the mystery of human life."[4] We now believe that there is no "external cosmic order . . . to which we must conform" but that truth can be "constructed according to the individual's will."[5] We have moved from the ancient understanding that we should "conform the soul to reality" all the way into an age where we "subdue reality to our [soul's] wishes."[6] What we have now is less a reversal of modernity than an intensification of its deepest patterns.[7] So it would be better to talk of our late-modern rather than our postmodern times.

In earlier modern times, religion was still seen as a good thing—or at least a benign one. There was still a general understanding that society should be built upon shared moral norms that people should submit to, and religion was one of the things that helped people live by those moral norms. That has changed. Columbia humanities professor Mark Lilla writes that when Jesus told Nicodemus in John 3 that he had to be "born again," what he "seems to be telling Nicodemus is that he must recognize his own insufficiency—that he will have to turn his back on his autonomous, seemingly happy life and be reborn as a human being who understands his dependency on something greater. . . . That seems a radical challenge to our freedom, and it is."[8] Lilla is assuming the autonomy on which late modernity pins its hopes. In the face of this, religion is now almost the ultimate enemy. That is why for many today religious faith seems so unimaginable as to be crazy.

How then do we preach to the late-modern mind? The key to preaching to a culture, as we have said, is to identify its baseline cultural narratives. To those we now turn.

The Hidden Belief Web of Secularity

The late-modern mind presents itself as something like this. We have come to realize that we don't need God to explain the world we see—science does that job for us. We don't need God or religion to be moral, to love and work for a better world, or to have meaning and fulfillment in life. What we need is to be free to live life as we see fit and to work together to make the world a better and more just place to live. Religion gets in the way of all this—it constrains our freedom to live as we wish and divides us so we can't work together.

Philosopher Charles Taylor calls this the "subtraction story" of secularity. Science and objective reason, it is said, have simply subtracted God from the imagination of modern people and left behind secularity. It operates objectively, without the need for faith and belief; frees us from value judgments, narrow-mindedness, and prejudice; offers moral support for equality, human rights, and the betterment of humankind; and promises a life of personal meaning, freedom, and peace of mind—all based on human resources alone. Taylor doesn't buy this at all. In *A Secular Age* he argues that secular people are not more objective but instead have embraced a new, constructed web of alternate beliefs about the nature of things that are not self-evident to all, are no more empirically provable than any other religious beliefs, require enormous leaps of faith, and are subject to their own array of serious problems and objections.[9]

It is not natural to disbelieve in God. Mark Lilla writes that to most human beings, deep interest in the supernatural, the afterlife, transcendence, and God "comes naturally—it's indifference to them that must be learned."[10] Consider the late-modern view of our humanity itself. Many secular people hold that people are a complex of chemicals without souls, that love itself is just a chemical reaction that helps people pass on their genes, that when loved ones die they simply cease to exist, and that there is no right or wrong outside of what we in our minds choose to feel. The universe is just a cold, immense mechanism and science merely a way to figure out how the giant clock works. "Reason [then] cannot offer us ecstatic fulfillment, a sense of community, or wipe away the tears of those who mourn."[11] This view of the cosmos contradicts many of our deepest intuitions about love, purpose, and the nature of human beings. We are to hold that we are products of an impersonal universe yet be committed to human rights. Taylor and others explain that it took many generations to construct a way for human beings to acclimate to such a counterintuitive way to live.[12]

What is unique about late modernity in history's marketplace of worldviews is this. Nonsecular cultures are overt about their faith, and their members acknowledge the faith nature of their convictions. Many late-modern secular people, however, don't see or grant the leaps of faith they are taking. Their commitments are, in Michel Foucault's terminology, "unthoughts"—beliefs that seem to be not beliefs but unchallengeable, self-evident common sense.[13] These unthoughts achieve currency in the

Christian mind differs from the late-modern mind. It does indeed, and yet we should acknowledge the reality that all Christians living in late-modern times are somewhat shaped by the following narratives. That is not necessarily all bad because, as we will see, the narratives are grounded to a degree in Christian ideas and therefore are partly right. Yet Christian believers in Western societies are generally too influenced by these narratives, and we know why—they are so pervasive, and felt to be so self-evident, that *they are not visible as beliefs to those who hold them*. So here we "make them visible," not only to engage and challenge them in nonbelievers but also to help us as believers avoid being too shaped by them.

The Narratives of Late Modernity

What, then, are the basic cultural narratives or "unthoughts" of the late-modern mind? I will describe five distinct narratives—particular beliefs or story lines about human rationality, history, society, morality, and identity. First, however, I'll sketch where they came from.

In his chapter "The Impersonal Order" Taylor shows that these five late-modern cultural narratives originally grew out of Christianity and its interaction with the classical paganism of antiquity.[17] In response to the Greek philosophers' views of the material world, of history, and of human nature, Christian teachers gave new answers on the basis of the Bible and Christian doctrine. The differences between Christianity and paganism ran along what Taylor called these five "axes."

Before Christianity emerged	After Christianity came to the West
The body and material world are less important and real than the realm of ideas.	The body and material world are good. Improving them is important. Science is possible.
History is cyclical, with no direction.	History is making progress.
Individuals are unimportant. Only the clan and tribe matter.	All individuals are important, have dignity, and deserve our help and respect.
Human choices don't matter; we are fated.	Human choices matter and we are responsible for our actions.
Emotions and feelings should not be explored, only overcome.	Emotions and feelings are good and important. They should be understood and directed.

The basic reason for the shift, according to many scholars, is that before Christianity virtually all cultures had a fundamentally impersonal view of the universe. The Greeks believed that the *logos* behind the universe was a rational, impersonal principle. Eastern cultures believed that all individual personality was a temporary illusion. Christianity, by stark contrast, saw the universe as the loving and creative act of a tripersonal God, who made people for personal relationship with him, as selves that last forever. All the Christian ideas above flowed naturally from the idea that the purpose of all things was "communion" with the personal God.[18]

None of these ideas—the goodness of the material, the progress of history, the dignity of individuals, the significance of choices, and the value of emotions—made any sense in an impersonal universe and therefore they had never arisen. Nietzsche's great critique of modern secular humanism strikes at the irony of this point: Though none of these (basically Christian) moral ideals rationally follows from an impersonal universe, late modernity has inherited them, intensified and absolutized them, and cut them completely loose from any transcendent grounding whatsoever. It has created a moral value matrix out of the fruit of Christian ideas and severed the root. Now all these ideals must be held in the face of what is thought to be a completely impersonal universe, even more impersonal than the ones believed in by ancient societies because it has no supernatural or spiritual aspect to it at all.[19]

The late-modern positions on these five issues comprise the late-modern baseline cultural narratives, or "unthoughts."

1. The rationality narrative. The Greek philosophers saw the material world (including the body) as subordinate, unimportant, and unreal, but Christianity saw them as the good creations of God, with a dependable, objective reality of their own. Many have recognized that this Christian view of a world crafted by a rational, personal being was an important foundation for the development of modern science.[20] Late modernity, however, picked up the Christian view and amplified it to say that the natural world is the *only* reality. It believes that everything has a physical cause and explanation—even love and moral feelings are functions of brain chemistry—and that material prosperity is the only prosperity there is. This view provides the basis of today's powerful consumer and technological culture—which holds that our problems will yield to technological solutions if we throw enough time, money, and effort at discovering them. This utopian narrative is still very powerful in our culture. Objective, detached human reason can solve what ails us. Psychology and medicine will help us adjust and overcome emotional and physical problems—we won't need spiritual resources for that. Sociology will help us create a just society—we won't need God-given divine virtue for that. Technology will figure out solutions to hunger, aging, poverty, and environmental calamity. Men and women can live healthy and just lives quite as well (if not better) without religion as with it, so religion should be kept private.

2. *The history narrative.* The ancients saw history as cyclical and endless, while Christians understood it to be under the control of God, who was moving it purposefully through light and darkness toward a great and irreversible climax. Late modernity picked up on the idea of historical progress (hence the term "progressive") but detached it from any idea of divine control. Now history is seen as automatically making progress in every stage. Today, therefore, we make judgments through what C. S. Lewis called "chronological snobbery," namely "the assumption that whatever has gone out of date is on that account [alone] discredited."[21] Many of our government officials now denounce actions or positions as "having no business in the twenty-first century," as if every chapter of history is by definition better than the one before. Whatever is new is automatically better.

3. The society narrative. The ancients saw the individual as less important than the tribe or clan and never entertained the thought that every individual of any race, class, or status deserved our help and respect simply as a human being. Christianity, however, saw every person to be created in the image of God and therefore possessing an inviolable dignity. Western secularism has gone far beyond that and is radically and increasingly individualistic. The highest purpose of a social order, under this narrative, is not to further the interests of any one group nor to promote any particular values or virtues but rather to set all individuals free to live as they choose without hindrance, regardless of any communal relationships, as long as they don't harm someone else's freedom to live as he wishes. Choice becomes the one sacred value and discrimination the only moral evil.

4. The morality or justice narrative. The ancients believed we were essentially fated. The order behind the universe was inexorable; we could either learn to submit to it stoically and bravely or be dashed upon its rocks. Oedipus was fated to kill his father and marry his mother, and that is what happened to him, despite all his efforts to the contrary. Christianity, by contrast, saw the universe not as an impersonal order but as one made by a personal God, who created human beings as responsible moral agents and who cared how we behaved. Late-modern secularism is intensely moral in many ways. It is more committed to social justice, universal benevolence, and human rights than any civilization has ever been. Yet it insists that in pursuing these aims we do not align with God's moral norms—we determine the norms for ourselves. Our moral ideals are not based on any absolutes in the universe; they are determined by our one else what is right or wrong for them?" "You have to be yourself and not care what anyone else says." "You don't want to be on the wrong side of history."

How, then, should Christian preachers and teachers engage these baseline cultural narratives? Integrity, humility, and love require us to sincerely and appreciatively affirm much of what they contain, since we see their clear origins in Christianity. Yet we must show their dangers and flaws, how they absolutize and essentially deify many good things in the absence of faith in the Author of all things. And we must offer the benefits of the gospel at the points where these narratives fail to deliver.

Engaging the Identity Narrative: The Sovereign Self

Many argue that the most fundamental of the late-modern narratives is that of identity—that we must discover our deepest desires and longings and then do all we can to realize them, regardless of constraint or opposition. Sociologist Robert Bellah has called this narrative "expressive individualism";[23] I will call it the "sovereign self."

We should start by recognizing the great good ushered in by the modern emphasis on the individual. In the past vast numbers of people were locked into a given social status in rigidly hierarchical societies where people had to remain forever on the lower rungs of the social ladder simply because that was seen to be their duty and their place.[24] My grandfather was born in Italy in 1880. He was told that his only options were to become a priest, go into the military, or pursue the family trade. He did not want to give his life to any of those. In response, he emigrated to the United States, coming through Ellis Island into a more individualistic society where he could shape a life that fit his personal aspirations.

Christianity has always seen the importance of the heart and its loves. Augustine's *Confessions* represented an innovation in the history of human thought: a thorough-going examination of inner motivations and desires. Unlike the thinkers of classical antiquity, Christians regarded emotions as something not to be ignored or simply suppressed but instead to be examined and redirected toward God. Much of the modern understanding of the feelings and the self has grown from these Christian roots.[25]

The new late-modern narrative, however, goes beyond merely understanding and directing our own passions to enthroning them. Its essence is captured by the words of the song "Let It Go" in the Disney movie *Frozen*. The song is sung by a character determined no longer to "be the good girl" that her family and society had wanted her to be. Instead she would "let go" and express what she had been holding back inside.[26] There is "no right or wrong, no rules" for her. This is a good example of the expressive individualism Bellah described. Identity is not realized, as in traditional societies, by sublimating our individual desires for the good of our family and people. Instead we become ourselves only by asserting our individual desires against society, by expressing our feelings and fulfilling our dreams regardless of what anyone says.

There are many severe problems with the sovereign self as a philosophy of life. To begin with, it assumes that we know what we want—that our inner desires are coherent and harmonious. Modernity tells you to discover your deepest desires and fulfill them, but our deepest desires often contradict one another. A desire for a stellar career will often be in conflict with the desire for a particular relationship. And our feelings constantly shift. So an identity based on our feelings will be unstable and incoherent.[27]

An even more serious problem is that an identity based on expressing ourselves—without listening to outside dictates—is actually an illusion. A popular exponent of the sovereign self was Gail Sheehy in books like the seminal *Passages* in 1976. She insists that you can become yourself only when you can look inside and express yourself apart from any "external valuations and accreditations."[28] This is patently impossible.

Imagine an Anglo-Saxon warrior in Britain in AD 800. He has two very strong inner impulses and feelings. One is aggression. He loves to smash and kill people when they show him disrespect. Living in a shame-and-honor culture with its warrior ethic, he will identify with that feeling. He will say to himself, *That's me! That's who I am! I will express that.* The other feeling he senses is same-sex attraction. To that he will say, *That's not me. I will control and suppress that impulse.* Now imagine a young man walking around Manhattan today. He has the same two inward impulses, both equally strong, both difficult to control. What will he say? He will look at the aggression and think, *This is not who I want to be,* and will seek deliverance in therapy and anger-management programs. He will look at his sexual desire, however, and conclude, *That is who I am.*

What does this thought experiment show us? Primarily

it reveals that we do not get our identity simply from within. Rather, we receive some interpretive moral grid, lay it down over our various feelings and impulses, and sift them through it. This grid helps us decide which feelings are "me" and should be expressed—and which are not and should not be. So this grid of interpretive beliefs—not an innate, unadulterated expression of our feelings—is what shapes our identity. Despite protests to the contrary, we instinctively know our inner depths are insufficient to guide us. We need some standard or rule from outside of us to help us sort out the warring impulses of our interior life.

And where do our Anglo-Saxon warrior and our modern Manhattan man get their grids? From their cultures, their communities, their heroic stories. They are actually not simply "choosing to be themselves"—they are filtering their feelings, jettisoning some and embracing others. They are choosing to be the selves their cultures tell them they may be. In the end, an identity based independently on your own inner feelings is impossible.

The reality is that we can no more bestow dignity on ourselves than identity. In fact, they go together. In "The Need for Recognition" Charles Taylor quotes Gail Sheehy's book and her counsel that we must not care what others think—but that we must bestow the verdict of significance on ourselves.[29] Taylor argues that this too is an impossibility.[30] You cannot get significance through self-recognition; it must come in great measure from others. In the end, you can't name yourself or bless yourself. You can't ultimately say to yourself, *I don't care that everyone I know thinks I'm a monster. I love myself and that is all that matters.* That would not convince us of our worth, unless we were mentally unsound. We need someone from outside to say we are of great worth, and the greater the worth of the person telling us so, the more powerful that recognition is to our identity formation. So if we try to authenticate and validate ourselves, we place ourselves in an infinite loop of delusion that will lead to either narcissism or self-loathing.

The unshakable need for external affirmation and recognition—along with the current denial of this fact of human nature—puts enormous pressure on the late-modern self. In traditional societies, if you were simply a good son or daughter, husband or wife, father or mother, you were doing all your society required. That could be smothering and confining, but the bar for recognition was not impossibly high. The modern process of identity formation, however, tells you to go out and create a self from scratch. You must identify your dreams, especially the most vivid ones, and fulfill them—or feel like a failure. That prospect crushes those in many segments of our society where money, looks, power, success, sophistication, and romantic love all become not just good things but necessary identity factors.[31]

And here is where Christianity's offer can be recognized as so liberating. In biblical terms we are socially interdependent and worthy beings because we were made in the image of the triune God—the *imago dei*. This means our value is both *inherent* (it comes simply from being human) and *contingent* (it reminds us how dependent we are upon God). It is an identity that is not achieved but received. Likewise in the gospel, in the work of Christ, that identity is baptized into something even greater. It is not achieved through our performance of social roles, or through our fulfilling of religious and moral standards, or through our success and achievement of status. It is the ultimate recognition—the approval of God as he sees us in Jesus Christ. It is to "be found in him, not having a record of my own that comes from my performance and effort, but that which is through faith in Christ—the righteousness that comes from God on the basis of faith" (Philippians 3:9, my paraphrase).

You can preach on the Christian approach to identity from many biblical texts and themes.

The most fundamental way is to draw out the implications of three of the crucial benefits of Christ's salvation—justification as legally righteous, adoption into God's family, and union with Christ, being "in him." Each of these great theological topics has massive implications for our identity as received rather than achieved, and each one challenges yet fulfills late-modern aspirations for identity. For example, a Christian, as it were, arrives at far higher self-esteem by getting much lower self-esteem. Only if we repent and admit we are far worse than we ever imagined can we become justified, adopted, and united with Christ, and therefore far more loved and accepted than we ever hoped. The Christian identity then creates a profound humility even as it bestows an infinite love and sense of worth upon us. In this way Christian identity both critiques yet completes modern desires for an identity.

There are other biblical themes that relate to this narrative as well. God puts his family name on us (Isaiah 43:7; 2 Chronicles 7:14; Matthew 28:19). The question of identity is not "who am I?" but "whose am I?" Since identity always comes from the acclaim and accreditation of someone outside us, who- or whatever that source is holds the title to our heart. We belong to them. We will get their approval only if we perform, and so our self-worth will vacillate wildly depending on how we are doing. We will be slaves. Only if God names us, and we serve him, will we be free from enslavement because he grants us love on the basis of Jesus' performance, not ours. If he names us—if we are his—we can finally rest in our identity as his child.

The modern interest in having a unique identity is also addressed in biblical teaching. The Bible teaches that God gives us our own personal name (Isaiah 62:2; Revelation 2:17), which unfolds through our lives as he shows us the distinct things he has called us to do for him in the world (Ephesians 2:10). There are some deeds that only we can do, some hands that only we can hold, some hurts that only we can heal, because of the unique person he is making us to be. In addition, all the biblical teaching about "putting off the old self" and "putting on the new self" (Ephesians 4:22–24) resonates with modern people in a way that might not be as true in other cultures. The simplistic cultural narrative is that we should simply express our deepest desires. In reality, we know that there are some deep things in our hearts that will thwart us from becoming the true selves we should be. The process of sanctification, of growth into the likeness of Christ, is also, then, the process of becoming the true self God created us to be.

Engaging the Society Narrative: Absolute Negative Freedom

What in the late-modern society narrative can we affirm from the Bible? A good deal. As Taylor argues, the fundamental Protestant doctrine that we are saved by faith alone—not just by church membership, nor by expressing cosmic order through dutiful participation in a social class or caste—meant that every person had to make a conscious and deliberate choice to believe. Therefore the importance in the West of individual freedom and personal choice (as opposed to culturally or tribally defined commitments) grew especially out of Protestant theology.[32]

However, the late-modern intensification of this narrative goes beyond the Bible's once-revolutionary conception of freedom. Freedom of choice without limits has become almost sacred. (Philosophers call this "negative freedom"—freedom *from* constraints—which they contrast with "positive freedom," the freedom *to* pursue some good aim.) Absolute negative freedom becomes the chief moral good, so that "the [only] sin which is not tolerated is intolerance."[33] This poses many problems both philosophical and practical.

One is that this narrative's sacralizing of personal choice erodes community and fragments society. Remember Taylor's quote that "to have any kind of livable society some choices have to be restricted, some authorities have to be respected, and some individual responsibility has to be assumed."[34] Sociologists have documented the growing civic and political disengagement of younger adults.[35] The more people are invested in the late-modern understanding of the sovereign self and in its younger brother, absolute negative freedom, the less they feel a loyal part of the greater body politic.

Another problem with this freedom narrative is the unworkability of what has been called the "harm principle." Taylor summarizes it as "no one has a right to interfere with me for my own good, but only to prevent harm to others."[36] The harm principle seems to make freedom of choice into a self-correcting absolute. In this view, a society does not need to lay down any moral principles at all—it can be "value free." Everyone is free to live in any way she chooses, as long as it doesn't curtail someone else's freedom. However, the Achilles' heel of this theory is the assumption that we all know what "harm" is or that it can be defined without recourse to deep beliefs about right and wrong.

One person says that it harms no one for a man to consume pornography privately in his own home. Others counter, however, that pornography will shape how he talks and acts with others, especially with women. Beneath these different conclusions about harm lie different understandings of the right and wrong way for individuals to relate to community. In other words, any decision about what harms others is rooted in specific views of human nature, happiness, and right and wrong—each of which is a matter of faith. So even if we all agree that freedom should be curtailed if it harms people, since we can't agree on what harm is, the principle is useless in practice.

The freedom narrative also thins out the pursuit of meaning in life. Harvard scientist Stephen Jay Gould once was asked "What is the meaning of life?" and responded,

"We are here because one odd group of fishes had a peculiar fin anatomy that could transform into legs for terrestrial creatures. . . . We may yearn for a 'higher' answer—but none exists. This explanation, though superficially troubling, is ultimately liberating. . . . We must construct these answers for ourselves."[37] If there is no God and we have not been put here for some purpose, then there is no "discovered" meaning in life—no purpose that is *there*, existing before us, for which we were built, and with which we are obligated to align ourselves. This absence frees us, Gould says, to decide what things are meaningful for us. We may find that building homes or painting pictures or raising a family gives us purpose. So those are the meanings we choose for ourselves.

Philosopher Thomas Nagel, however, says that created meanings are less *rational* in principle than discovered meanings. Most of us would agree, Nagel argues, that we only have meaning if we feel we are making a difference, that what we do matters. But, he argues, if there is no God and you write a "great work of literature that continues to be read thousands of years from now," nevertheless "eventually the solar system will cool or the universe will wind down and collapse and all trace of your effort will vanish. . . . If you think about the whole thing . . . it wouldn't matter if you had never existed."[38] In other words, if there is no God or anything beyond this material world, then whether you've been good or cruel or murderous will make no final difference. No one will be around to remember anything. That means you can live a meaningful life only if you are *careful to not think out* the implications of your view of the universe. That's not a very rational way to live. Religious believers, however, draw greater meaning in life the *more* they think out the implications of their view of the universe. In their view, right actions now count literally forever.

Luc Ferry, another atheist, makes a related argument—that these created meanings are not just less rational but more selfish. We may decide to give our lives to serve the medical needs of poor people; but why, within a secular framework, is that significant? The proper answer according to the freedom narrative is that we are doing it not because we are obligated to do it but because we freely choose to find this activity significant for us. However, Ferry argues, that means we are actually helping sick people for *our* sake, not theirs. We are doing it because it makes us feel worthy and significant.[39] Self-created meanings come terribly close to simply living for oneself.

The final reason that this narrative does not ultimately work is that the modern idea of freedom itself is an illusion. Remember that the modern concept of freedom is absolute negative freedom, the absence of any constraint. The fewer limits or boundaries I have on my desires, choices, and actions, it would seem that the freer I am. However, this does not do justice to the complexity of the dimensions of freedom and the realities of incarnate and communal life.

A sixty-year-old man may have a strong desire to eat fatty foods, but if he regularly exercises his freedom to give in to that desire, his life will be curtailed in some way. He must choose to lose a lesser freedom (to eat these foods he enjoys) for a greater freedom (health and long life). If you want the freedoms that come with being a great musician—the ability to move people with your music and to make a good living for your family—you will have to give up your freedom to do other things in order to practice eight hours a day for years. Freedom is not, then, simply the absence of restrictions, but rather consists of finding the right, liberating restrictions. Put another way, we must actively take tactical freedom losses in order to receive strategic freedom gains. You grow only as you lose some lower kinds of freedom to gain higher kinds. So there is no absolute negative freedom.

The ultimate proof that the freedom narrative does not work—is love. No love relationship can grow unless each person sacrifices some freedom in order to serve the other, yet these restrictions, if accepted mutually, lead to the various liberations of mind and heart that only love can bring. Most people will say they feel most like "themselves" when they are truly loved and loving another—but that requires the surrender of complete self-determining freedom. As we have seen, the late-modern freedom narrative undermines human community in general. But it is especially corrosive of marriage. A late-modern person, controlled by both the freedom and identity narratives, wants a spouse who "accepts me as I am" and neither demands that you change nor requires you to sacrifice any of your own substantial desires, interests, and dreams. This kind of marriage is a fiction—it doesn't exist.[40]

This is the main way to engage the freedom narrative in your preaching. Show that at the human level love does not grow or even survive alongside the self-absorption of the late-modern understanding of freedom and choice. This will come out as you preach on love relationships in places like 1 Corinthians 13 and Colossians 3. And if we experience this at the human level, it will be more so in our relationship with God. In marriage, we might say, we lose our independence in order to gain new freedom, so if we give ourselves to our God, our True Love, we will become more free than we can imagine. We will be free from fears, insecurity, and shame. We will be free to forgive, to love others, to face suffering in a way we could not before.

The very theme of the kingdom of God, when preached properly and fully, directly challenges yet fulfills the late-modern desire for freedom. We can see in daily life how the disciplines—freedom "losses" like practice and dieting—lead to other kinds of freedom gains. We also see how when employees submit to the leadership of a great CEO or team members to that of a great coach, everyone on the team realizes his potential and everyone thrives. Submitting to the right rules and the right leader can bring all sorts of great freedoms. If we see this to be the case, then how much more liberating will it be to submit to the true king of our souls? When the Bible talks about God's returning to judge the earth, even the created order is liberated from decay (Psalm 96:11–13; Romans 8:20–23).

All of this supports the famous claim by Jesus that knowing him sets you "free" (John 8:31–36), meaning "The ultimate bondage is . . . rebellion against the God who has made us. The despotic master is not Caesar, but shameful self-centeredness, an evil and enslaving devotion to created things at the expense of worship of the Creator."[41] Passages on freedom from sin in Romans 6–8 and Galatians 4–5 can cover the same themes, as can teaching in James 1–2 on how freedom comes from obedience to

be the most problematic of all of late modernity's baseline narratives. It does not have the moral sources or foundations in which to ground its ideals. This leads to three major difficulties.

The first is the problem of moral *motivation. Why* should we care about the poor and do justice? Christians' motivation for the alleviation of poverty, inequality, and suffering is *agape,* the extension of the radical love we have received from God and offer to others. The moral source of Christian benevolence lies there. What, however, is the motivation for secular benevolence?

One common motivation, says Luc Ferry, is "a feeling of satisfaction and superiority when we contemplate . . . illiberal societies."[46] In other words, we base our moral self-worth on being more liberal in our values than others. This not only is a selfish and fragile motivation but also makes our philanthropy "vulnerable to the shifting fashion of media attention and the various modes of feel-good hype."[47] Because we are doing good for others in order to bolster our sense of worth and superiority, our benevolence easily turns to contempt when faced with the disappointments of real-life human service and helping.[48] By contrast, Christian *agape* motivates benevolence through humbling us, showing us that we are loved sinners, so that spending ourselves for others is not to be based on a sense of superiority but on having been shown our own lack.

Another possible secular motivation for benevolence is not in the register of paternalistic charity but is simply anger over injustice. "We fight against injustices that cry out . . . for vengeance. We are moved by a flaming indignation against these: racism, oppression, sexism . . ."[49] This, of course, requires the demonization of some people in order to help others. Any philosopher in the tradition of Nietzsche will have a field day exposing this motivational engine. Nietzsche insisted that benevolence and social-justice activism in modern society is largely powered by hatred and contempt for others.[50]

The second problem is that of moral *obligation*. A slogan that expresses this cultural narrative is "God isn't necessary for you to live a moral life that includes working for the good of all." Two recent books arguing this case are *Good Without God: What a Billion Nonreligious People Do Believe* and *Atheist Mind, Humanist Heart*.[51] They strongly assert that atheists and secular people can be, and are, highly moral—people who live with integrity, help others sacrificially, and live lives of love and justice.

When secular people claim that moral behavior is possible without God, they are certainly right. From a Christian point of view, someone who does not believe in God is capable of loving her neighbor and doing many things that God's law requires. This is true not just in theory but in everyday experience—we all know irreligious people who are very generous, moral, and loving. From a secular point of view, moral feelings may come from many sources. They may be the product of my evolutionary biology or a function of my cultural background, or they may simply be the product of my distinct temperament and choices.

Yet while there are certainly moral feelings and moral behavior without God, how can there be moral *obligation*? On what basis can you say: "You ought not to do X, even if you feel like it"? In self-authorizing morality, you may feel X is wrong and refrain from it but, then, for example, on what basis can you tell governments in some other hemisphere that they need to give women equal rights? Why should your feelings and inward moral intuitions about a given issue overrule theirs? We all have inner moral evaluators. What happens when yours differs from those of people in other cultures? Or from those of neighbors or siblings? The only way to get from moral feelings to moral obligation is to appeal to some moral source or norm of right and wrong outside of both cultures or individuals that validates, invalidates, or revises their competing internal moral feelings. Every culture until ours has had such a mechanism, a way to appeal to people to live as they ought, because every culture until ours had some consensus on a moral source outside the self. But the late-modern system does not.

At this point, secularity is defenseless against Friedrich Nietzsche's main message. He argued that the world was full of destruction, chaos, suffering, exploitation, and brutality. Now, if this natural world is all there is, then there cannot be anything "above" this life, no standard by which we judge some parts of life good and right and other parts bad and wrong. There cannot be anything higher than this life, which means there are no moral ideals that can bring anything in this life under judgment and correction. Nietzsche argued tirelessly that secular humanism was simply too cowardly to recognize the implications of its secular view of the universe. If all our moral beliefs are really just the product of evolutionary biology, then while some things may *feel* wrong, they aren't actually truly wrong. We may feel that it is wrong to starve the poor in order to accrue wealth and power for yourself, but there's no way to say that it actually *is* wrong to do so—even for people who don't feel it to be wrong. You might say it is impractical (although many people would contest that) but not that it is inherently wrong in and of itself. Without a moral source outside the self, the only way to resolve these inevitable conflicts among moral ideals, according to Nietzsche, is to exercise power. It means to say to others, this is right simply because I say so and I have the power to force you to comply.

This leads us to the last serious problem of the modern moral narrative. Mari Ruti, a professor at the University of Toronto, concisely expresses the deep tension in secular moral thought. She writes: "Although I believe that values are socially constructed rather than God given . . . I do not believe that gender inequality is any more defensible than racial inequality, despite repeated efforts to pass it off as culture-specific 'custom' rather than an instance of injustice."[52] Notice that she says that all moral values are socially constructed by human beings, not grounded in God. Yet she is saying that her (Western) culture's understanding of equality *must* be followed by everyone. She gives no reason for it—she just asserts it.

This is a signal example of what Taylor calls the "extraordinary inarticulacy . . . of modern culture," which comes from the view that "moral positions are not in any way grounded in reason or the nature of things but are ultimately just adopted by each of us because we find ourselves drawn to them."[53] If you are proposing a position that some behavior is wrong and should be stopped, there is no way to justify or even have a conversation about it with someone who disagrees. All you can do is shout the other person down.

In his article "Conditions of an Unforced Consensus on Human Rights" Taylor shows this Western dilemma. Since secular modernity believes that its values have not come from Christianity but are simply the deliverances of objective reason, it cannot appeal to any other society to adopt human rights without first telling them they are regressive and need to jettison Hinduism or Islam or Buddhism or their tribal religion and become secular. Taylor writes, "An obstacle in the path to . . . mutual understanding comes from the inability of many Westerners to see their culture as one among many."[54] Western secularists insist that their view of equal rights is simply self-evident to any rational person, but non-Western cultures do not agree. The secular ideals of universal benevolence and rights are "far from self-evident."[55] Because truly secular people can't admit the source of their main moral values in their Christian history, it makes them imperialistic.

One of the main ways that a Christian preacher can engage this narrative is to identify the Christian moral understandings from which so many of the secular moral ideals have come. For instance, the biblical emphasis on care for the poor and marginalized is pervasive. The wisdom literature of Job, the Psalms, and Proverbs constantly talks about living justly, disadvantaging yourself for others, caring for the rights and needs of the poor.[56] Prophets such as Amos show that God holds all nations responsible to standards of social justice (Amos 1:1–2:3). Genesis 1 and 9 show that every human being is made in the image of God. It is always good to show how the rhetoric and action of the civil rights movement were heavily based on the concept of every person's being made in the *imago dei*.[57] At every juncture, however, it is crucial to show how this Christian moral idea flows from and fits in with the nature of God and of the world he has made. In this way you are doing Nietzsche's work(!) of reminding people where all these ideas came from and how they make sense only in a personal universe, created by God.

It is also important for the Christian preacher to show his listeners that the experience of *agape*—the unmerited grace of God in Christ—inevitably leads to a just and compassionate life. James 2:14–17 tells us that you cannot have been truly saved by grace through faith and yet have no compassion for the poor. James 1:9–11 tells us that wealthier people will be humbled out of arrogance by the gospel and poorer believers affirmed out of self-loathing by the gospel. The gospel is socially and motivationally transformative.[58] Secular listeners will be startled to hear this, and often will recognize that by comparison their own motivations for doing justice are relatively thinner and more negative.

One more important biblical theme that engages this narrative is the teaching on the Resurrection. Christians not only have a deeper motivation for doing justice but also a stronger hope. In the end of time, according to the Bible, we will not live forever in a nonmaterial realm, but this world will be renewed; we will get resurrected bodies; and all injustice, suffering, disease, and death will be wiped away. As we noted earlier in the writings of Miroslav Volf, a belief in Judgment Day, when all wrongs will be put right, can be a powerful incentive for eschewing violence and vengeance and living at peace now, in the knowledge that ultimately justice will be done on the earth.

Finally, there will be some times in which, as we noted in the last chapter, there can be a place to use apologetic sidebars. At those times you can briefly but clearly point out that secular accounts of justice have no moral sources outside the self; that, if there is no God, Nietzsche is right and there is no good reason to tell someone else they should live unselfishly.

Engaging the History and Rationality Narratives: Science as the Secular Hope

The history and rationality narratives are linked in some ways. There is still a powerful narrative in our culture that science and technology will bring us a better future. Silicon Valley is the epicenter of this kind of thinking, with many "prophetic voices" talking about a future in which the problems of aging, disease, poverty, and inequality are all solved or transformed.

However, there is a strong reaction in our culture against this kind of hopefulness. A remarkable number of recent films depict a dystopian future in which civilization is largely decimated. There is a widespread pessimism that technology is destroying our privacy, dehumanizing us, and making us vulnerable to future terrorism and to exploitation on an unprecedented scale.

The Christian answer to this is that the modern idea of historical progress has been too optimistic about both history and human nature. It assumes that the new is always better, which common sense tells us is not the case. History is completely inadequate as a moral guide. The Nazis were sure that they were on "the right side of history," as were the communists. Indeed, in the first half of the twentieth century it may be that most of the Western intelligentsia thought socialism or communism was "the way history was going." On the other hand, many in our present time are too pessimistic. They have rejected the idea of inexorable progress for the opposite idea that history is, in Macbeth's words, "a tale / Told by an idiot, full of sound and fury, / Signifying nothing."

The Christian answer to the overly optimistic or overly pessimistic late-modern view of history is to point to the Resurrection. Christianity is at the same time *both* far more pessimistic about history and the human race than any other worldview *and* far more optimistic about the material world's future than any other worldview. Our future is a renewed material universe with resurrected bodies—but of course resurrection always comes after death and destruction. There is no reason for Christians to believe that every decade and stage in history will be better than the stage before, but we believe that all is being brought infallibly to a glorious end.

So the Christian view of history avoids the utopianism and overoptimism of modernity but also the pessimism and ennui of dystopianism.

The rationality narrative should be engaged in a similar way by Christian preachers. The belief that everything has a scientific explanation and that every problem has a technological solution is hopelessly naive, and in the past such utopian dreams have always been disappointed. Nearly every place that Christian preachers or teachers come to a passage on the depth and complexity of evil—corporate and systemic evil ("the world"), internal evil ("the flesh"), or supernatural evil ("the devil")—they should take the opportunity to engage this cultural narrative, showing that psychology and sociology and technology alone will never deal with all that is wrong with us, nor can reason alone discern the meaning of things.[59]

Wisdom is another biblical theme for Christian preachers to introduce at this point. Job 28 is a magnificent poem that engages the modern technology narrative head-on. It celebrates the human technology of mining and metal craft but then asks, "But where can wisdom be found? . . . It cannot be found in the land of the living" (Job 28:12–13). Knowledge is not the same thing as wisdom. Knowledge is data and facts, but wisdom is knowing what is the good and right way to live. Wisdom is a kind of understanding about the nature of reality that science cannot possibly give you. The wisdom literature of the Bible provides Christian preachers with many rich themes and passages for thoughtfully engaging the late-modern faith in science.

Don't Be Daunted

The idea of "taking on" the baseline cultural narratives of late-modern secularism may sound intimidating. Those who promote the wisdom of this age, who disdain Christians as being "on the wrong side of history," seem supremely confident. However, Christian preachers and teachers should not be abashed or threatened. Try to remember that you are at odds with a system of beliefs far more than you are at war with a group of people. Contemporary people are the victims of the late-modern mind far more than they are its perpetrators. Seen in this light the Christian gospel is more of a prison break than a battle.

Paul cries out, "Where is the wise person? Where is the teacher of the law? Where is the philosopher of this age? Has not God made foolish the wisdom of the world?" (1 Corinthians 1:20). In his day the cross and the atonement made no sense within any of the reigning worldviews. The philosophers treated Paul with disdain on Mars Hill in Acts 17, and hardly anyone believed his message. But answer the question. Where now is the wisdom of that world? It's over, gone. No one believes those worldviews anymore. Such will always be the case. The philosophies of the world will come and go, rise and fall, but the wisdom we preach—the Word of God—will still be here.

SIX

PREACHING CHRIST TO THE HEART

For where your treasure is, there your heart will be also.

—Matthew 6:21

The Importance of the Heart

It is fundamental to preach biblically, and to preach to cultural narratives, but these are not enough. Unless the truth is not only clear but also *real* to listeners, then people will still fail to obey it. Preaching cannot simply be accurate and sound. It must capture the listeners' interest and imaginations; it must be compelling and penetrate to their hearts. It is possible to merely assert and confront and feel we have been very "valiant for truth," but if you are dry or tedious, people will not repent and believe the right doctrine you present. We must preach so that, as in the first sermon on Pentecost, hearers are "cut to the heart" (Acts 2:37).

Modern readers of the Bible will almost always misunderstand the term "heart." They run it through their

[*157*]

contemporary grid and conclude that it means the emotions. But the Bible often talks about *thinking* with the heart or *acting* with the heart, which does not fit with our modern concept at all. Nor did the ancient Greeks have a biblical understanding of the heart. Virtue was to them a matter of spirit over body, and that meant reason and will triumphing over unruly bodily passions. Today, we continue to pit the mind and the feelings against each other, but we have radically reversed the ancient order. Emotions are the "true" self, not the rational thoughts.

The biblical view of the heart is "none of the above." In the Bible the heart is the seat of the mind, will, *and* emotions, all together. Genesis 6:5 says about the human race that "every inclination of the thoughts of the human heart was only evil all the time." One commentator writes: "*Leb* 'heart' is the center of the human personality in biblical anthropology, where will and thought originate; it is not merely the source of emotions as in English."[1]

Of course, the heart does produce emotions, such as joy in Deuteronomy 28:47, sorrow in 1 Samuel 1:8, anger in 2 Kings 6:11, anxiety in John 14:1, and love in 1 Peter 1:22. However, the heart also thinks (Proverbs 23:7; Daniel 2:30; Acts 8:22) and wills, making plans and decisions (Proverbs 16:1, 16:9). It is the source of all our words (Matthew 12:33–34; Romans 10:9). Most fundamentally, the heart puts its trust in things (Proverbs 3:5). Biblically, then, the heart's "loves" mean much more than emotional affection. What the heart most loves is what it most trusts and commits itself to (Proverbs 23:26).

The Bible knows no dualism between "head" and "heart." Genesis 6:5 says that the heart's thoughts, acts, and feelings arise out of the heart's "inclination." Matthew 6:21 is a key verse here: "For where your treasure is, there your heart will be also." One commentator on this verse says that the heart is therefore the "center of a person's attention and commitment."[2] Whatever we most value and cherish in our hearts "subtly but infallibly controls the whole person's direction and values."[3]

No wonder the Bible says that God ignores outward matters and looks supremely at the heart (1 Samuel 16:7; 1 Corinthians 4:5; Jeremiah 17:10). No wonder the prophets said obedience to the law and even praising God with the mouth meant nothing if you didn't have a heart for God (Isaiah 29:13; Jeremiah 12:2). That is why they said that the goal is not mere compliance with the law but heart change, having the law "written on the heart" through spiritual rebirth (Jeremiah 31:33).

Whatever captures the heart's trust and love also controls the feelings and behavior. What the heart most wants the mind finds reasonable, the emotions find valuable, and the will finds doable. It is all-important, then, that preaching move the heart to stop trusting and loving other things more than God. What makes people into what they are is the order of their loves—what they love most, more, less, and least. That is more fundamental to who you are than even the beliefs to which you mentally subscribe. Your loves show what you actually believe in, not what you say you do. People, therefore, change not by merely changing their thinking but by changing what they love most. Such a shift requires nothing *less* than changing your thinking, but it entails much more.

So the goal of the sermon cannot be merely to make

the truth clear and understandable to the mind, but must also be to make it gripping and real to the heart. Change happens not just by giving the mind new arguments but also by feeding the imagination new beauties.[4]

Preaching and the "Affections"

One of Jonathan Edwards's most enduring contributions is the religious psychology found in his *The Religious Affections*. Instead of accepting the typical Western division of "will" versus "emotions" (and thus the division of the soul into three parts—thinking, feeling, willing), Edwards posits only two faculties. The first is the "understanding," which is our ability to perceive and judge the nature of things. The second he calls the "inclination" to either like or dislike, to love or reject, what we perceive. Edwards calls this inclination the "will" when it is involved in action and the "heart" when it senses the beauty of what is being perceived by the understanding. The "affections" are what Edwards calls the most "vigorous and sensible exercises" of this faculty. In the Bible they are called "the fruit of the Spirit"—love, joy, zeal, thankfulness, humility.

These affections are, of course, filled with emotions, but they are not identical to them. Affections are the inclination of the whole person when sensing the beauty and excellence of some object. When our heart inclines toward the object in love, it propels us to acquire and protect it. Emotions can be caused by a variety of physical and psychological stimuli and often are fleeting, resulting in little or no changed behavior. Affections, however, are more enduring and involve both the convictions of the mind and changes in action and life. Edwards refused to suppose an opposition between the understanding and the affections. In other words, if a person said, "I know God cares for me, but I am still paralyzed by fear," Edwards would reply, "Then that means you don't truly *know* that God cares for you. If you did, then the affection of confidence and hope would be rising within you."[5]

We are now in a position to see how important these concepts of the heart and the affections are for preachers. If Edwards is right, then there is no ultimate opposition between "head" and "heart." We must not assume, for example, that if our people are materialistic they need only to be exhorted to give more. That would be to act solely on the will. That will produce temporary guilt—which might help the offering that day—but it will not bring about a long-term change to the people's life patterns because their hearts have not been reached. Nor should we simply tell stories of people's lives being changed through acts of generosity. That will act directly on the emotions, creating pity or inspiration and (perhaps) leading to a passing impulse to give some money to a cause but, again, the emotion will fade and there will be no long-term change.[6]

If people are materialistic and ungenerous, it means they have not truly understood how Jesus, though rich, became poor for them. It means they have not understood what it means that in Christ we have all riches and treasures. They may subscribe to this as a doctrine, but the affections of their hearts are clinging to material things, finding them more excellent and beautiful than Jesus himself. They may have a superficial intellectual grasp of Jesus' spiritual wealth, but they do not truly grasp it. Thus in preaching we must re-present Christ in the particular way that he replaces material things in their affections. This does not simply take rational argument and doctrinal teaching—though it does indeed include those; it also requires the presentation of the *beauty* of Christ as the one who gave up his riches for us.

Edwards believed that at the root of every heart's affections is "excellency"—that which is appreciated and rested in for its own sake.[7] Edwards defined a nominal Christian as one who finds Christ useful (to get those things the heart found "excellent" or beautiful), while a true Christian is one who finds Christ beautiful for who he is in himself. In perhaps his best discussion of this dynamic, Edwards says:

> There is a twofold knowledge of good of which God has made the mind of man capable. The first, that which is merely notional . . . and the other is, that which consists in the sense of the heart, as when the heart is sensible of pleasure and delight in the presence of the idea of it. In the former is exercised merely . . . the understanding, in distinction from the . . . *disposition* of the soul. Thus there is a difference between having an *opinion* that God is holy and gracious, and having a *sense* of the loveliness and beauty of that holiness and grace. There is a difference between having a rational judgment that honey is sweet and having a sense of its sweetness. A man may have the former that

knows not how honey tastes; but a man cannot
have the latter unless he has an idea of the taste
of honey in his mind.[8]

Many years ago, in my first pastorate, I met with a
teenage girl in our congregation. She was about sixteen
at the time, and she was discouraged and becoming depressed. I tried to encourage her, but there was a revela-
tory moment when she said, "Yes, I know Jesus loves me,
he saved me, he's going to take me to heaven—but what
good is it when no boy at school will even look at you?"

She said she "knew" all these truths about being a
Christian, but they were of no comfort to her. The attention (or the lack of it) of a cute boy at school was far more
consoling, energizing, and foundational for her joy and
self-worth than the love of Christ. Of course this was a
perfectly normal response for a teenage girl. Nevertheless
it was revealing of how our hearts work. Edwards would
say that she had the opinion that Jesus loved her, but she
didn't really *know* it. Christ's love was an abstract concept while the love of these others was real to her heart.
That was the reality that had captured her imagination.

In Ephesians 3, Paul prays for his readers and asks that
"Christ may dwell in your hearts through faith . . . and . . .
know this love that surpasses knowledge . . . [and] be
filled [with] . . . all the fullness of God" (Ephesians 3:17–
19). He is talking to Christians, and elsewhere says that if
you are a Christian, Christ is already dwelling in your
heart, that you already know about God's love and have
come to fullness of life. Why isn't this a contradiction?
Because what is objectively true of Christians isn't

automatically subjectively true. That's why he prays that they would be strengthened by the Spirit in their "inner being"—their hearts—to "grasp" the love of God (Ephesians 3:18). Paul is praying for the very thing that you're supposed to be aiming at every time you preach. There are many things Christians know but they don't really know. They know these things in part, but they haven't grasped them with the heart and had the imagination so captured that it has changed them thoroughly from the inside out.

This understanding of the affections profoundly affected Edwards's own preaching. In one of his sermons (on Genesis 19:14) he argues: "The reason why men no more regard warnings of future punishment, is because it don't seem real to them."[9] This is, essentially, the main spiritual problem and the main purpose of preaching. Though people may have a superficial understanding of a truth, God's truth is not spiritually real to them. If it were, their affections would be engaged and their actions accordingly changed. In the case of materialism, the security of money is more spiritually real to people than the security of God's loving and wise providence. We don't live as we should—not because we simply know what to do but fail to do it but rather because what we think we know is not truly real to our hearts.

Changing Them in Their Seats

How can we go about making truth real to hearts as we preach?

According to Edwards, there are two ways that "the

prejudices of [human] nature" can be overcome in order to have divine truth become real. "There are these two things in realizing a thing, or necessary in order to things seeming real to us: [1] believing the truth of it, and [2] having a sensible idea or apprehension of it."[10] The first aspect requires us to be convincing and persuasive. The biblical concept of the heart includes the mind and the thinking. Preaching must not simply tell stories or try to work on the emotions. It must be what D. M. Lloyd-Jones often called "logic on fire." We must reason and argue strenuously, but that is only the first step. Then, second, we must help listeners form "sensible ideas" as we preach, a deep preoccupation of Edwards's. As we will see below, this means to bring abstract concepts into connection with the listeners' actual sense experience in order to engage their imaginations and not just their intellects.

The implications of this shift for preaching are great. If it is true that we are the product of our loves, so that what we most love is what shapes us, then preaching to the heart can change people right in their seats. A sermon that just informs the mind can give people things to do after they go home, but a sermon that moves the heart from loving career or acclaim or one's own independence to loving God and his Son changes listeners on the spot.

It has been said that D. M. Lloyd-Jones wasn't always excited by people taking notes on his sermons. He felt that that was more appropriate to a lecture. The job of the preacher, he believed, was to make the knowledge *live*. Lloyd-Jones and Edwards believed preaching should aim to make an impression on the listener, and that impression is more important than "information takeaways." I would

to heart-manipulating ones) reveal their own affections without really trying to. What is required is that as you speak it becomes evident in all sorts of ways that you yourself have been humbled, wounded, healed, comforted, and exalted by the truths you are presenting, and that they have genuine power in your life.

The alternatives to affectionate preaching are three: You could preach with flat affect. It's obvious your own heart isn't engaged. You are just getting through your material—perhaps nervously, perhaps perfunctorily, but in either case there's no note of joy, awe, or love. A second possibility is mere excitability. You psych yourself up, "putting on your game face" like an athlete before a big game. Here we could say your emotions are more engaged, but your motive is excitement to be "on stage" and a desire to perform well, to be dynamic and focused and poised so that people think well of you. The third and worst alternative is to consciously put on an act, to adopt a grand, spiritual-sounding tone and style. Any intentional effort to appear joyful or humbled or filled with love will be obvious to all and will have the opposite effect on hearers of the one you are seeking.

People can tell the difference. Teachers and preachers of the Bible are often so focused on preparing and presenting their content that they don't realize the degree to which people are not just listening to what they are saying but are also looking at who they are as they preach. People are examining motives without even being aware that they are doing it. They can sniff out if you are more concerned about looking good or sounding authoritative than you are about honoring God and loving them.[11]

Even people who are moved on one level by your performance will subconsciously resist it at another level, the same way many feel cynical at sentimental advertising even as they fight back tears.

So if you *try* to be affectionate as you preach, you will be putting on an act. You have to simply *be* affectionate as you preach. Your heart needs to be soft toward God and toward the people. How can affectionate preaching come naturally? I think there are basically two things needed.

One is to know your material so well that you aren't absorbed in trying to remember the next point. If your material is not at your fingertips, you will expend energy just to remember it, or else you will be simply reading from your notes. You won't be personally tasting and enjoying the spiritual food you are presenting to people—you will be too distracted by the mechanics to do so. You need to have confidence in your material and to know it cold or you won't be able to preach from the heart. For me, this kind of confidence and mastery comes not only from sufficient time in preparation but also from going over the entire message in my mind three or four or more times before getting up to speak. Whatever your preparation approach, people can tell the difference between your trying to remember what you should say and your just saying it.

The other necessity for preaching affectionately is a deep, rich, private prayer life. If your heart isn't regularly engaged in praise and repentance, if you aren't constantly astonished at God's grace in your solitude, there's no way it can happen in public. You won't touch hearts because your own heart isn't touched.[12] What happens when you preach should be something like what happens when you pray. In prayer you don't just say, "I confess my sins," but you experience sorrow. You don't just say, "You are great, Lord," but you experience joy and awe. You don't just say, "Thank you," but you experience love and gratitude. You get a sense of the heart of the holiness, the glory, and the love of God. If this happens to you in prayer, then it can happen to you in preaching. Of course, if nothing like that happens to you in prayer, then it can't happen when you preach.

Imaginatively

To engage the heart is also to engage the imagination, and the imagination is more affected by images than by propositions. Here we are talking about what are usually termed "sermon illustrations." Over the past generation preachers have recaptured the importance of story. Common sense tells us that stories capture interest and stick in the mind, and so preachers are often advised to lace their sermons liberally with narratives. However, we should think a bit more deeply about why these are so effective. An illustration is anything that connects an abstract proposition with the memory of an experience in the sensory world. Here again we can learn much from Jonathan Edwards. Edwards knew well the preacher's great challenge—that people could subscribe to many propositions of Christian doctrine with their minds that did not influence how they actually lived their lives. Why?

He argued that human beings are body-bound creatures, and because of our fallenness, spiritual realities are simply not as real to us as sense experiences—things we actually see, hear, touch, smell, and taste. Objects that we can experience through our senses are real to us—they are memorable and make impressions that last. While people can agree that "abstractions are true . . . Only images [things they have experienced with the senses] seem real."[13]

Most people know that they are going to die, but it is only if they have an actual physical brush with death that their mortality becomes real to them and influences how they live their daily lives. For Edwards preaching is an "attempt to construct a verbal correlative to such a brush."[14] A sermon is a place to wake people up to realities they have assented to with the mind but have not grasped with the heart. The way to do it is to connect a spiritual truth to the memory of a vivid sense experience the listener has had, "representing the spiritual in concrete language implying an almost physical tangibility."[15]

When Edwards says in "Sinners in the Hands of an Angry God" that "all your righteousness would have no . . . influence to uphold you and keep you out of hell," he offers an abstract proposition. It is one of the cardinal doctrines of Protestant Christianity that you cannot be saved by your good works. However, he does not leave it there. Having stated the proposition he then adds, "[Any more] than a spider's web would have to stop a falling rock."[16] What did he just do? All of us have seen with our eyes and felt with our hands how flimsy a spiderweb is. We know that if a rock falls on it, it doesn't give and bounce on the web but cuts right through it almost as if it wasn't there at all. This is a sense experience we have all had or can easily imagine.

By bringing the proposition together with that experience Edwards gives the listeners a remembered sense impression, not merely a rational thought. At the statement of the proposition we may nod in assent, but the image of the rock and spiderweb is more striking. Edwards is bringing two fields of discourse together: the logical and the experiential. Your good deeds are like a spiderweb, and your sin is like a rock. The image grabs the imagination and illumines the mind at the same time. It helps you understand the doctrine in a new way. It shows *how impossible* it is to earn our way to heaven. The futility of it grabs you and settles the truth more deeply in your heart.

It is also possible for an illustration to construct a sense experience you have not had out of experiences that you have had. In 2 Samuel 11 David has an affair with Bathsheba, then arranges for her husband, Uriah, to be killed in battle, and finally marries her. Though doubtless having some pangs of conscience, David justifies his behavior to himself in some way. It is likely he does so through self-pity, telling himself that the burdens of his office and the sacrifices they require mean that he deserves this indulgence. In the next chapter Nathan the prophet comes to challenge the king over his sin. But he does not do so immediately. He begins with an illustration and adds the ethical proposition only at the end.

Nathan tells the king a story of a rich man with many possessions and a poor man who owned only one little lamb. "He raised it, and it grew up with him and his children. It shared his food, drank from his cup and even slept in his arms. It was like a daughter to him" (2 Samuel 12:3). Nathan then explains that the rich man throws a feast but refuses to supply his guests with food out of his own abundant herds of livestock and instead steals the poor man's lamb and prepares it as the main course for the dinner. What should be done about this rich man, Nathan asks the king? David "burn[s] with anger" at this story and says that the man who did this should die, "because he did such a thing and had no pity." Nathan immediately responds, "You are the man!" (2 Samuel 12:5–7).

David is filled with rationalizations that blind him to the injustice in his own life story. So Nathan takes him (through his imagination) into someone else's life experience, where he can see injustice in its true colors and be outraged. Finally Nathan connects the proposition about injustice to the sense experience David has just had. He says, essentially, "You see the outrageous injustice in this story? Well, what you have done is just like that." The feeling of horror David had in the imagined sensory experience now becomes attached to his own behavior. He is cut to the heart—and repents.

Let me give you another example from the Bible of how illustrations work. God says to Cain, "Sin is crouching at your door; it desires to have you, but you must rule over it" (Genesis 4:7). The Hebrew word used here connotes an animal that is coiled low, perhaps off in the shadows, ready to spring, rend, and kill. God does not simply say, "Sin will get you into trouble, Cain." That would have been an abstraction. By likening sin to a dangerous, predatory animal, God is not only gripping the heart but also conveying a great deal of information about sin—much more than a mere proposition could do. God is saying, for example, that if Cain sins, his own sin will eventually consume him. Sin is the suicidal action of the human soul against itself. The image also implies that sin isn't simply a passing action; sinful actions create a dark reality in your life that stays with you. Sin creates bad habits; it creates distorted affections. These things control you, and you start to lose control of yourself. You're surrendering to something that wants to kill you.

Here, then, is God himself using an illustration—bringing two fields of discourse together, connecting an abstract proposition and sense experience in order to make the truth real to the heart and influential in the whole life. God says sin is like a panther or a leopard ready to spring on you, and you think, *Wow,* because it illuminates the mind even as it engages the emotions.

The essence of a good illustration, then, is to evoke a remembered sense experience and bring it into connection with a principle. That makes the truth real both by helping listeners better understand it and by inclining their hearts more to love it.

It is crucial to keep in mind that this is the goal and purpose of an illustration. Often speakers tell stories that don't do this. Sometimes stories stir the emotions but don't illumine the mind. Make sure that your stories are true illustrations, in that they do both.

One kind of illustration is the analogy. An analogy is mainly concerned with clarifying the truth for the mind, but with a sensory wallop.[17] You might say, "Christ's justification is like being in a law court, where you are about to be sentenced to pay a financial penalty you cannot pay, but then the judge himself says that *he* will personally pay the entire sum." This helps people grasp the concept of justice being satisfied by someone else's taking the burden of the debt. It also shows you that the one who condemns you is also the one who saves you. All this sheds light on the mind, but it engages the heart because it is easy to construct how you would feel in that situation from memories of similar experiences. The listener not only gets information about the doctrine of justification but also feels the relief and joy of a defendant who is being cleared of all charges. Analogies can also be used to convince. If you say, "If someone stole your car and totaled it, you wouldn't want the judge to say, 'Let's just forgive and forget.' You'd want justice. So why should God overlook all the things we've done that are wrong?" Here you are saying, "If you agree to A, why not to B, since B proceeds from A?"

A somewhat different kind of story is the example. Unlike the analogy, which likens two things to each other, the example gives hearers a more digestible "slice" of what you are talking about. Examples can be used to clarify the practical implications of what you are saying. If you are encouraging honesty, you could list common examples of not telling the truth. If you are encouraging generosity, you could give examples of specific generous acts and deeds.

The danger with example stories is that they can be ways to simply work on the emotions and not also to illumine the understanding. You could, for example, tell the touching story of "a poor family, huddled around a fire, whose last ounce of food has just been eaten, but then in comes . . ." Stories can work directly on our fears, our guilt feelings, or our prejudices.

The simplest and most overlooked form of illustration is the brief word picture—using just a phrase or even a word to link an abstraction to concrete sense experience. Rather than just saying, "This means freedom," you might say, "This is God's trumpet call of freedom." Rather than just "The Resurrection proves your sins are forgiven," say, "The Resurrection has stamped 'paid in full' across history." This fills your speaking with sense appeal, evoking pictures, sounds, and even smells and tastes in the listeners. Edwards himself did not tell that many stories. He worked much more with word pictures and extended metaphors, in which God was likened to the sun or his love to a fountain or a fire.

Wondrously

If we are going to preach to the heart, we need also to evoke wonder. Tolkien's famous essay "On Fairy Stories" argues that there are indelible, deep longings in the human heart that realistic fiction cannot satisfy. Fantasy fiction—fairy tales and science fiction and similar literature—depict characters who

- get outside of time altogether;
- escape death;
- hold communion with nonhuman beings;
- find a perfect love from which they never part;
- triumph finally over evil.

Of course readers and viewers know that fairy stories are fiction, but when the story is well told and these things are depicted vividly, it provides a peculiar kind of comfort and satisfaction. What we call "fantasy fiction" is massively popular and continues to be consumed by audiences numbering in the billions. The enduring appeal of stories that represent these conditions is unquestionable. But why? As a Christian, Tolkien believed that these stories resonate so deeply because they bear witness to an underlying reality.

Even if we do not intellectually believe that there is a God or life after death, our hearts (in the Christian view) sense somehow that these things characterize life as it was and should be and eventually will be again. We are so deeply interested in these stories because we have intuitions of the creation/fall/redemption/restoration plotline of the Bible. Even if we repress the knowledge of that plotline intellectually, we can't not know it imaginatively, and our hearts are stirred by any stories that evoke it.

The English word "gospel" comes from the Middle English word *Godspell* which derives from two Old English words: *good* and *spell* (story). In Old English "to tell a story" was "to cast a spell." Stories capture the heart and imagination and give us deep joy. The Gospel of Jesus Christ is *the Goodspell*. It is *the* story that all other joy-bringing, spell-casting, heart-shaping stories only point to. What's special about this one? It is the one story that satisfies all these longings—yet is historically *true*.

If Jesus Christ was really raised from the dead—if he is really the Son of God and you believe in him—all those things that you long for most desperately are real and will come true. We will escape time and death. We will know love without parting, we will even communicate with nonhuman beings, and we will see evil defeated forever. In fairy stories, especially the best and most well-told ones, we get a temporary reprieve from a life in which our deepest desires are all violently rebuffed. However, if the gospel is true—and it is—all those longings will be fulfilled.

Christian preachers and teachers must preach in such a way as to show people the profound good news of that truth. They must point these things out at every turn and have the sense of wonder appropriate to such astonishing claims. Even those of us who believe in the gospel cannot take it in. We do not preach with the tears of joy we should so often have. As we preach we should always open ourselves to let the wonder sink in. In that way we may, like Moses, preach with radiant countenance (Exodus 34:29–35; 2 Corinthians 3:13).

Memorably

Some modern expository preachers spend so much time on understanding and explaining the text that they have little time to think about two other things: practical application and striking, memorable, fluent use of language. One thing that makes a sermon memorable is its insight. Rather than telling the listeners things they already know in terms they know, a memorable address is filled with fresh, insightful ways of conveying concepts—concepts the listeners may already know at one level but find new and interesting. "I never heard it put that way before" is what they say or think afterward. How will you do this? I'm afraid the answer is volume. If you read a couple of books on a subject or text, you will have only one or two great, surprising insights. If you read a dozen books, you'll have a lot more. I don't see any shortcut here. Insightful preaching comes from depth of research and reading and experimentation.

A second thing that makes preaching memorable is orality. Many preachers tend to speak (at least during sermons and talks) as they write. However, oral communication differs from written communication. Oral presentations must not contain as many ideas—they should be more repetitious because listeners cannot stop and pause over words as readers can. They usually do not need to have as many steps in an argument in order to feel compelling. Oral communicators must use simpler vocabulary. They can effectively begin sentences with "but" or "and." They can use contractions without sounding too colloquial.

Culturally appropriate rhetoric also makes sermons memorable. It is easy for preachers to fall either into a stiff, written style of speaking or a distractingly conversational style. Neither will be as memorable as communication marked by rhetorical devices that fit your culture. There are scores of these, and they are better picked up and "caught" (from other speakers) than "taught" and deliberately used.[18] They include assonance, alliteration, and other kinds of parallelism. "He doesn't just talk the talk—he walks the walk." And there are a large number of less obvious but striking ways to use language memorably and movingly. However, different cultures and different generations will respond to various devices in different ways. Some will seem too florid or too highbrow or too stuffy or too manipulative.

Christocentrically
I won't belabor this point, because earlier chapters addressed at length the importance of moving beyond moralistic exhortation to gospel-motivated change, of not preaching just biblical principles but preaching Christ, the one to whom all the principles and narratives point. Here I need only say that preaching Christ is not only the ultimate way to fully understand a text, nor just the best way to simultaneously reach those who don't believe and those who

do, but also the way to be sure that your address moves beyond a dry lecture and becomes a real proclamation of the truth that reaches the heart.

We have said that sermons may be nothing but good lectures until we "get to Jesus," at which point they often move from being a Sunday-school lesson to being a sermon. This is because, so often, a biblical theme such as kingdom or covenant or atonement for sin is essentially an abstract proposition until we show how that theme climaxes in Christ. When we lift up Jesus as the King, as both Lord and servant of the covenant, and as our atoning sacrifice—suddenly these abstractions become heart-gripping realities. Jesus himself, then, is the ultimate way to move from informing the mind to capturing the heart, from merely giving out information to showing everyone a Beauty.

Resist ending your sermon with "live like this," and rather end with some form of "You can't live like this. Oh, but there's one who did! And through faith with him you can begin to live like this too." The change in the room will be palpable as the sermon moves from primarily being about them to being about Jesus. They will have shifted from learning to worship.

Practically

Finally, preaching to the heart is to preach practically. In the prologue to this book we said that the preacher has two great responsibilities: to the truth of the text and to the lives of the hearers. The first requires *exposition* in a broad sense (which we addressed in part one); the second requires *application* in a broad sense (which we have addressed earlier in part two). I want to close part two by offering suggestions for application in the narrow sense. This is where you seek to help your listeners apply a gospel dynamic, aligned with the text of your sermon, to make practical changes in their lives.

1. Diversify Your Conversation Partners

When we study the Bible, we tend to extract answers to the questions that we implicitly or explicitly have on our hearts as we read it. Because we are limited human beings in a particular time and place, for us there is no such thing as a "view from nowhere." We have certain questions, problems, and issues on our minds, and as we read the Bible, we mainly "hear" what it teaches us about those questions, problems, and issues.

Therefore, one of the natural dynamics in preaching is that you will tend to preach to the people you listen to most during the week. Why? The people you are most engaged with fill your mind with their questions, which become added to your own grid as you read the Bible, and you will learn to notice biblical truth that speaks to them. Thus your sermons will tend to aim at the people whom you already have most on your heart. Over time they will be the people who are most interested in and satisfied by your preaching. They will come and bring others like themselves. Because they are coming, you will meet more of them, speak more to them, and thus (semiconsciously) tailor your sermons more to them. The more you listen to them, the more they pull the sermon in their direction; the more you aim the sermon to them, the more they come to church; and so on.

This pattern can be a vicious or a virtuous cycle. At the very worst, evangelical preachers read and engage only other evangelical preachers and writers. They read, speak to, and engage online almost exclusively with those thinkers who support their own views. Then their sermons are really helpful only to other students, practitioners, and devotees of their particular theological or political stripe. It is not, as is often thought, that some sermons born from this pattern are too academic and thus lack application. Rather, the preacher is applying the text to the questions of the people he most understands: other academics.

Most preachers read and engage other Christians. That's better, but then their sermons are really helpful only to other Christians, who may love the messages and feel they are being "fed" but know instinctively that they cannot bring non-Christian friends to church. They never think, *I wish my non-Christian neighbor could be here to hear this.*

There is no abstract, academic way to preach relevant, applicatory sermons. Application will naturally arise from your conversation partners. If you spend most of your time reading instead of with people, you will apply the Bible text to the authors of the books you read (which is fairly unhelpful). If you spend most of your time in Christian meetings or in the evangelical subculture, your sermons will apply the Bible text to the needs of evangelicals (which is far more helpful but still incomplete). The only way beyond this limitation is to deliberately diversify your people context.

How? First, vary what you read across the political spectrum. You might read the *New Yorker* (liberal), the *Nation* (very politically liberal), the *Weekly Standard* (very politically conservative), and the *Atlantic* and the *New Republic* (liberal but eclectic). Read the *New York Times* as well as the *Wall Street Journal*. Also read book reviews in *Books and Culture* (more conservative) and the *New York Review of Books* (more liberal). Reviewing periodicals will help you stay on top of thought trends.

You also need to vary whom you talk to. Pastors find this difficult, because we're busy, and because most people won't be themselves with us. Nevertheless, through being very careful with your appointment schedule and through being creative with your community and neighborhood involvement, you can spend time with people from a variety of spiritual conditions and traditions.

2. Diversify Whom You Picture as You Prepare

When you read the text and write the sermon, think specifically of individuals you know with various spiritual conditions (non-Christian, weak/new Christian, strong Christian), with various besetting sins (pride, lust, worry, greed, prejudice, resentment, self-consciousness, depression, fear, guilt), and in various circumstances (loneliness, persecution, weariness, grief, sickness, failure, indecision, confusion, physical handicap, old age, disillusionment, boredom). Now, *remembering specific faces,* look at the biblical truth you are applying and ask: *How would this text apply to this or that person?* Imagine yourself personally counseling the person with the text. This sounds arduous, but it can become second nature. The effect of this exercise is to be sure that your application is specific, practical, and personal. It will also make you a better pastoral counselor.

A simpler version of this is to ask yourself: *What does this text say to the groups represented by the "four soils" of the Mark 4 parable?* The four groups are conscious skeptics and rejecters of the faith; nominal Christians whose commitment is shallow; Christians who are divided in their loyalties and upside down in their priorities; and mature, committed Christians.[19] You can also make longer lists to prompt your own thinking.[20]

3. Weave Application Throughout the Sermon

The traditional Puritan sermon consisted of "doctrine," in which the text was studied and the doctrinal propositions laid out, and then "application," in which the doctrine's implications for practical life were drawn out. In general, that is still the best order. You lay out what the text means and then bring it home to the heart, calling for a changed life.

However, preachers should not follow this model too rigidly. You don't need to wait to the very end of a sermon for application—it can and usually should run throughout, because you should state every biblical principle in somewhat practical terms. Also, you may touch briefly on some subjects to which you will not return later in the message, so short application is warranted at that time.

Still, as the sermon progresses, you should move to more direct and specific application. As the sermon winds to a close, it is appropriate for you to collect and recap the applications and then drive them home by moving at least one step deeper in specificity. Push yourself to be as vivid and specific as possible without referring to individual people. Here is an example from one of my own sermons on integrity and honesty.

> There are political lies. "I would love to go, but I'll be out of town that day," when you won't be. "I think your writing is a little too sophisticated for your readers," when it's actually just terrible. Then there are Watergate lies: "The little people won't understand." There are business lies. Don't say publicly, "We're for equality," when privately you make unreasonable demands on your employees, so that everybody knows you really don't care about equality. Don't take friends to company box seats when you all know that you should be bringing only clients there. Don't say publicly everything is fine, when all your employees know things aren't. Don't put in a big number of orders right before the end of the quarter, because even though you know they'll all be canceled, it'll look good in the figures for the quarter.

Remember this, however. While you can and should spend much time doing application in the final stages of the sermon, it is usually best at the very end to stress not "This is what you must do" but rather "Here's the one who did everything for you, so that you could know God," that is, Jesus himself.[21]

4. Use Variety

Ask direct questions. The best preachers speak to each type of listener very personally. You can do this by posing direct questions to the audience, inquiries that call for a response in the heart. Ask, "How many of you *know* that this past week you twisted the truth or omitted part of the truth in order to look good?" and follow it with a pause. This is far more personal and attention riveting than a mere statement like "Many people twist the truth or tell half-truths to reach their own ends." Talk to the people; ask direct questions. Be ready for the occasional person who really will answer you back! But the goal is to give people the space to answer in their minds/hearts— in effect, carrying on a dialogue with you.

Provide tests for self-examination. Do not underestimate our human ability to avoid conviction of sin. Every heart has scores of time-tested subterfuges and excuses by which it can somehow rationalize away any direct confrontation with its own wickedness. If you are preparing well, you will have been convicted of many of these for yourself in the week before the sermon. As you preach, these are the kinds of thoughts going on in the minds of the listeners:

> *Well, that's easy to say—you don't have my husband!*
> *I suppose that may be true of others, but not of me.*

I sure wish Sally were here to hear this—she really needs that.

Therefore, it is important to provide brief tests for your listeners. For example:

Perhaps you agree with me that pride is bad and humility is good, but you think, *But I don't have much of a problem with pride.* Well, look at yourself. Are you too shy to tell others about your faith? Are you too self-conscious to tell people the truth? What is that but a kind of pride, a fear of looking bad?

Use a balance of the many forms of application. Application includes, at least, (a) warning and admonishing, (b) encouraging and renewing, (c) comforting and soothing, and (d) urging, pleading, and "stirring up." Most preachers have a dangerous tendency to specialize in just one of these as a manifestation of their temperament or personality. Some are temperamentally gentle and reserved, others are lighthearted and optimistic, and still others are serious and intense. These temperaments can distort our application of the biblical truth so that we are always majoring in one kind of application and exhortation. But over the long haul that hampers our persuasiveness. People get used to the same tone or tenor of voice. It is far more effective when a speaker can move from sweetness and sunshine to clouds and thunder! Let the biblical text control you, not your temperament. Learn to communicate "loud" truth as loud; "hard" truth as hard; and "sweet" truth as sweet.

5. Be Emotionally Aware

Don't pass by the "pliable" moment. Occasionally there comes a point in a sermon when it is evident that the audience's attention is riveted and they are having a heightened communal experience of the truth. Often you can sense that people are coming under conviction. One sign is an absence of fidgeting, foot shuffling, and throat clearing. The audience gets more silent and still. This is a "pliable" or teachable moment. Don't let it go past! Don't be so tied to your outline or notes that you fail to take time to drive home the truth directly and specifically. Perhaps you could pause and look people in the eye as they process what you have just given them.

Be affectionate as well as forceful. Be sure, when you deal very specifically with people's behavior and thoughts, that you combine an evident love for them with your straight talk about sin. Be both warm and forceful when dealing with personal questions—never scolding, never even disappointed. If you ridicule a listener for a question he or she may have just posed inwardly, you will make yourself appear haughty and unapproachable (and maybe you are!).

PART THREE

In Demonstration of the Spirit and of Power

SEVEN

PREACHING AND THE SPIRIT

My message and my preaching were not with wise and persuasive words, but with a demonstration of the Spirit's power, so that your faith might not rest on human wisdom, but on God's power.

—1 Corinthians 2:4–5

We have said that your listeners will be convinced by your message only if they are convinced by you as a person. There is no escaping this. People do not simply experience your words, arguments, and appeals as disembodied messages; they are always sensing and evaluating the source. If they don't know you, they are (usually unconsciously) gathering evidence to determine whether they like you, can relate to you, and respect you. They're noticing whether you're a happy or dour person, whether you are poised or nervous, whether you seem kind or hard or smug. They are looking for love, humility, conviction, joy, and power—for some integrity and congruence between what you are saying and who you are. Audiences are able to sense what kind of energy—or lack thereof—lies behind the speaking. They may see insecurity, the desire to impress, a lack of conviction, or self-righteousness—any of which closes their minds and hearts to the words.

To be sure, your listeners are responding to your skills, preparation, character, and conviction in a general sense. And these are critical elements of any good communication, including good preaching and teaching. But for the act of preaching in particular, there's something even more central to persuasion: your listeners' sense of the Holy Spirit working in and through you. How can we invite the Holy Spirit's work into our preaching?

The Spirit and the Preacher

It has been reported that when George Whitefield was first approached with the idea of publishing his sermons, he agreed, but noted, "You'll never be able to put down the thunder and lightning on the page."[1]

Remember from the prologue that an older Christian minister once said Whitefield often produced great preaching without always delivering a good sermon (in the sense of its craft and structure). This man was referring not to Whitefield's oratorical prowess but to how the Spirit attended his preaching. In Colossians 1:24–29 we read about this.[2]

> [This is] the commission God gave me to present to you the word of God in its fullness. . . . He is the one we proclaim, admonishing and teaching everyone with all wisdom,

so that we may present everyone fully mature in Christ. To this end I strenuously contend with all the energy Christ so powerfully works in me (Colossians 1:25–29).

Paul's commission encapsulates the two great tasks of preaching we have been exploring in this book: preaching the whole Word of God and preaching to the heart. But Paul's description of his preaching does not stop there. He speaks of an intense, churning spiritual power within him that generates a fierce internal yearning as he preaches: "To this end I strenuously contend with all the energy Christ so powerfully works in me." For Paul preaching is no detached, clinical exercise, and it is even more than a satisfying climax to a creative endeavor. He says that he literally *agonizes* as he speaks. The same Greek term Paul uses here, *energia*, will be used just a few verses later to describe God's power in raising Jesus from the dead.[3] Those who heard Paul must have been impressed that the gospel truth he was proclaiming was already operating as a deep power in Paul's own life. He did not merely reason and engage but moved people to life change—"everyone fully mature in Christ"[4]—through who he was as he spoke, not just through what he said.

What was it about Whitefield and Paul that invited the Holy Spirit to work through them like this?

First, it was *what they did*—they didn't just talk about Christ but lifted him up, showed him to be glorious, and expressed their own wonder and joy as they did so. Earlier we looked at 1 Corinthians 2:4, which spoke of a "demonstration of the Spirit's power." Anthony Thiselton writes that, as becomes clear in the passage immediately following (1 Corinthians 2:16–3:4), the role of the Spirit is to be "self-effacing," pointing away from himself to the beauty of Christ (cf. John 16:12–15).[5] When preachers do this as well—when instead of merely giving information or showing their learning they lift up Christ and show people his loveliness—then they are aligning themselves with the Spirit and they can expect him to accompany their message.

Second, it was *who they were*—their spiritual grace and character. Often it is said that great preachers are so because they have strong gifts of public speaking and preaching. That is true, but for the "demonstration of the Spirit and of power" it is our spiritual *fruit*—love, joy, patience, humility, and kindness—that is more important than talents and abilities. Gifts are things we *do*, but spiritual fruit or graces are things we *are*.

Gifts and talents can operate when the speaker is spiritually immature or even when the preacher's heart is far from God. If you have a gift of teaching, for example, the classroom situation draws out your gift, and you may be very effective. But that can happen in the absence of a strong walk with God. Jonathan Edwards, in a sermon on 1 Corinthians 13, says:

> Many bad men have had these gifts [for preaching and ministry]. Many will say at the last day, "Lord, Lord, have we not prophesied in thy name? and in thy name cast out devils? and in thy name done many wonderful works?" [Matthew 7:21]. Such as these, who have had . . . gifts of the Spirit, but no special and saving

[work] of the Spirit. . . . They are excellent things, but . . . not properly any quality of the heart and nature of the man, as true grace and holiness are. . . . Extraordinary gifts of the Spirit are, as it were, precious jewels, which a man carries about him. But true grace in the heart is, as it were, the preciousness of the heart, by which . . . the soul itself becomes a precious jewel. . . . The Spirit of God may produce effects on many things to which he does not communicate himself. So the Spirit of God moved on the face of the waters, but not so as to impart himself to the waters. But when the Spirit by his ordinary influences bestows saving grace, he therein imparts himself to the soul. . . . Yea, grace is as it were the holy nature of the Spirit of God imparted to the soul."[6]

This distinction between "gift operations" and "grace operations" or fruit is a vital one. Gifts will usually be mistaken for spiritual maturity, not just by the audience but even by the speaker. If you find people attending eagerly to your addresses, you will take this as evidence that God is pleased with your heart and your level of intimacy with him—when he may not be at all. If anything, we Christians living today are in greater danger of this misperception than at any other time in history, for our era has been called the "age of technique." No civilized society has put more emphasis on results, skills, and charisma—or less emphasis on character, reflection, and depth. This is a major reason why so many of the most successful ministers have a moral failure or lapse. Their prodigious gifts have masked the lack of grace operations at work in their lives.

The dynamic works in reverse as well. Strong spiritual character, grace operations, can make up for modest gifts. A Christian minister has three basic roles or functions— preaching, pastoring/counseling, and leading. No one is equally gifted in all three areas, and yet we must do them all. The greatest factor in the long-term effectiveness of a Christian minister is how (or whether) the gift-deficient areas in his skill set are mitigated by the strong grace operations in his character. The leadership literature advises us to know our weaknesses, our gift-deficient areas. It usually tells us to surround ourselves with a team of people with complementary gifts, and that is certainly wise if you can do it. But even if you can, that is not sufficient, for your gift-deficient areas will undermine you unless there is compensatory godliness. What do I mean?

You may not have strong public-speaking gifts, but if you are godly, your wisdom and love and courage will make you an interesting preacher. You may not have strong pastoral or counseling gifts (e.g., you may be very shy or introverted), but if you are godly, your wisdom and love and courage will enable you to comfort and guide people. You may not have strong leadership gifts (e.g., you may be disorganized or cautious by nature), but if you are godly, your wisdom and love and courage will mean that people will respect and follow you.

The grace operations that produce godly character are primary because they can make up for certain shortcomings in gifts, and also because there is such enormous pressure in the Christian ministry toward hypocrisy. Church or ministry leadership means telling people every day, "God is so wonderful!" This is not the sort of thing you have to do in most other walks of life. But in the ministry you are daily pointing people in one way or another to God to show his worth and beauty.

Often your heart will not be in a condition to say such a thing with full commitment and integrity. You then have two choices. Either you have to watch your heart far more closely, warming it up continually so you can preach to people what you are practicing; or you have to learn to put on a ministerial air and become something on the outside that you are not on the inside. The statesman Abraham Kuyper somewhere said that Phariseeism (spiritual hypocrisy) is like a shadow—deepest and sharpest closest to the light. I continually observe that ministry amplifies people's spiritual character. It makes them far better or far worse Christians than they would have been otherwise, but it will not leave anyone where he was!

Combining Warmth and Force

Deep godly character, or spiritual maturity, combines qualities that cannot be united in the natural man apart from the transforming power of the Holy Spirit. This is the theme of Jonathan Edwards's masterful discourse, "The Excellency of Jesus Christ."[7] In it, Edwards claims that there is a striking and "admirable conjunction of diverse excellencies in Jesus Christ." He shows how Jesus combines infinite majesty and glory with the lowest humility and meekness; infinite justice with boundless grace; absolute sovereignty and dominion with perfect submission and obedience; transcendent self-sufficiency with utter trust and reliance upon the Father. He is the Lamb and the Lion of God, proclaims Edwards. Approach him as the Lamb of God, and he will become a Lion *for* you, defending you. But reject him as the Lamb of God, and he will become a lion against you. "Kiss the Son, lest he be angry, and ye perish from the way" (Psalm 2:12, King James Version).

It is no coincidence that in Western literature and thought the ideal hero has always been depicted as gracious and kind, yet bold and strong. In Sir Thomas Malory's ancient history of King Arthur, Sir Ector says of Launcelot, "Thou wert the meekest man that ever ate in hall among ladies; and thou wert the sternest knight to thy mortal foe that ever put spear in the rest."[8] C. S. Lewis, an expert in medieval literature, explains that this was an expression of the Christian ideal of heroism applied to knighthood.

> The important thing about this ideal is, of course, the double demand it makes on human nature. The knight is a man of blood and iron, a man familiar with the sight of smashed faces and the ragged stumps of lopped-off limbs; he is also a demure, almost maidenlike, guest in hall, a gentle, modest, unobtrusive man. He is not a compromise or happy mean between ferocity and meekness; he is fierce to the nth and meek to the nth. . . . What is the

relevance of this ideal to the modern world? It is terribly relevant. . . . The Middle Ages fixed on the one hope of the world. It may or may not be possible to produce by the thousand men who combine the two sides of Launce-lot's character. But if it is not possible, then all talk of any lasting happiness or dignity in human society is pure moonshine.[9]

Lewis shows in his essay that it is not normally possible for human nature to combine these two sides. He knew that only as the Holy Spirit reproduces the excellency of Christ can this human ideal be realized—the man of humility and power, of justice and grace, of authority and compassion.

What does this have to do with preaching? Everything. It is the secret of the power of all the great preachers. People could sense in them the startling and striking union of love, humility, and gentleness with power, authority, and courage. The sermons and biographies of Spurgeon, Whitefield, and M'Cheyne reveal this character. There was a compassion, even a weakness and vulnerability, about them. They were transparent, willing to talk about their own frailty, able to show their concern and love and even anxiety for their people. Yet in the pulpit they thundered away with towering authority as well.

No better example of this can be found than the apostle Paul. His impact on the Thessalonians, for example, flowed out of his character. Read 1 Thessalonians 2, in which Paul recounts his ministry among them. First there was intensity and courage born of urgency. Paul "appeals" (verse 3) to the Thessalonians, and he "dared to tell you his gospel in the face of strong opposition" (verse 2). We sense a kind of solemnity and nobility that command respect yet are humble, not pompous or cold. "We were not looking for praise from people, not from you or anyone else" (verse 6). "We worked night and day in order not to be a burden to anyone while we preached the gospel of God to you" (verse 9). In Paul we see honesty and plainness of speech ("You know we never used flattery, nor did we put on a mask to cover up greed") (verse 5) and affection ("Instead, we were like young children among you. Just as a nursing mother cares for her children, so we cared for you. Because we loved you so much, we were delighted to share with you not only the gospel of God but our lives as well") (verses 7–8).

When a preacher has this same loving boldness, his preaching will be accompanied by power. This beautiful Christian marriage of character traits can be neither hidden nor faked. In summary, a good preacher will combine warmth and force. Without the help of the Holy Spirit, I believe all of us tend naturally toward being mainly warm and gentle or mainly forceful and authoritative in the pulpit. We must recognize our imbalance and seek the Lord for growth into the fullness of his holy character.

The Test of the Third Text

One way to think about preaching is through the framework of three "texts"—the biblical *text,* the listeners' *context,* and the *subtext* of your own heart. Most of this book has dealt with the text (preaching the Word) and the context (preaching to the heart and the culture). As we've seen in this chapter, your gifts alone can lead you a long way toward creating sermons that deal properly with the Word and understand the heart of the listener. But one excellent test of your spiritual maturity—of the presence of the Holy Spirit in your preaching—is to examine the subtext of your preaching.

The subtext is the message under your message. It is the real, intended meaning (conscious or unconscious) of a message, which is deeper than the surface meanings of the words. For example, the statement "No, I'm just fine" may have the subtext of "I have no concerns; please proceed with what you are doing," or it may mean "I have a concern but I don't want to have to say it directly." Your tone of voice, facial expression, posture, and gestures will do a lot of work to signal your real goal to the audience, and that goal can hijack the communication regardless of your stated message.[10] The following subtexts are not the only ones that appear in preaching, but they are the most typical.

A Subtext of Reinforcement

One kind of subtext is "Aren't we great?" This is ritual and stylized communication, which is used to reinforce boundaries and contribute to a sense of security and belonging. It is ritual in the sense that its main goal is to furnish a sense of self-reinforcement to a group. When reinforcement is the subtext of preaching, the real message is "We are gathered here with people of like mind to share this presentation with each other as a symbol of our common commitment to each other, to God, and to this organization. We are the kind of people who believe these kinds of things and live in this kind of way."[11] Of course, it is a good goal to give a community a sense of identity and belonging. But if that becomes the main goal, the true subtext, it will destroy the sermon's ability to change lives. It will turn us not into Christlike but into smug people.

This communication is stylized in that real information transfer is not asked for or offered. The most common example of stylized communication in our culture is the interchange "How are you?" and "I'm fine." Ordinarily that is not meant to be a real exchange of information. Rather, the subtext is "I'm friendly to you and you are friendly to me." When a doctor asks the same question in a hospital, however, it is not stylized—real information is requested and given. If, in a greeting situation, the receiver gives a long inventory of physical condition, he has probably misunderstood the sender!

Many churches are committed to this reinforcement subtext, which functions as a kind of *gatekeeping*. These churches do not want to be challenged or convicted or stretched. They may feel they are "standing up for the truth"; but as they are addressing insiders who already believe, there is scarcely anyone being engaged, let alone confronted, with that truth. The motive and focus of such communication is to build up and protect insiders from those outside the boundary. The main skill needed to operate in this subtext is a mastery of the tribal dialect.

A Subtext of Performance

A second kind of subtext is "Aren't I great?" The speaker is seeking to exhibit his or her skills and promote the products of the church. The message is "Don't you think I'm a great preacher, and don't you think this is a great church? Don't you want to come back, bring friends, and give money?" The performance goal is "Look at me; listen to me. See how worthy I am of your respect." The problem here is that every communicator *does* need to establish credibility with an audience, but if this becomes the main goal, it destroys the sermon's ability to change lives. Self-conscious preachers draw attention to themselves, not to Christ. At some level the audience members realize that the speaker is not really concerned about them. He or she is concerned with delivering the message well and getting on their good side.

This subtext does rely on real teaching and information transmission, as the goal is to get across a body of information that the hearers do not have. However, the purpose of the teaching is mainly to win people over to the organization or the church as an institution.

This performance subtext is fundamentally a form of *selling*. This kind of communication is more directed to newcomers and outsiders—but the motive is still, indirectly, the benefit of the insiders (to grow their church). The communicator needs far more rhetorical skills for arousing and keeping interest than in the first kind of communication.

A Subtext of Training

A third kind of subtext is "Isn't this truth great?" The goal is to increase the knowledge of the receivers, so that they can live in a desired way. The subtext is "news you can use." Like the performance subtext, this relies heavily on real information transfer—though its aim is less selfish.

Many churches are committed to this training or *teaching* subtext. People in these churches want to be shown new things they have not seen before. They would like to be inspired, but they consider that less central. They want to be fed "solid food." The focus of such communication is still completely on insiders (for non-Christians can't be changed until they believe). The skills needed here are research and communication abilities.

A Subtext of Worship

A last kind of subtext is "Isn't Christ great?" This is the most complex and complete of all, and it takes the most skill. It aims beyond information, beyond capturing the imagination, and even beyond behavior change to the goal of changing what our heart most sets its affections on. The message: "Look at how Christ is so much grander and more wonderful than you thought! Don't you see that all your problems stem from failing to see this?"

I believe all churches should be committed to this worship subtext, which I believe is the heart of true *preaching*. The focus is on both insiders and outsiders (since you are calling both to worship Christ rather than those things they are worshipping instead), and the motive is to build up everyone. This kind of subtext requires research, rhetorical, and contextualization abilities.

There is no way to convey this right and true subtext through technique; it comes down to your spiritual life as a preacher. Are you "sensing Christ on your heart" as you preach? Are you, in a way, meditating and contemplating him during the very act of preaching? Are you actually praising him as you talk about his praiseworthiness? Are you actually humbling yourself as you talk of your sin? The answer will be very evident to any attentive listener. And these things will happen in your preaching only if you are regularly cultivating them during routine prayer and meditation, beyond the task of sermon preparation.

In short, the temptation will be to let the pulpit drive you to the Word, but instead you must let the Word drive you to the pulpit. Prepare the preacher more than you prepare the sermon.

Preaching from the Heart

Half this book is dedicated to preaching to the heart. You certainly understand by now that you cannot hope to do that unless you are consistently preaching *from* the heart. What you are calling people to experience you must be experiencing yourself. What the Holy Spirit is to do in the hearts of your listeners he will normally do first in and through you. You must be something like a clear glass through which people can see a broken but gospel-changed soul in such a way that they want it for themselves.

Some final thoughts on what it looks like when you preach from the heart:

• *You preach powerfully.* You will have poise and confidence, striking a note of authority without swagger, without any indication that you enjoy authority for its own sake. You will not be insecure or nervous. You have confidence in your material and will not try to please or perform.

• *You preach wondrously.* There will be unmistakable awe and wonder at the greatness of the One you point people to. It is evident to listeners that you are "tasting" your salvation even as you offer it to others.

• *You preach affectionately.* You exhibit an unselfconscious transparency devoid of artifice. This doesn't come by telling personal stories about yourself; it comes only from having had a broken heart mended by the truth of the gospel. You can't fake that.

• *You preach authentically.* One paradox of preaching from the heart is that it bypasses all of the counterfeit mannerisms and emotional affectations that preachers have learned to adopt and that listeners have come to expect. Your language and tone of voice will be simple and unaffected.

• *You preach Christ-adoringly.* When you describe Jesus, you aren't reciting facts or abstractions but enacting a vivid presentation of him. Many hearers will feel they can almost see him, so they cannot help but admire and worship him.

Feel overwhelmed? Me too. However, a key to developing these traits is not to directly try to have them.

Instead, glory in your infirmities so his power may be made perfect in weakness (2 Corinthians 12:9). This is a discipline by which you constantly remind yourself of what you are under your own power. It leads to desperate dependence on the Spirit—but along with this desperation will come the joyful freedom of knowing that in the end nothing in preaching rests on your eloquence, your wisdom, or your ability. Nothing ever has! Every success and blessing and fruit you have ever borne has been from him.

Tremendous freedom comes when we can laugh at ourselves and whisper to him, "So! It's been you all along!" In some ways that day will be the true beginning of your career as a preacher and teacher of God's Word.

Becoming a Voice

John the Baptist was a popular preacher. Lots of people were coming to hear him, and he was telling people that the Messiah was coming. This bothered the religious authorities of the time. They were concerned that John might declare himself to be the Messiah—or the Elijah figure of Malachi 4 or the "prophet" of Deuteronomy 18, both of whom many scholars thought might be messianic forerunners. The Jewish leaders sent out an investigative team to see who John thought he was. They asked him a series of questions in John 1:19–26.

Now this was John's testimony when the Jewish leaders in Jerusalem sent priests and Levites to ask him who he was. He did not fail to confess, but confessed freely, "I am not the Messiah."

They asked him, "Then who are you? Are you Elijah?"

He said, "I am not."

"Are you the Prophet?"

He answered, "No."

Finally they said, "Who are you? Give us an answer to take back to those who sent us. What do you say about yourself?"

John replied in the words of Isaiah the prophet, "I am the voice of one calling in the wilderness, 'Make straight the way for the Lord.'"

Now the Pharisees who had been sent questioned him, "Why then do you baptize if you are not the Messiah, nor Elijah, nor the Prophet?"

"I baptize with water," John replied, "but among you stands one you do not know. He is the one who comes after me, the straps of whose sandals I am not worthy to untie."

What we see in John is a remarkable mixture of humility and boldness, all at once. He refused to believe he could be Elijah, the great forerunner of the Messiah, even though Jesus himself later said that John was indeed "the Elijah who was to come" (Matthew 11:14). John couldn't see himself as such a formidable person. No, he was "not worthy" to even untie the straps of the Messiah's sandals.

John was too humble to see in himself the greatness that Jesus and we can see. Yet at the same time he showed astonishing boldness and courage. He was clearly undaunted by the investigators. They asked him about why he baptized. The baptism that John was doing was a radical act. When a Gentile wanted to convert to Judaism, he was baptized with water to symbolize that a spiritually unclean pagan was coming into the true people of God. But John demanded that everyone, Jews as well as Gentiles, be baptized to be ready for the Messiah. He was saying that everyone is unclean and undeserving. It was a bold public stance.

The question is how someone that humble and unaware of his own greatness could be that confident and fearless. He gives us the answer by evoking Isaiah 40. He is saying: "I am a *voice.* I am just a voice, pointing to the one who is to come." That explains how he can be so humble and bold at the same time. He is saying: "In myself I am nothing, but the one I serve is the greatest in the world." He is confident because he is looking not at himself but at "the lamb of God, who takes away the sin of the world" (John 1:29). The greatness of Jesus, in a sense, flowed through John because he was like Paul, who wrote, "For what we preach is not ourselves, but Christ Jesus as Lord, and ourselves as your servants for Jesus' sake" (2 Corinthians 4:5).

We can still hear John's voice today. I love that part in the movie *The Greatest Story Ever Told* when John the Baptist is taken away from Herod's presence to be executed. You can hear him off in the distance shouting, "Repent! Repent!" Then you hear offstage the sickening thud of the ax coming down on his neck to behead him.

But then, as the camera zooms in on Herod sitting on his throne in silence, suddenly you hear a whispered voice

ACKNOWLEDGMENTS

I want to first thank the members of West Hopewell Presbyterian Church, in Hopewell, Virginia, whom I served in my first pastoral charge from 1975 to 1984. I arrived in Hopewell at the age of twenty-four, fresh from seminary, where I had received a deserved C in preaching. At West Hopewell I was expected to preach three different Bible expositions a week—Sunday morning, Sunday evening, and Wednesday night. In addition I preached on average two other messages a month at weddings and funerals, in nursing homes and local school chapels, and on retreats. It was a remarkable challenge, and over nine years I wrote and delivered about 1,500 expository messages, all by age thirty-three. Along with this challenging schedule, however, the people of the congregation provided me with a loving, supportive community in which my very weak early efforts were received with appreciation. Ministries in small churches in small towns are highly relational. I had ample opportunity to talk with almost everyone about how they were hearing my sermons. I saw where I was confusing people, or missing people's real needs, or failing to deal with their objections or questions. In the pastor's counseling office I also could see where some of my preaching was bearing fruit in changed lives—and where it wasn't. This combination of practice with feedback and loving support made me a far better preacher than I could have ever been had I gone to another place where I was not worked as hard or loved as well.

I also should thank both the students and faculty of Westminster Seminary in Philadelphia, where I was able to teach preaching for five years, 1984–89.

As a working preacher I've wanted to write a book on this subject for a long time, but it has proven to be a hard task. Like many other practitioners I am full of advice about details. It has taken the labors of my colleague at Redeemer City to City, Scott Kauffmann, and my longtime editor at Penguin Random House, Brian Tart, to help me discern the most important broad contours of what the preaching task entails today.

As usual, I want to thank the people who enable me to write several weeks of the year in lovely and secluded settings—Lynn Land, Mary Courtney Brooks, Janice Worth, John and Carolyn Twiname. Finally, I thank my wife, Kathy, my best critic and the most ardent supporter of my work and life as a preacher of the Word.

APPENDIX: WRITING AN EXPOSITORY MESSAGE

This volume is far from a complete textbook on preaching. You will have noticed that I've spent most of my time on *why* a certain kind of preaching is needed and *what* that preaching looks like in principle and in example but relatively little time on *how* to prepare a good sermon. A manifesto, not a manual, as I told myself many times in the writing of this book.

Yet I couldn't completely resist the urge to provide more practical support. In this appendix I offer a mini manual to the first great task of preaching—to faithfully preach the Word. There are many good books that describe in detail how to write and deliver an expository message on a text of the Bible.[1] A survey of dozens of these—some very old, some brand-new—reveals a surprising consensus on method. When you organize those top-level points of agreement, you're left with a very helpful set of irreducible essentials of how to preach a sound expository sermon. Though the sources call for varying steps and stages, they all include following four directives in one form or another.[2]

1. Discern the *goal* of the text by itemizing all the things that it says and looking for the main idea that all the other ideas support.

2. Choose a main *theme* for the sermon that presents the central idea of the text and ministers to your specific listeners.

3. Develop an *outline* around the sermon theme that fits the passage, with each point raising insights from the text itself, and has movement toward a climax.

4. *Flesh out* each point with arguments, illustrations, examples, images, other supportive Bible texts, and, most important, practical application.

DISCERN THE GOAL OF THE TEXT[3]

First you must discern the *goals* of the biblical author. What does the author of the text want his original hearers to learn, think, feel, and do? This requires digging deeply into the text, spiraling down through multiple rounds of reading and analysis, keeping a running commentary on it, and itemizing all the things that the text says or implies. You must ask them which of the thoughts are major and which are minor—which are the main concepts that the other ideas explain or support. Here is a simplified approach, again distilled from the most useful books on expository preaching and seasoned with my own experience.[4]

Round One: Read the English text[5] over at least a couple of times, beginning to write your own running commentary, noting anything that strikes you or raises a question.[6]

Round Two: Now read it over another two or three more times. This time look for three basic categories of things in the text: repetitions of words, ideas, or grammatical forms; connector words such as "therefore," "because," "for," "since," "if," and "then"; and finally any metaphors or images. As you note these, add to your commentary by asking questions about each repetition, connector, or image: Why did the author use this? What was he conveying with this? How would the meaning of the passage be changed if this weren't here?

In this round the connector words will not only make visible the text's component parts (the parts being the clauses, sentences, and paragraphs that come before and after the connectors) but also show you the way the parts relate to one another. The relationship could be one of cause and effect, showing the results or consequences of something. Or it could be one of general to particulars, with one part of the text serving as an elaboration or elucidation of something said earlier. That relationship could also be reversed, with a later part of the text being a summary or generalization based on earlier parts.

Round Three: Read the passage through again, this time using commentaries and other tools that help you look at the text in the original language. Because of the various software programs available for Bible study, this is now possible in at least a limited way for people without academic training in the original languages.[7] I try to do five main things in this round.

1. Determine the meaning of each significant word, learning what the term means here and elsewhere in the Bible.

2. Be sure to see if there is some repetition in the text that has been masked by the English translations. Often a Greek or Hebrew word repeated within the passage is given different English renderings by translators for reasons of style and variety.

3. Use the commentaries to seek answers to things in the text that puzzled you. The best ones take plenty of time to explain obscure and difficult passages.

4. Use reference tools to closely examine the images in your text and see their use and meaning in the rest of the Bible.[8]

5. Look for anything in your text that alludes to or quotes from other places in the Bible, especially in the other testament.[9]

These last two lines of study will reveal how your text points to Christ. Add all these insights to your running commentary on the passage.

Round Four: Now ask the context questions about your text. To begin, look at the context within the biblical book. Ask: How does this passage fit in with the rest of the book? What is the message of the whole book, and how does this particular passage contribute to it? Why is it here? How would the message of the book be diminished or changed if this were not here?

You must also, however, ask how this text (and the book in which it sits) fits in with the rest of the Bible and its message. What doctrines does it touch on that are laid out in the rest of the Bible? What themes in the text run through the whole canon? Most crucially, in what way do the biblical themes running through your text point to or find their fulfillment in Christ? Your use of the reference tools in round three will have given you a lot of the answers to these context questions already. Add all new ideas to your commentary.

Finally, you should have one concluding "goal of the text" question that helps you pull all your findings together. J. Alec Motyer asks: "What is the one thing that all the other things are about?"[10] Haddon Robinson asks the question as a two-parter: "Subject: what is this talking about? Complement: what is this saying about what it is talking about?"[11] Some formulate the question like this: What is the central thing the author wanted his original listeners to learn, feel, and/or do? What is the goal or point of the passage? You should choose one of these heuristics to begin with, though you can certainly formulate your own version over time.

However you choose to pose the "goal question" of the text, the answer can usually be found in one of two patterns. One is in the repetitions and their relationship to one another. When "courage" or "fear" is mentioned four or five times in a passage, that is probably the central subject. The other is in the answers to the context questions of how the passage relates to the chapter, book, and Bible. The 1 Corinthians 13 "love chapter" is read and preached upon at weddings, but a look at its context between 1 Corinthians 12 and 14 shows that it was not about romantic love but about how to create peace in a community torn apart by dissension. Jesus' statement "I am the light of the world" in

John 8 can be understood best when we see that in John 7 he was making this claim during the Festival of Tabernacles, commemorating God's glory cloud leading Israel through the wilderness. Jesus is, therefore, not speaking about some general power of illumination. He is identifying himself as the glory of Israel, the God of Moses, who has become a human being.

Write down the answer to the goal question in a sentence or two. This should be the "freshly-squeezed essence of the passage."[12] To force yourself to distill all your material, give your passage a title and, if it is a longer passage with paragraphs and parts, give each of them a title as well.

CHOOSE YOUR THEME FOR THE SERMON

Then choose a main *theme* for the sermon that presents the central ideas of the text while also addressing your listeners in particular. You may want to highlight different aspects of the biblical teaching depending on whether you have a homogeneous group of believers or a mixture of believers and those who do not believe. The occasion may be a worship service, a retreat, or a wedding.

Even if the central idea of the text is unambiguous (and it is not always so), that does not mean there can be only one theme for the sermon. The central textual idea can usually be faithfully presented through any of a variety of sermon themes. Sinclair Ferguson writes: "Alongside this objective exercise [discerning the central idea of the text] there is an exercise in spiritual sensitivity. . . . The preacher is not a systematic theologian. . . . He is a pastor. . . . Our preaching is not to be *need-determined,* but it must be *people-oriented.*"[13] Ferguson is saying that we must look at both the main idea of the text (our first responsibility) and the needs and capacities of the listeners (our second) to determine the sermon theme. Alan Stibbs says the same thing. He writes: "Some passages are very fertile. They are capable of a number of selective treatments according to the points in them chosen for emphasis and according to the corresponding particular aim and application which the preacher may have in view."[14] In another volume David Jackman says that the preacher should have not only a statement of the text's big idea but also an "aim sentence," by which he means "what you are praying the Holy Spirit will be pleased to do in the lives of the hearers as a result of the sermon."[15] The central text idea and the pastoral aim together produce the sermon theme.[16]

To illustrate the development of the theme, Stibbs takes one text: John 2:1–11, Jesus turning the water into wine at the wedding feast in Cana. The main idea of the text is found in verse 11—the miracle showed Jesus' glory by pointing to his death, which purifies us and secures our festal joy. The plot tension in the little narrative revolves around Jesus' enigmatic, brusque response to Mary when she tells him they have run out of wine, followed by his subsequent miracle that saves the joy of the feast. Jesus does the miracle by using jars of water normally used for purification of sin, pointing to the purpose of his own shed blood. Jesus is signaling that he must lose all joy so that we can receive it.

The miracle reveals the glory of who Jesus is and what he came to do. However, we see a number of aspects to that glory in the passage, and Stibbs shows how we can high-light this main idea through different sermon themes, de-pending on the context and the people we are addressing. Stibbs suggests that at a wedding his main focus would be verse 2 ("Jesus . . . had also been invited to the wedding") and the sermon theme could be "Jesus should be invited into your marriage." At a prayer meeting the main focus could be verse 3 ("Jesus' mother said to him, 'They have no more wine'") and the sermon theme could be "why and how to pray." In an address to Christian leaders and work-ers the main focus could be on verse 5 ("'Do whatever he tells you'") with the theme of "how to be useful in Christ's work." In a Sunday-morning sermon to a broad audience, including people all across the faith spectrum, the main fo-cus could be on verse 10: "You have saved the best [wine] till [last]." The theme could be "the joy Jesus brings."

In each case the same central idea of the glory of his saving death in particular is brought to the fore in a dif-ferent way. The sermons begin with Jesus offering to come into our marriage, answering prayer, blessing the work of obedient colaborers, and bringing you the joy you have been looking for all your life. How? Through his death, which is glorious.[17]

Bible scholar Alec Motyer uses 1 John 2:1–2 to dem-onstrate the same process of moving from the central text idea to the theme:

My dear children, I write this to you so that you will not sin. But if anybody does sin, we have an advocate with the Father—Jesus Christ, the Righ-teous One. He is the atoning sacrifice for our sins, and not only for ours but also for the sins of the whole world.

Motyer says that there are at least six ideas or truths about Jesus stated in the two verses: (1a) Jesus' goal is that sin diminish and disappear from our lives. (1b) Yet Jesus will not abandon us if we do sin. (1c) Jesus is an ascended advocate for us before the Father. (1d) Jesus is righteous. (2a) Jesus makes propitiation for our sins through the atonement (Greek *hilasmos*). (2b) Jesus secures forgiveness of them and makes this available to us and to the whole world.

Motyer thinks that the central idea, on which the others hang, is the second—that Jesus will never abandon or give up on us. The point of the passage is that we should not sin, but "if anyone *does* sin," Jesus will still be our advocate, the Father will still love us, we will still be forgiven. "Each of the six truths breathes heavenly security. . . . As we battle with sin and constantly lose the battle [we can] credibly claim to be heirs and possessors of this great salvation."[18]

Motyer echoes Ferguson and Stibbs when he says that the central idea of the text must be put into a sermon theme "tailored to the congregation to whom we are ministering." He reminds us that we have not one but two responsibilities when we preach: "First to the truth, and secondly to this particular group of people. How will they best hear the truth? How are we to shape and phrase it so that it comes home to them in a way that is palatable, that gains the most receptive hearing, and . . . avoids needless hurt?"[19] Motyer says, therefore, that there is never just one possible sermon theme. Even though the main idea of the text could be phrased as "the assurance of our salvation," that does not necessarily have to be the theme of the sermon. If the congregation needs more instruction in Christian theology, the preacher could focus more on the fact that Jesus is our advocate and heavenly intercessor because he has ascended. The theme could be "the reality and meaning of the Lord's ascension," in which the emphasis is on that biblical teaching and what it means for believers. There could also be a variety of pastoral reasons that the preacher would want to focus on the important word "propitiation" in the text, which refers to the taking away of God's wrath.[20] This gives more attention to how thorough and deep our forgiveness is as a result of the cross. That theme could be "how Jesus saves us (the meaning of propitiation)." A third approach could be a more personal one, making the theme "how to deal with recurrent sin." In each case you would draw out and present the main idea of our infallible security and assurance yet, depending on how familiar the people are with doctrine or what sorts of things they are facing in their lives, the sermon theme could differ.

As we've seen, many writers suggest crafting a sermon theme combining the main text idea and the pastoral aim. However, since you can't preach a text rightly unless you put it into its whole Bible context and show how it points to Christ, we might want to choose our sermon theme after answering three questions:

> *Main text idea question:* What is this text talking about, and what is it saying about what it is talking about?

    Pastoral aim question: What practical difference did this teaching make to the author's readers, and what difference should it make to us?

    Christ question: How does the text point us to Christ, and how does his salvation help us change in line with the pastoral aim?

After answering these questions, formulate a main theme for your sermon. It should be a people-oriented use of the text's main idea. It is helpful if the sermon theme can be an active, declarative sentence. For example, suppose you have studied John 16:16–23 and determined that the text's "big idea" is "Jesus comforts his disciples with teaching about his second coming." Your sermon theme could be "Christians, through the hope Christ gives, can face anything."

DEVELOP AN OUTLINE AROUND THE THEME

Once you have chosen the theme, develop an *outline* around that theme that unfolds the meaning of the passage—with each point arising from insights from the text itself—and creates narrative tension toward a climax. One kind of outline is much like a case in court—a statement of facts, a thesis, and an argument for the thesis. Another kind of outline is more like the telling of a story, with a statement of something that has knocked life out of balance, a history of the struggle to rectify things, and the description of the plotline's resolution.

Many expository preachers of the earliest centuries did not develop outlines per se but instead proceeded to give commentary on consecutive verses. There was, of course, an implicit outline in this method. The preacher would break the text into logical units of ideas, treating three or four verses as a unit, followed by another unit, and when he reached the end of the passage, he might summarize the main themes and teachings. In other words, the outline of the sermon was simply the consecutive structure of the passage, and the preacher did very little to suggest any other organization of the ideas. It was not until the Middle Ages that the sermon outline became customary for preachers.[21] Though John Calvin sought to revive the consecutive, running-commentary method of Chrysostom and other early Christian preachers, most of his early Protestant contemporaries were more interested in recovering the rhetorical methods of the Greeks and Romans and adapting them for the church. The Puritans and their heirs went on to develop a very Scholastic, classical outline for each sermon, with a single proposition, a rigorous analysis of it, and an exhaustive defense and application of it.[22]

Over the last two hundred years, some consensus has developed about the qualities of a sermon outline. It should have *unity,* with each point supporting the main theme. It should have *proportion,* with each point given roughly equal time and importance, so the pace and progress of thought do not seem too slow or too fast. It should have *order.* That is, each point should not merely be related to the theme but should build upon the other points, carrying the thought forward, not merely repeating what was said before. Finally, it should have *movement*. The sermon outline should not just present data in an orderly way, nor just offer a "case" for a proposition. It should give people the sense they are being taken somewhere, building toward some kind of climax and finally being brought face-to-face with God. (And yes, this includes expository sermons on nonnarrative texts as well. I'll address movement in the next section.)[23]

Every point in your outline should progressively clarify or justify your theme, so that it becomes clearer, richer, and more compelling as the sermon goes on. In this way the outline provides not only order but also discipline—it forces you to practice the crucial art of knowing what to leave out. Recently you may have found some quotes and examples that would make great sermon illustrations, but if they don't fit your outline, each part of which serves the theme, you should save them for another sermon.

The outline also helps you ensure that your main points in an expository sermon come from the text itself. In your study you have gathered a host of interesting ideas that you have seen in the text. Then you asked the goal-of-the-text question and determined which of the ideas was, as it were, the trunk (the central idea) and which ones were the branches. Having done that, you can arrange the secondary ideas to form the points of the sermon, each one explaining or elaborating on the main idea.

It is not too difficult to see that Mark 2:1–12, the healing of the paralytic, is about the forgiveness of sins. The word "forgiven" or "forgiveness" occurs four times, and all the narrative tension in the passage is around Jesus' assuming the right to forgive sins and the scribes' challenge of that right. There are, however, numerous other things to notice in the text. Jesus doesn't at first give the man the primary thing his friends were seeking for him, namely physical healing. Another key observation is that Jesus seems to intuit the man's inward state, since forgiveness requires repentance and the man never verbalizes this. Another key issue in the text is Jesus' question: "Which is easier: to say to this paralyzed man, 'Your sins are forgiven,' or to say, 'Get up, take your mat and walk'?" (verse 9). It is a trick question because, while it may seem harder to heal physically than to forgive, in the end it will require Jesus' death to secure remission of sins.

All these items and ideas can become points in the outline. The sermon theme could be "the true healing of forgiveness." The outline could be: (1) the need for forgiveness; (2) the grace of forgiveness; and (3) the cost of forgiveness. Verses 1–4 show the need of it. When Jesus forgives before he heals, he indicates that our spiritual need for a right relationship with God is more basic than the need for physical healing or anything else at all. Verse 5 shows the grace of it. Jesus responds even to the inarticulate longings of the man, showing that you don't have to have it all together in order to merit God's forgiveness. You just have to want it. All you need is need; all you need is nothing. Verse 9, the enigmatic question, puts us into the shadow of the cross. It takes only great power to heal a man physically, but it will require infinite suffering, death, and astonishing love for Jesus to be able to forgive us. However, when we receive that, we will be healed indeed of the only disease that can really, finally kill us.

Alec Motyer uses Psalm 51 as another example.[24] He points to nine significant words in the text (New King James Version): "mercy, loving kindness, tender mercies, blotting out, transgressions, wash thoroughly, iniquity, cleans, and sin." The central idea of the passage is how God deals with our sin. Motyer examines each word to see what it means in the rest of the Bible. He learns that three of the words define what sin is, three describe what we need from God for it, and three describe what we should say to God in order to receive that. Motyer then observes that all these may be presented as grounding points in the sermon, but the sermon theme will determine how to do that. Is this a sermon to Christians on an important aspect of prayer? Then the sermon theme would be how to confess our sins. The outline could be: (1) why we must confess; (2) what we must confess; and (3) how we must confess. In that case each triad of words could be used to fill out each of the points.

Or is this a sermon to an audience with many people who don't believe or who don't know what they believe? Then a possible sermon title could be "When Life Blows Up." The outline could be: (1) we aren't what we ought to be; (2) why we aren't what we ought to be; and (3) what we can do about it. This sermon would give more background on the setting for Psalm 51, recounting how David—the best king Israel ever had—nonetheless had a deeply flawed heart and "blew up his life" through an extramarital affair. The first point could establish that we are weaker and more prone to disaster than we want to admit. The Hebrew word translated as "sin" means to miss the mark. It goes beyond mere violation of rules to signify failing to be all we know we should be. The second point, on why we miss the mark, could be built from two subpoints: our self-absorption, our being curved in on ourselves ("iniquity" means to be bent or twisted); and our self-will ("transgression" refers to stubbornness and willfulness). These two things make the world a miserable place. The third point does not need to use all six remaining keywords, but it must at least focus on the Hebrew word translated as "blot out," meaning that there is a kind of spiritual-cosmic detergent, as it were, that can remove sin down to the last fiber (Hebrews 9:14), which could bring us to Hebrews 9 and to the work of Christ.

THE MOVEMENT OF THE SERMON

Your outline has to have movement, progression, tension.[25] I hear many sermons that are simply a string of good thoughts that could almost be set forth in any order—even if they are all faithfully taken from the text and in general accord with the sermon theme. That is actually a series of mini sermons, and it is invariably tedious, even when delivered with conviction. Each point in a compelling sermon must contribute something new to the theme, building on previous ones, sometimes making use of clues and undeveloped thoughts mentioned earlier but opened at just the right moment later on. In your sermons you must build some suspense that creates an eagerness to hear what is coming next and a sense of traveling to a destination. Skillful preachers can state earlier points in such a way that it will cause questions to be raised in listeners' minds: *If this is true, doesn't it contradict that?* or *Won't this create a problem with that? If that is what the Bible says, how do you answer those who object to it like this? If that is what we must do, where do we get the resources to do it?* That way the preacher can answer the questions in the hearts of the listeners as he or she moves through the sermon.

Eugene Lowry argues that even if preachers are not preaching on a biblical story, the points of the sermon should nevertheless feel like the parts of a narrative.[26] A narrative begins when something knocks life off balance. Life is now not the way it ought to be. For example, "Little Red Riding Hood took her grandmother some goodies" is just a fact. However, "Little Red Riding Hood was going to her grandmother's, but a big bad wolf was waiting to eat her" is a narrative. As the story proceeds, the plot thickens as central characters fight to restore the initial balance. There are always protagonist figures and forces struggling toward the restoration of balance as well as antagonist figures and forces struggling against the restoration and against the protagonists. Finally, the story ends as the struggle results in either restoration of the balance—in which the desires of the protagonists (and the listeners) are reunited with objective reality—or the failure to restore balance. So every story consists of an assumption about how life ought to be, a problem or force that prevents life from being that way, and a pathway through which that life can be restored.[27]

Lowry believes that the general flow and movement of the sermon (though not necessarily embodied in explicit headings or points) should follow this general pattern. First, present the problem, showing the particular way indicated in the text that sin has knocked life out of whack, what Bryan Chapell calls "the fallen condition focus."[28]

Then develop tension by looking under the surface at the reasons that the problem is so difficult and enduring. Crucial to this step is going beneath personal and social behavior down to the motivations of the heart.[29] We may be selfish with our money, but mere exhortation won't work, because money is more than money to us; it is identity and security. This second move must always recapitulate the gospel message that we do not have the resources to save ourselves. It seems hopeless (because it is).

Next, show how Jesus, his salvation, and faith in him solve the problem before us, objectively and subjectively. Jesus is the exemplar, who lives the human life we should be living. He dies to save us from the guilt and consequences of our failure. But in addition to all this, faith in Christ always perfectly solves the heart problem that is at the root of the difficulty. We can't give our money away until we get new security and identity in Jesus. We can't love our spouses rightly until we fill our inner neediness with the spousal love of Christ. The second and third moves of the sermon are intimately tied together. If, when analyzing the fallen-condition focus, you depict the problem as a matter of behavior, then the only solution will be some exhortation to try harder. Unless you get down to the level of heart dynamics and motivation, the transforming power of the gospel in the work of Christ won't be seen as the unique, direct solution to the problem.

This is why the sermon, if it moves like a narrative, with a thickening plot and little hope—can at this point produce what Tolkien calls "the turn" that is present in all good stories. There is a reversal, an upending of normal expectations, and a sudden plot resolution that is counterintuitive and satisfying.[30] This is where the gospel and the person and work of Christ are brought to bear on the problem, and he is proclaimed as the unique solution to this issue, unlike anything the world has to give. This is how Jesus is assured to be the "hero" of every well-crafted sermon.[31]

Here is another way to look at the underlying movement of the sermon to give it a gospel shape, a fall-redemption-restoration plotline. Remember that these are seldom or never the announced headings or even the points of your outline. I think of it as the metaoutline, the deep gospel pattern, of every sermon I preach:

Intro	What the problem is; our contemporary cultural context: *Here's what we face.*
Early points	What the Bible says; the original readers' cultural context: *Here's what we must do.*
Middle points	What prevents us; current listeners' inward heart context: *Why we can't do it.*
Late points	How Jesus fulfills the biblical theme and solves the heart issue: *How Jesus did it.*
Application	*How through faith in Jesus you should live now.*

Here are the assumptions behind this deep pattern. One is that the Bible addresses heart issues that are true for all human beings everywhere in every century. So the heart issues of the original readers will overlap with those of the preacher's listeners. Also, in every text of the Scripture there are imperatives, moral norms for how we should live. That norm may be seen in what we learn about the character of God or Christ, or in the good or bad example of characters in the text, or in explicit commands, warnings, and summonses. The next assumption is that this moral imperative always presents a crisis, for when properly understood, the practical and moral obligation of the Scripture is impossible for human beings to meet. If the preacher does not bring that out, the sermon is headed for moralism, for implicitly or even explicitly asserting that our moral efforts could be sufficient to please God. If instead the preacher makes the crisis clear, then the listeners who have followed the path of the sermon to this point are led to a seemingly dead end. Then, when we point to the gospel, a hidden door opens and light comes in. Jesus has fulfilled the law's requirement in our place and so protects us from condemnation. But more than that, when we put our faith in that saving fulfillment, it changes the structure of our hearts, melting them where they are icy, strengthening them where they are weak. Faith in Jesus is our only hope—but it is a sure hope.

The sermon now moves definitively out of argument and teaching toward worship and wonder when it shows how only Jesus Christ has fulfilled the requirement. If the text is a narrative, you can show how the characters in it point to Christ as the ultimate deliverer, sufferer, prophet, priest, king, and servant. If the text is didactic, you can show how Christ is the ultimate embodiment of the moral norm and the only way to become people who can begin to follow it. Finally, the sermon can take time to spell out practical ways that faith in Christ should shape our lives in this area.

CASE STUDY #1: EXPOSITORY

Here's an example of applying this deep pattern to the story of Abraham and Isaac in Genesis 22.

1. What you must do: We must put God first in every area of life, as Abraham did. (This is where the traditional sermon ends!!)

2. But you can't: We can't! We won't! So we deserve to be condemned.

3. But there was one who did: Jesus put God first, on the cross. His was the ultimate and perfect act of submission to God. Jesus is the only one to whom God ever said, "Obey me, and as a result I will judge you and condemn you." Jesus obeyed anyway—just for truth's sake, for God's sake. The only perfect act of submission.

4. Only now we can change: Only when we see that Jesus obeyed as Abraham did—*for us!*—can we begin to live like Abraham. Let your heart be shaped by this.

Only when I see that God has already accepted me can I even begin to try to live like Abraham. I would never even start down this road of Abraham-like obedience. I'd be so discouraged by my failures. But God has already set his love on me, prior to my obedience. Without knowing that, I'd never have the heart to start or keep going.

Only when I see that God has already accepted me can I deal with the real reasons I fail to live like Abraham. I put my "Isaacs" ahead of Christ because I think they will give me more security and worth than he will. Only by rejoicing in my acceptance will these Isaacs lose their power over me. Without doing that, I'd not have the ability to make any progress at all.

Only when I see that God has accepted me can I really want to live like Abraham for the right, nondestructive reason. As I listen to this sermon about Abraham, I realize I may try to obey God so that he will give me a happy life and family. But if I obey like that, I'm really not obeying him for his sake. I'm using the law of God to control him, not praise him. Without joying in, seeing, resting in Christ's obedience for *me,* I'll never be obeying for the right reason, nor even truly obeying at all.

CASE STUDY #2: TOPICAL

Here's an example of an outline for a sermon on the power of beauty and sexual attraction in our culture.

1. What you must do: The power of physical beauty over us must be broken. Look at the devastation it has wrought in our society and in our lives. (1) It distorts women's view of themselves (leading to self-loathing and eating disorders); (2) it demoralizes aging people; (3) it distorts men's lives by making them reject great spouse prospects for superficial reasons and turn to pornography. What must we do? Don't judge a book by its cover. Don't be controlled by something superficial.
2. But you can't: You know quite well we won't be able to escape its power. Why? (1) We desire physical beauty to cover our own sense of shame and inadequacy

(Genesis 3). "When you look good, you feel good about yourself" really equals "When you look good, you feel yourself to be good." (2) We are afraid of our mortality and death. Evolutionary biologists and Christians agree that the drive to possess physical beauty is a desire for youth. We'll never overcome our problem by just trying.

3. But there was one who did: There was one who was beautiful beyond bearing yet willingly gave it up (Philippians 2). He became ugly that we might become beautiful (Isaiah 53).

4. Only now we can change: Only as we see what he did for us will our hearts be melted and freed from the belief that we can judge a book by its cover. Only when we can be in him will we be freed from our sense of shame and fear of mortality.

FLESH OUT EACH POINT

Finally, you must *flesh out* each of your outline's points with a great variety of arguments, illustrations, examples, images, other supportive biblical texts, and other forms of practical application and rhetorical devices. The number and character of these things depends on the choices you have made previously about the goal of the passage, your theme, and the structure of your outline.

I will focus my suggestions here on one aspect of fleshing out the structure of the outline. In chapter 6 we looked at how to *prepare* for effective application; here I give some *examples* of applications that move along gospel-centered lines rather than (as is far more common) moralistic lines. How do we call people to obey on the basis of the text without being moralistic? How do we change their hearts so they want to obey rather than beat on their wills just to get compliance?

Faithfulness

In Genesis 12 (Abram's call) Abraham leaves his comfort zone and follows God's call despite having to go it alone, without his family, and having to leave his home culture. He can become a blessing to others only if he is willing to leave the normal sources of human security. Jesus, however, was the ultimate example of someone who heard a call away from security. He left heaven itself and his glory (Philippians 2) all in order to die for us. Jesus lost his security so we could have the ultimate security—his love and salvation. When we have that, we will have the ability to take the risk to reach out to other individuals and other cultures. Only then do we become people, or disciples, "on mission."

Caring for the Poor

It is remarkable how much God *identifies* with the poor. Proverbs 19:17 says that if you are kind to the poor, you are kind to the Lord; Proverbs 14:31 says that if you insult or are unkind to the poor, you insult the Lord. A remarkable example of this is in Matthew 25, where Jesus says that when you feed the hungry, clothe the naked, shelter the homeless—you are feeding and sheltering "me." It is tempting to preach these passages moralistically, telling people that therefore *we* should identify with the poor and care for them. But we often find that when we try to do this, things go wrong. We are filled with insensitive pride and we offend the poor. Or we get our feelings hurt when they don't respond with gratitude. Or we get impatient that they seem not to be responding well. There is too much pride and too little love on our part. It's because we tried to directly apply the biblical teaching without letting faith in Jesus restructure our hearts.

Yes, you can see that God in the Old Testament identifies with the poor; but not until Jesus do we see how *far* he went to do so. In Jesus he both figuratively and literally came among the poor! He was born in a manger to poor parents. He lived virtually homeless, saying, "Foxes have holes, but the son of man has nowhere to lay his head" (Luke 9:58).[32] When he died they cast lots for his robe, his only possession, and he was buried in a borrowed tomb. Not only that, but he was also the victim of a miscarriage of justice. He knew what it was like to be poor, marginalized, and oppressed. Finally he was stripped naked and died of thirst and exposure on the cross. So on the last day when people say to Jesus, "When did we see you thirsty, naked, in prison?" Jesus could say, "On the cross! There I, who deserved exoneration, got condemnation so that you, who deserve condemnation, can go free. That is the true basis for living a life of justice and care for the poor." Seeing Jesus embrace you when you are spiritually poor helps you see that you are no better than the poor in any meaningful way. It should remove condescending attitudes and impatience.

Adultery and Marital Love

When preaching to spouses about being faithful to their mates, at some point you must show them that the selfishness of their hearts will keep them from doing so unless they have the love of their true spouse, Jesus. He was faithful to us at infinite cost to himself. That moves us to be faithful to our spouse. And he loves us so much that we don't need our spouse's love as the ultimate affirmation in our lives. If it is, we will be too emotionally dependent on our spouse and won't be able to cope with his or her ups, downs, or flaws. In Christ we have the affirmation we need—so we don't have to look elsewhere, even when our spouse is imperfect. In Ephesians 5 Paul is speaking to spouses but especially, it seems, to husbands. Many of them had brought from their pagan backgrounds (as we bring from our own cultures) dehumanizing attitudes toward marriage. In Paul's time marriage was seen as mainly a business relationship (you had to marry as well as you could). Paul wants to encourage husbands not only to be sexually faithful but also to cherish and honor their wives. In Ephesians 5 Paul does not present unloving husbands a simple moral example but (again) shows them the salvation of Jesus, who was the ultimate spouse to us in the gospel. He showed sacrificial love toward us, his bride. He did not love us because we were lovely but in order to make us lovely.

Tithing and Generosity

If you preach about tithing, at some point you must get to the ultimate giver, Jesus, who at infinite cost gave us not just a tithe of his wealth but all of it. This gives us the security and joy to give away our wealth, since the only real long-term security is to be rich in him. In 2 Corinthians 8 and 9 Paul wants the people to give an offering to the poor. But he says, in effect, "I don't want to order you. I don't want this offering to simply be the response to my demand." He doesn't put pressure directly on the *will* (for example, by saying, "I'm an apostle and this is your duty to me!") or on the *emotions* (by telling them stories about how much the poor are suffering and how much more they have than the sufferers). Instead, Paul vividly and unforgettably says, "You know the grace of our Lord Jesus Christ, that though he was rich, yet for your sake he became poor, so that you through his poverty might become rich" (2 Corinthians 8:9). When he says, "You know the grace," he is, of course, spiritually reminding them of that grace using a powerful image, bringing Jesus' salvation into the realm of money and wealth and poverty. He moves them by a spiritual recollection of the gospel.

In applying texts like these concerning ethics and commandments, there is a theological, a rhetorical, and a practical reason to base your application around the work of Jesus instead of around our merit or effort. In theological terms, sanctification proceeds only as we grow in faith—as the reality of what Christ has done for us personally loosens our hearts' need for idols. The sin under every sin is the failure to believe the gospel at the point where we turn instead to an idol. So listeners' hearts can be softened and reprogrammed only by bringing them to Jesus. Otherwise we will believe we can be sanctified on the basis of our own effort. So the theological reason is that it's not Christianity otherwise.

The rhetorical reason is that moralistic preaching is boring. Every family, every culture, every age has its favored forms of motivational speech. At one level these can

NOTES

INTRODUCTION: THREE LEVELS OF THE MINISTRY OF THE WORD

1. Peter Adam, *Speaking God's Words: A Practical Theology of Preaching* (Vancouver, British Columbia: Regent College Publishing, 1996), p. 59.
2. Ibid., p. 75.
3. Here I follow most commentators in viewing "speaking" and "serving" not as two specific spiritual gifts but as two broad categories containing the more specific gifts listed in Romans 12 and 1 Corinthians 12 and 14: word gifts (prophecy, teaching, exhortation, wisdom, knowledge) and deed gifts (giving, mercy, healing, administration, governance). See, for example. J. Ramsey Michaels, *1 Peter* (Nashville, TN: Word Publishing, 1988), pp. 250–51.
4. P. H. Davids, *The First Epistle of Peter* (Grand Rapids, MI: Wm. B. Eerdmans, 1990), p. 161.
5. Ibid.
6. Ibid., p. 59.
7. E. P. Clowney, *The Message of 1 Peter: The Way of the Cross* (Downers Grove, IL: InterVarsity Press, 1988), pp. 184–85.
8. Ibid., p. 84.
9. This book will not be a complete "preachers' manual." It will serve as a foundation for thinking about Christian communication of the Bible in a skeptical age and it will lay out the basic tasks—preaching the Word, preaching the gospel, preaching to the culture, preaching to the heart, all by preaching Christ. In

this book there will be slightly more time devoted to preaching to the culture than to some of the other tasks. This is not because this is more important but because other books on preaching today provide so little on that subject. So this volume is more a charter for preaching today than a guide on how to go about it. It should be supplemented by other training resources for preachers. Many of these are being prepared for preachers' use and equipping at City to City. See redeemercitytocity.com.

PROLOGUE: WHAT IS GOOD PREACHING?

1. D. M. Lloyd-Jones, *Preaching and Preachers,* 40th anniversary ed. (Grand Rapids, MI: Zondervan, 2011). The testimony came from David Jones of Llangan (1736–1810). Because he had heard both Rowland and Whitefield preach in person, he was asked to compare them. His answer: "'As regards . . . the act of preaching, as regards the soaring to the heights and the lifting of the congregation to the heavens I really could detect very little difference between them; the one was as good as the other. The one big difference between them,' he continued, 'was this, that you could always be certain of getting a good sermon from Rowland, but not always from Whitefield.'" Lloyd-Jones, p.67-68.

2. Quoted in Scott Manetsch, *Calvin's Company of Pastors* (New York: Oxford University Press, 2013), p. 156.

3. The manual is found in Augustine's *On Christian Doctrine,* book IV, and is printed in full with helpful annotations and analysis in *The Rhetorical Tradition: Readings from Classical Times to the Present,* Patricia Bizzell and Bruce Herzberg, eds. (New York: St. Martin's Press, 1990), pp. 386–422. Books I through III essentially lay out "hermeneutics," how to understand the Bible. Book IV then explains how to communicate what has been learned from the Bible.

4. George A. Kennedy, *Classical Rhetoric and Its Christian and Secular Tradition from Ancient to Modern Times,* 2nd ed. (Chapel Hill, NC: University of North Carolina Press, 1999), p. 1.

5. Ibid., p. 2.

6. John Calvin, *1 Corinthians,* in *Calvin's Commentaries,* electronic ed. (Albany, OR: Ages Software, 1998).

7. Ibid.

8. Ibid.

9. See Anthony C. Thiselton, *The First Epistle to the Corinthians: A Commentary on the Greek Text,* The New International Greek Testament Commentary (Grand Rapids, MI: Wm. B. Eerdmans, 2000); Roy E. Ciampa and Brian S. Rosner, *The First Letter to the Corinthians,* Pillar New Testament Commentary (Grand Rapids, MI: Wm. B. Eerdmans, 2010); Gordon D. Fee, *The First Epistle to the Corinthians,* The New International Commentary on the New Testament (Grand Rapids, MI: Wm. B. Eerdmans, 1987). See also D. A. Carson, "The Cross and Preaching," in *The Cross and Christian Ministry: Leadership Lessons from 1 Corinthians* (Grand Rapids, MI: Baker, 1993), pp. 11–41.

10. "Yes. In our world too, a Stable once had something inside it that was bigger than the whole world." C. S. Lewis, *The Last Battle* (London: Geoffrey Bles, 1956), p.143.

11. See Paul Barnett, *The Second Epistle to the Corinthians* (Grand Rapids, MI: Wm. B. Eerdmans, 1997), pp. 277–83. See especially note 8 on p. 280. Barnett reads Paul's statement that "we try to persuade others" as a description of his evangelistic ministry.

12. See Thiselton, pp. 216–23.

13. Ibid., p. 218.

14. Ibid., p. 222.

15. Carson, *Cross and Christian Ministry,* p. 20.

16. Article XX, "Of the Authority of the Church," in the Thirty-Nine Articles of Religion of the Anglican Church.

17. Alec Motyer, *Preaching? Simple Teaching on Simply Preaching* (Ross-shire, Scotland: Christian Focus, 2013), p. 65.

18. Charles Spurgeon, "Christ Precious to Believers" (sermon no. 242, March 13, 1859), in *The New Park Street Pulpit,* vol. 5 (repr., Pasadena, TX: Pilgrim Publications, 1975), p. 140.

CHAPTER 1: PREACHING THE WORD

1. William Perkins, *The Art of Prophesying with the Calling of the Ministry* (first published in English 1606; repr., Edinburgh, Scotland: Banner of Truth, 1996), p. 9.

2. Hughes Oliphant Old, *The Age of Reformation* (Grand Rapids, MI: Wm. B. Eerdmans, 2002), p. 359.

3. Perkins, *Art of Prophesying,* chapters 1 and 2, pp. 3–11.

4. Ibid.

5. Hughes Oliphant Old, *The Reading and Preaching of the Scriptures in the Worship of the Christian Church,* vol. 1, *The Biblical Period* (Grand Rapids, MI: Wm. B. Eerdmans, 1998); vol. 2, *The Patristic Age* (Grand Rapids, MI: Wm. B. Eerdmans, 1998); vol. 3, *The Medieval Church* (Grand Rapids, MI: Wm. B. Eerdmans, 1999); vol. 4, *The Age of Reformation* (Grand Rapids, MI: Wm. B. Eerdmans, 2002); vol. 5, *Moderation, Pietism, and Awakening* (Grand Rapids, MI: Wm. B. Eerdmans, 2004); vol. 6, *The Modern Age* (Grand Rapids, MI: Wm. B. Eerdmans, 2007); vol. 7, *Our Own Time* (Grand Rapids, MI: Wm. B. Eerdmans, 2010).

6. Old, *Reading and Preaching of the Scriptures,* vol. 1, *Biblical Period,* p. 9.

7. Timothy Ward, *Words of Life: Scripture as the Living and Active Word of God* (Downers Grove, IL: InterVarsity Press, 2009), p. 157.

8. The three volumes I would urge all preachers to read on the doctrine of Scripture are J. I. Packer, *"Fundamentalism" and the Word of God* (Grand Rapids, MI: Wm. B. Eerdmans, 1958); Ward, *Words of Life;* and Kevin DeYoung, *Taking God at His Word* (Wheaton, IL: Crossway, 2014). These three books abridge and distill expertly the work of the four best historical expositions of the doctrine of the Scripture: John Calvin, *Institutes of the Christian Religion,* book 1; B. B. Warfield, *The Inspiration and Authority of the Bible* (Phillipsburg, NJ: Presbyterian and Reformed, 1980); Francis Turretin, *Institutes of Elenctic Theology,* vol. 1, J. T. Dennison, ed., G. M. Giger, trans. (Phillipsburg, NJ: Presbyterian and Reformed, 1992), "Second Topic: "The Holy Scriptures"; and Herman Bavinck,

Reformed Dogmatics, vol. 1, ed. John Bolt, trans. John Vriend (Grand Rapids, MI: Baker Academic, 2003), part 4: "Revelation." (The first two titles are readily available in multiple editions.) In addition, the following works are helpful in that they connect the authority of the Bible directly to preaching method: Peter Adam, *Speaking God's Words: A Practical Theology of Preaching* , part 1, "Three Biblical Foundations for Preaching," and chapter 5, "The Preacher's Bible," pp. 13–56 and 87–124; John R. W. Stott, "Theological Foundations for Preaching," in *Between Two Worlds: The Art of Preaching in the Twentieth Century* (Grand Rapids, MI: Wm. B. Eerdmans, 1982), pp. 92–134; J. I. Packer, "Why Preach?" in *Honoring the Written Word of God: Collected Shorter Writings on the Authority and Interpretation of Scripture* (Vancouver, British Columbia: Regent College, 2008), pp. 247–67. See also D. A. Carson, "Recent Developments in the Doctrine of Scripture," in *Collected Writings on Scripture* (Wheaton, IL: Crossway, 2010), pp. 55–110. I should add that having a good grasp of the evangelical doctrine of the Scripture not only gives the preacher confidence that these are God's words but also prevents the mistakes that come from a naive belief in the Bible's divinity that excludes its also being a human book, written by actual human beings in historical, sociocultural contexts. Packer is particularly good in distinguishing the historical doctrine from "divine dictation" and other such views.

9. God's Word is "God's active presence in the world." Ward, *Words of Life,* p. 25. "When God's Word goes out to act it means God himself has gone out to act. Thus (we may say) God has *invested* himself with his words, or we could say that God has so *identified* himself with his words that whatever someone does to God's words . . . they do to God himself. . . . God's . . . *verbal actions are a kind of extension of himself.*" Ibid., p. 27. These are Ward's italics.

10. Ibid., p. 156.

11. Ibid., p. 158.

12. See Hughes Oliphant Old, *Worship That Is Reformed According to Scripture* (Louisville, KY: John Knox, 1984), chapter 5 ("The Ministry of the Word") and pp. 171–72.

13. A sample of Dick Lucas's sermon series from the late 1980s and 1990s includes eleven weeks of messages through 1 Peter 1 and 2, five weeks through Titus 3, six weeks through 1 John 1, and seven weeks through Luke 12. The themes include the attributes of God, the new birth, generosity and financial stewardship, and the character of the Christian church.

14. Here is what I did at Redeemer Presbyterian Church over the years. On the one hand I made sure that every twelve months we "covered the waterfront," from the nature of God (usually more in the fall, when Old Testament texts are especially appropriate) to the incarnation and person of Christ (December) to the nature and reality of sin (in the bleak midwinter) to the death and work of Christ as a remedy (late winter, early spring, climaxing at Easter) and finally to the power of the Holy Spirit to help us live as we ought (after Easter and into and through the summer). I wanted to be sure to cover this "core curriculum" of gospel Christianity every year, hitting all the main themes. There were many, many people coming who would be there only through one or two of these annual preaching cycles. If a person was at the church for only a year, the new person coming in the fall would be exposed to the whole biblical "plotline"—the gospel. The person would learn about who God is in the fall, ideally come to faith in Christ during the winter, and then have the spring and summer preaching to help him or her begin to lead the Christian life.

   I generally did *short* series (four to twelve weeks, though some ran as long as half a year), usually from one book of the Bible or from one section of a book or from one author. It is important with this approach for each message to be thoroughly expository—really digging down and getting out the meaning of the author rather than finding a text that loosely resembles something you want to say anyway. This way, even though you are preaching the same basic "gospel curriculum" each year, you are doing it from fresh texts and learning new things from the Bible every year. That way your longtime members—who *are* there year after year—will be growing. If you don't do exposition, you won't actually learn new things from the Bible yourself. I also have had a general goal of preaching through every part of the Bible over a ten-year period.

So, for example, a two-year preaching course might look like this.

Fall: Attributes of God (all texts taken from the Prophets); Apostle's Creed (all texts taken from the Gospel of John)

December: The Songs of Christmas (Luke's Songs: Zechariah, Mary, Angels)

Winter: The New Birth (texts from Peter and Paul on regeneration and rebirth); Why Did Jesus Die? (St. Matthew's Passion, chapters 26–28)

Spring: Living a Life of Faith in a Pluralistic World (Daniel and Esther)

Summer: The Lord Praying (John 17 and the Lord's Prayer)

Fall: Our Struggles and God's Grace (Jacob: Genesis 25–32, 48)

Winter: What Did Jesus Come to Do? (the "amen" statements of Jesus in the gospels)

Spring: Life of Faith (Abraham: Genesis 12–22)

Summer: Arguing with Jesus (Mark 11–12)

Fall/Winter/Spring: Knowing God (Proverbs); St. John's Passion; Living in Wisdom (Proverbs)

15. The "big idea" movement in preaching is not new. In one of the most influential nineteenth-century works on preaching, *On the Preparation and Delivery of Sermons* (1870), John A. Broadus wrote that every sermon must have one very definite subject. "Whether a sermon has two points or ten points it

must have one main point: it must be about something. This definite subject . . . guides [the preacher] in his preparation. It is the key to his organization. It also helps him choose and arrange the material . . . [and] it will tell the listening people what they are to hear." John A. Broadus, *On the Preparation and Delivery of Sermons,* 4th ed. (1870; repr., New York: Harper & Row, 1979), p. 38. Robert Dabney's *Sacred Rhetoric* also drew on classical rhetoric to insist that the preacher "must, first, have one main subject of discourse, to which he adheres with supreme reference throughout." Robert Dabney, *Sacred Rhetoric; or, a Course of Lectures on Preaching* (Anson Randolph, 1870, or Edinburgh, Scotland: Banner of Truth, 1979, reprinted as *R. L. Dabney on Preaching*), p. 109. And in the early twentieth century prominent preacher John Henry Jowett stated this concept even more forcefully: "No sermon is ready for preaching, nor ready for writing out, until we can express its theme in a short, pregnant sentence as clear as crystal. . . . I do not think any sermon ought to be preached or even written, until that sentence has emerged, clear and lucid as a cloudless moon." J. H. Jowett, *The Preacher: His Life and Work* (Philadelphia: Doran, 1912), p. 133. The landmark midcentury book on preaching, *Design for Preaching* by H. Grady Davis (Minneapolis, MN: Fortress, 1958), called for one "central thought." "It is one thought catching others up into itself" (p. 20). In more recent times it has been Haddon Robinson who has made the "big idea" the heart of evangelical expository preaching. Haddon Robinson, *Biblical Preaching: The Development and Delivery of Expository Messages,* 2nd ed. (Grand Rapids, MI: Baker, 2001), pp. 33–50. The principle is that "a central, unifying idea must be at the heart of an effective sermon" (p. 35). Robinson quotes Jowett and others to hammer home his thesis: "Every sermon should have a theme, and that theme should be the theme of the portion of Scripture on which it is based" (p. 34, quoting Donald G. Miller). In other words, any text of Scripture has a central theme—and the sermon on that text must have the same central theme. The "big idea" of the sermon must be the "big idea" of the text.

16. In the book *The Big Idea of Biblical Preaching*, Duane Litfin lists a number of "challenges" to this view, and he bases these challenges on New Testament texts. See Duane Litfin, "New Testament Challenges to Big Idea Preaching," in *The Big Idea of Biblical Preaching: Connecting the Bible to People*, ed. Keith Wilhite and Scott M. Gibson (Grand Rapids, MI: Baker, 1998). One challenge is that the main idea of a text depends on what we believe to be the main idea or purpose of the entire book. Sometimes this is quite clear, as when John tells us that he wrote so the reader could believe in Jesus and receive eternal life (John 20:31). But what is *the* central message and purpose of the book of Acts? Or (in particular) *the* central message of each of the final chapters of Acts—all the hearings and trials of Paul? Commentators cannot even agree if these were written for non-Christians for apologetic purposes or for Christians in order to encourage them to be strong under persecution. Conclusions about the author's specific motives and intent often have to be tentative. And that means that it is hard to be absolutely certain what the central, main, primary intended point is of an individual chapter.

A second challenge is that few of the Bible's books and chapters were themselves written along the lines of classical rhetoric, with one central proposition. Few passages have clearly demarcated theme or thesis statements, and so identifying what *the* theme is can be fairly subjective. Litfin gives the book of James as a classic example. It deals with temptation, the tongue, and worldliness, but the text often shifts back and forth among these. As Litfin says, most of us, when writing letters, do not take the trouble to organize all we say around a central main idea. We ramble. Why couldn't James do that? He does! And there are many others among the Bible's genres—such as poetry, narrative, and legal documents—that are similarly hard to distill into a single, central statement because they aren't literary forms that require it. Indeed, it could be that the whole point of narrative, story, and parable is to convey meaning richly—beyond that which can be condensed into a simple proposition or even a sequence of them. In addition, there are sometimes lists of exhortations at the ends of the epistles. Almost every sentence introduces a different major subject. (See Hebrews 13:1–7, for example.) Finally, there are places like the book of Proverbs, in which it is notoriously difficult to see unifying themes in the chapters and in which often every verse provides a new "big idea."

The concept of a "big idea" within the text is, therefore, a bit artificial. It is more true for some passages than for others. The richness of the Bible often defies such reduction. Any preacher who has preached the same text two or three times over several decades knows that when you return to the text and listen to it, you almost inevitably see new things and hear new messages. And even when you think you have discerned a primary theme or subject (and usually the main subject *is* clear), because this is the inspired Word of God, even the more tangential statements and the semideveloped assumptions of the inspired author are rich sources of instruction. Not only the author's major points but also his minor points should be attended to, since they are also from God.

Summary: We must be careful of a kind of "expository legalism"—in which it is assumed that there can be only one exegetically accurate sermon and sermon theme on any one passage.

17. I should make it clear that to say that biblical texts talk about more than one subject and do not always have one central theme is *not* to say that the biblical text itself has multiple or indeterminate meanings. Neither I nor Alan Stibbs is here proposing the postmodern idea that no text has any inherent meaning, that the meaning of language is always indeterminate. Many people influenced by contemporary philosophy, with its skepticism about human language, apply this to the Bible and teach "polysemy"—the coexistence of many possible meanings of any text, some contradictory to one another, that the interpreter is free to draw out. This of course means that there is no way to say, "This is what the Bible teaches"— we would all be free to interpret it in our own way, with many interpretations contradicting others and no way to say which was the right one and therefore what God says in the Scripture. This view would turn preaching toward mere suggesting, musing, and open-ended storytelling (which in many

quarters is precisely what it has become). For a strong defense of the clarity of the Scripture, see Mark D. Thompson, *A Clear and Present Word: The Clarity of Scripture* (Downers Grove, IL: IVP Academic, 2006), and Benjamin Sargent, *As It Is Written: Interpreting the Bible with Boldness* (London: Latimer Trust, 2011). Both authors argue that each scriptural text has one meaning—the intended meaning of the biblical author—and that it is possible to discern this often enough in the Bible to speak of it with confidence. Despite this ringing, important affirmation, we must not fall into the mistaken belief that every biblical text is always clear, nor that discerning the Bible's meaning is easy, nor should we believe even that we ever see any text with complete and final clarity, because of the limits of our vision. A good, sober presentation of the complexity of biblical interpretation is an older but still helpful history of biblical interpretation: Moises Silva, *Has the Church Misread the Bible? The History of Interpretation in the Light of Current Issues* (Grand Rapids, MI: Zondervan, 1987). Silva rightly shows that as interpreters we never come to the text without a host of "background" (unconscious) assumptions that influence our interpretation. We are never as objective and neutral as we feel we are, and so the clarity of Scripture means we can be confident in our preaching, but the sinfulness of the interpreter means we should be humbly open to criticism. Also, Silva and others point out the tension between the Protestant principle that the intended meaning of the biblical author (the *sensus literalis*) *is* the meaning of the text and the way in which the New Testament authors often interpret Old Testament authors' statements as referring to Christ when the original authors did not seem to be aware of that meaning. There are good ways to understand how to do justice to both the *sensus literalis* and the Christocentric interpretation of the Bible, but we cannot go into that here, not even in the end notes! See the reading list in the Chapter 3 notes below on preaching Christ.

18. *Westminster Confession of Faith*, chapter 1, part 6: "The whole counsel of God concerning all things necessary for his own glory, man's salvation, faith and life, is either expressly set

down in Scripture, or by good and necessary consequence may be deduced from Scripture."

19. Alan M. Stibbs, *Expounding God's Word: Some Principles and Methods* (Chicago: InterVarsity Press, 1960), p. 17. Italics in this quote are mine.

20. Elsewhere Stibbs advises that a sermon be "given . . . unity" by developing the exposition of the text "in relationship to a single dominant theme" (ibid., p. 40). He does not recommend the "discursive comment of the so-called 'Bible reading,'" which meanders through multiple topics and subjects. He means he does not recommend verse-by-verse commentary and counsels that a main idea be isolated and that the points of the message support and develop it.

21. Preachers like Calvin and Chrysostom were masters at quickly handling some of the details of the text and bringing in rich insights without losing the main train of thought. And often there are some very rich nuggets in a text that are not at all part of the main idea of the passage. Your listeners will be poorer if you take no time to point them out. For example, look at 1 Timothy 6:12–16:

> Fight the good fight of the faith. . . . In the sight of God, who gives life to everything, and of Christ Jesus, who while testifying before Pontius Pilate made the good confession, I charge you to keep this command without spot or blame until the appearing of our Lord Jesus Christ, which God will bring about in his own time—God, the blessed and only Ruler, the King of kings and Lord of lords, who alone is immortal and who lives in unapproachable light, whom no one has seen or can see.

The main point of this passage is obviously to "fight the good fight of the faith" (verse 12). That is the "this command" Paul refers to in verse 14. So Timothy is not only told to do this but then is charged solemnly before God to do it. In order to expound the meaning of "fight the good fight of the faith," the preacher would have to go back into the rest of the book, since this is a final charge, a conclusion and summary of what had gone before. However, notice that there are some remarkable things said along the way about the attributes of God. He gives life to everything (verse 13) and he lives in unapproachable light that no man can see (verse 16). Should we not say anything in the sermon about these wonderful statements, made with divine authority? Of course we can. In fact, the skillful preacher should be able to make this part of the reason we should fight the good fight. After all, Paul brought these attributes of God in to make this exhortation to Timothy. It would surely be wrong to say little about fighting the good fight of the faith and turn the sermon into a reflection on the attributes of God. But it would also be too rigid a definition of exposition to insist that you cannot enlarge at all on these subsidiary points.

22. Fred Craddock, *As One Without Authority* (Nashville, TN: Abingdon Press, 1971); John Blake, "A Preaching 'Genius' Faces His Toughest Convert," CNN.com, December 14, 2011, www.cnn.com/2011/11/27/us/craddock-profile/.

23. "The Bible: Speech at Annual Meeting of the British and Foreign Bible Society, May 5, 1875," in *Speeches by C. H. Spurgeon at Home and Abroad,* ed. G. H. Pike (London, 1878). This quote was made popular, I believe, by a reference to it in D. M. Lloyd-Jones, *Authority* (Chicago: InterVarsity Press, 1958), p. 41: "The authority of the Scriptures is not a matter to be defended, so much as to be asserted. I address this remark particularly to Conservative Evangelicals. I am reminded of what the great Charles Haddon Spurgeon once said in this connection: 'There is no need for you to defend a lion when he is being attacked. All you need to do is to open the gate and let him out.' We need to remind ourselves frequently that it is the preaching and exposition of the Bible that really establish its truth and authority." It would be wrong to interpret the contrast I draw between Fred Craddock and Charles Spurgeon to mean that Craddock did not hold that the Bible had any authority at all or to mean that I don't believe we can learn from Craddock's contribution, which has been called "inductive" or "narrative" preaching. I

do indeed believe that Craddock has much to teach us, and there are many forms of expository preaching that are (as I have indicated in the rest of this chapter) too cognitive, rationalistic, dry, and authoritarian.

CHAPTER 2: PREACHING THE GOSPEL EVERY TIME

1. This chapter should be read in conjunction with "The Essence of Gospel Renewal" and "The Work of Gospel Renewal" in Timothy Keller, *Center Church: Doing Balanced, Gospel-Centered Ministry in Your City* (Grand Rapids, MI: Zondervan, 2012), pp. 63–84.
2. John Colquhoun, *A Treatise on the Law and Gospel*, D. Kistler, ed. (Edinburgh, 1859; Soli Deo Gloria, 1999), pp. 143–44.
3. Important works on this subject include the following: Peter Adam, "Part 1: Three Biblical Foundations of Preaching," in *Speaking God's Words: A Practical Theology of Preaching* (Vancouver, British Columbia: Regent College Publishing, 2004); E. Clowney, *Preaching and Biblical Theology* (Phillipsburg, NJ: Presbyterian and Reformed, 1973); E. Clowney, "Preaching Christ from All the Scripture," in *The Preacher and Preaching: Reviving the Art in the Twentieth Century*, S. Logan, ed. (Phillipsburg, NJ: Presbyterian and Reformed, 1986); Graeme Goldsworthy, *Preaching the Whole Bible as Christian Scripture* (Grand Rapids, MI: Wm. B. Eerdmans, 2000); David Murray, *Jesus on Every Page: 10 Simple Ways to Seek and Find Christ in the Old Testament* (Nashville, TN: Thomas Nelson, 2013); Sidney Greidanus, *Preaching Christ from the Old Testament* (Grand Rapids, MI: Wm. B. Eerdmans, 1999); Gary Millar and Phil Campbell, "Why Preaching the Gospel Is So Hard (Especially from the Old Testament)," in *Saving Eutychus: How to Preach God's Word and Keep People Awake* (Sydney, Australia: Matthias Media, 2013); Bryan Chapell, *Christ-Centered Preaching: Redeeming the Expository Sermon* (Grand Rapids, MI: Baker Academic, 1994); Sinclair Ferguson, *Preaching Christ from the Old Testament: Developing a Christ-Centered Instinct* (London: Proclamation Trust Media, 2000), available at https://docs.google.com/viewer? url=http%3A%2F%2Fwww

.proctrust.org.uk%2Fdls%2Fchrist_paper.pdf; and Iain M. Duguid, *Is Jesus in the Old Testament?* (Phillipsburg, NJ: Presbyterian and Reformed, 2013). I would propose that beginners first read Duguid, Ferguson, and Clowney's article in *The Preacher and Preaching*.

4. Sinclair Ferguson, *The Whole Christ: Legalism, Antinomianism, and Gospel Assurance* (Wheaton, IL: Crossway, forthcoming), p. 81 of manuscript.

5. William Perkins, *The Art of Prophesying*, p. 54: "The basic principle in application is to know whether the passage is a statement of the law or of the gospel. . . . The law exposes the disease of sin . . . but it provides no remedy for it. However, the gospel not only teaches us what is to be done, it also has the power of the Holy Spirit joined to it." For a Lutheran view see C. F. W. Walther, *Law and Gospel: How to Read and Apply the Bible* (St. Louis, MO: Concordia Publishing, 2010).

6. Ibid., p. 55.

7. Ferguson, *Whole Christ*, p. 42.

8. Ibid, p. 47.

9. Ibid., pp. 51–52.

10. Ibid., p. 52.

11. Ibid., p. 51.

12. Ibid., p. 52.

13. Ibid., p. 55.

14. Ibid., pp. 43 and 101.

15. George Whitefield, "The Method of Grace," www.biblebb.com/files/whitefield/gw058.htm.

16. The key Greek word is *anti*. Jesus died as a ransom *anti* ("in the stead of") many.

17. Ferguson, "Preaching Christ from the Old Testament."

18. Ibid.

CHAPTER 3: PREACHING CHRIST FROM ALL OF SCRIPTURE

1. For help with specific ways to preach Christ from different parts of the Bible, see D. A. Carson and G. K. Beale, *Commentary on the New Testament Use of the Old Testament* (Grand Rapids, MI: Baker, 2007); Leland Ryken, ed., *Dictionary of Biblical Imagery*

(Downers Grove, IL: IVP-US, 1998); Tremper Longman and Raymond B. Dillard, *An Introduction to the Old Testament,* 2nd ed. (Grand Rapids, MI: Zondervan, 2006); Edmund P. Clowney, *The Unfolding Mystery: Discovering Christ in the Old Testament,* 2nd ed. (Phillipsburg, NJ: Presbyterian and Reformed, 2013); Edmund P. Clowney, *How Jesus Transforms the Ten Commandments* (Phillipsburg, NJ: Presbyterian and Reformed, 2007); Alec Motyer, *Look to the Rock* (Nottingham, UK: InterVarsity Press, 1996); Christopher J. H. Wright, *Knowing Jesus Through the Old Testament* (Downers Grove, IL: InterVarsity Press, 1995); Simon DeGraaf, *Promise and Deliverance* (Grand Rapids, MI: Paideia Press, 1977, 1978, 1979, 1981). See also the work of particular Old Testament commentators on books of the Bible who are strong on Christocentric interpretation, such as Alec Motyer, Iain Duguid, Tremper Longman, and Ray Dillard. In addition to this, see the entire set of volumes in D. A. Carson, ed., *New Studies in Biblical Theology* (IVP Academic). Also see the many volumes of Sidney Greidanus, especially his *Preaching Christ from the Old Testament: A Contemporary Hermeneutical Method* (Grand Rapids, MI: Wm. B. Eerdmans, 1999), and of Graeme Goldsworthy, particularly his *Preaching the Whole Bible as Christian Scripture: The Application of Biblical Theology to Expository Preaching* (Grand Rapids, MI: Wm. B. Eerdmans, 2000.)

2. Ferguson lists four ways to preach Christ from the Old Testament across the genres (law, prophets, poets) and stages in redemptive history (Creation, Fall, Abrahamic family, Israel under Moses, Israel with a King, Jesus' ministry, the apostles' ministry): (1) Relate promise and fulfillment, (2) relate type and antitype, (3) relate the covenant and Christ, and (4) relate proleptic participation in salvation and subsequent realization. Greidanus does the same thing at greater length. He lists (1) the way of redemptive-historical progression, (2) the way of promise and fulfillment, (3) the way of typology, (4) the way of analogy, (5) the way of longitudinal themes, (6) the way of New Testament references, and (7) the way of contrast.

   In contrast with Ferguson and Greidanus, Goldsworthy concentrates on how to preach Christ from *within* each genre and stage of redemptive history, discussing how (1) the historical narratives, (2) the law, (3) the prophets, (4) the wisdom literature, (5) the Psalms, and (6) the apocalyptic texts point to Christ. Then he shows how to be sure the saving work of Christ is brought out when preaching from (7) the gospels and (8) the Acts and the Epistles. Finally he discusses tracing out an intercanonical theme across the genres and stages in a chapter titled "Preaching Christ from Biblical Theology."

David Murray mixes both the genre and the longitudinal theme categories. He lists ten ways to preach Christ: (1) in creation, (2) in Old Testament characters, (3) in God's appearances, (4) in God's law and commands, (5) in Israel's history, (6) in the prophets, (7) in the types, (8) in the covenants, (9) in the proverbs, (10) in the Biblical poets.

Gary Millar is perhaps the most imaginative, distilling the categories but coming at them in a more practical rather than abstract manner. He counsels getting to Jesus by (1) following out a theme through every stage to Jesus, (2) jumping immediately to fulfillment in Christ, (3) exposing a human problem and showing Jesus as the solution, (4) highlighting a divine attribute and showing Jesus as its ultimate embodiment, (5) focusing on the divine saving action in the text and pointing to how this comes to its ultimate form in Christ's salvation, (6) explaining a theological category and tying it to Christ, (7) pointing out sin's consequences and finding the only remedy in Christ, (8) describing an aspect of human godliness and goodness and showing Christ as the epitome of it, or (9) seeing a human longing and pointing to Christ as its satisfaction.

Bryan Chapell's list is helpful and the briefest, and all his categories are filled out by the other authors. He says that if there is not a clear reference to Christ or a clear type of Christ in the text, then find a pointer to Christ that is (1) predictive (as in prophecy), (2) preparatory (as in law and command), (3) reflective (as in key aspects of salvation), or 4) "resultant," showing how the life called for by the text could only come through faith in Christ.

Some ways to preach Christ fall into more than one category. For example, the "divine warrior" motif explored by Tremper Longman is a prophecy (Genesis 3:15) but is also an attribute of God (Exodus 15) and includes a number of human figures that are "types" of Christ (e.g., David before Goliath). So the categories are artificial in the end, just ways of forcing us to observe Scripture very carefully.

3. Once you decide *what* to connect to Christ—an intercanonical theme, a major figure or image, a grace story line, etc.—you must also determine *how* you are going to introduce this connection. Here are several ways to do that. (Some of the categories mentioned below are named by authors as "ways to preach Christ," but upon reflection I believe they are not really parallel to the others but rather are "how to connect to Christ" methods that work across several of the "what to connect to Christ" categories.)

1. Follow the plan? Gary Millar believes that sometimes a text points forward in time along a biblical theme but does not refer explicitly to Christ. In such a case it would be most appropriate to "follow the whole plan," taking the time to trace out the various forms the theme takes through the different stages in redemptive history. For example, when Jacob meets God at Bethel at "the stairway," he says it was "the house of God"—*Beth-el*. It makes sense to trace the history of "sanctuaries," places of God's presence, through redemptive history. During the times of the patriarchs God's presence comes down temporarily, dwelling in a tabernacle, then a temple, finally in Jesus himself, and through him with the Body of Christ. This takes a bit more time, but it teaches the listeners to see the unity of the Bible. "Following the plan" often works well within the categories of intercanonical themes, images and symbols, and God's attributes.

2. Jump to fulfillment? Millar thinks, however, that if Jesus is directly referred to by the text, you don't have to trace things through the stages but can more abruptly "jump to the fulfillment." For example, in 2 Samuel 7 God tells David that he will not build God a temple but that God will establish David's throne forever, without end. That invites us to look past David's son Solomon, who builds the temple and establishes David's throne, and jump all the way to Jesus Christ, who is the ultimate temple and truly establishes David's line forever. We don't need to trace out the history of the kingship in Israel. Passages like Daniel 7 and Isaiah 53 are similar, as they clearly refer to or predict a figure whose description fits only Jesus.

The upshot of distinguishing these two approaches is that sometimes the "coming to Christ" part of the sermon warrants more time and development and other times the move to Christ can be more sudden and take less time. This is a subjective call, but it is good to consider that there can be variety here. "Jumping to fulfillment" often works well within the categories of prophecies, promises, deliverance story lines, and theophanic appearances. Most of these features do not consist of longitudinal themes that reappear in every stage of history.

3. Develop the "narrative tension"? The heart of a story, of a narrative, is the plot tension. Some kind of problem develops that creates suspense and interest, as listeners want to find out if and how the tension is resolved. It is "narratively coherent" to set up a conflict in the early part of the sermon outline and then resolve it with Christ. This makes Christ, in a sense, the hero of every sermon. But this "tension" can be of very different kinds, depending on what it is that you are connecting to Christ.

• One tension is *God acting complexly or inexplicably*—which only ultimately makes sense in the coming of Jesus. For example, how can God be both holy and loving—both just and faithful—to us? (attributes of God). Are God's covenant promises conditional or unconditional? (intercanonical theme). In both cases only Christ and the cross resolve the tension.

• Another tension is a *prophecy, promise, blessing, or human longing that seems impossible to fulfill*. For example, in Ezekiel 34 how can God come himself to shepherd his people yet send "David"? How can someone be a descendant of David and yet God himself? (prophecy). How can God truly work good things out of evil? (promises). Again, only Jesus' incarnation and unjust suffering can solve the problem. Look at the prophecies of Isaiah in chapters 54 through 56 and elsewhere where he says eunuchs and foreigners will be allowed in the temple, in God's presence, and will become part of God's people. How can this be? Only the work of Christ as seen in the book of Hebrews makes sense of the breadth of such a promise. We all dread death, and Isaiah says the "shroud" (death) will be taken away (Isaiah 25:7). How? Only through the death and resurrection of Jesus Christ is death destroyed.

• A third tension comes from presenting a *breathtaking command or virtuous character* in which we highlight some great example or command of how to live and show the inner workings of the human heart that seem to make this impossible. Then we see how faith in Jesus' work changes the heart and is the only way to become like that example. (This works within the categories of command or godly example and major figure.)

• A fourth tension comes from *a divine curse or consequence of sin.* Many passages develop the particular, devastating consequences of sin. Many texts show how selfishness constantly leads to broken relationships. How will we escape? Jesus judicially takes the consequence himself (he is rejected by all his loved ones). Many texts show how meaningless life is without God (e.g., Ecclesiastes: "meaninglessness!"). But Jesus on the cross experiences the lostness of "life without God"—he gets the curse we deserve.

• A fifth tension can simply come from the simple question, *Where do we get the power or procure the right to do or to be this?* The answer is that the motives or other conditions of the heart (fear, anger, pride) that make it ordinarily impossible to do what is required come from faith in the finished work of Christ. The freedom and joy that come from a new relationship with God through grace and faith remove the motives of the heart that lead to the particular sin. Or through the finished work of Christ we have the *right* to this even though in ourselves we don't deserve it.

I don't believe, however, that direct plot "tensions" are the only way to preach Christ. Symbol fulfillment (#4), for example, is often a simple presentation of the wonder and beauty of Christ and has its own appeal. "Faceting" sermon outlines—not based on problem solution—are another way to preach toward a climax without using plot tensions. For example, take Jonathan Edwards's sermon "Christian Happiness." His outline (not in his own words) is that Christians should be happy because (1) our bad things will turn out for good, (2) our good things can't be taken away from us, and (3) our best things are yet to come. This is taking a simple truth and explaining it in such a way that still builds toward a climax. But no "tension" is used.

4. New Testament use of the Old Testament? Another way to preach Christ is to take Greidanus's helpful counsel that you should always check to see if an Old Testament text is being cited, referred to, or alluded to in the New Testament. (This could work whether you are preaching on a New Testament text and want to see if the Old Testament background gives you an intercanonical theme or you are preaching on an Old Testament text and you see how the New Testament writers understand the Old Testament passage in the light of Christ.) Then you can "follow the thread" of the idea through the stages of redemptive history and see how it connects to the saving work of Christ. An extremely useful textbook for this is Carson and Beale, *Commentary on the New Testament Use of the Old Testament.* But it is not a category alongside, say, identifying types or finding promises and fulfillment. It works for all those categories. The New Testament can use the Old Testament either through direct quote, through a reference that is pretty obvious, or—though it is more speculative—through indirect allusions. So, for example, commentators believe Jesus' talk about the new birth being "by water and the spirit" alludes to Ezekiel's discussion of regeneration using the same terms (Ezekiel 36).

4. There are at least a dozen places in the Old Testament where, in order to bring his presence near somebody, God sends the

"angel of the Lord." There are other angels; for example, in the New Testament, Gabriel gives the Annunciation to Mary. But when Gabriel and the other angels speak, they say, "This is what the Lord says." Gabriel speaks *for* the Lord. But when the angel of the Lord speaks, it *is* the Lord. This is an incredible mystery because the angel of the Lord seems to be a figure that is different from the Lord and yet at the same time actually is the Lord. Alec Motyer, in his commentary on Exodus, points out that

> The angel is revealed as a merciful accommodation of God, whereby the Lord can be present among a sinful people, when were he to go with them himself, his presence would consume them. We can put it this way. The angel suffers no reduction or adjustment of his full deity, yet he is that mode of deity whereby the holy God can keep company with sinners. Alec Motyer, *The Message of Exodus: The Days of Our Pilgrimage* (Downers Grove, IL: InterVarsity Press, 2005), p. 51.

You see this again and again in the Old Testament: When God brings his presence near in mercy and blessing, not to consume and destroy, he does it through the angel of the Lord. One of the most moving places is in the book of Genesis, the story of Abraham, Sarah, and Hagar. Abraham and Sarah are husband and wife, but Sarah is barren and getting older. She doesn't see herself having any children, so she gives her young, fertile Egyptian slave girl, Hagar, to Abraham. He lies with her, and she has a son. But when Hagar has the son, everything breaks down. Hagar is vain and proud and she taunts Sarah: "You old bat. I am young. I am fertile. I have a boy." Sarah is so furious that she goes to Abraham and says, "Send her and the child out into the desert," which of course means send them out to die. And Abraham (though he is unhappy and he wrings his hands) does it.

They are all victims but they are also all villains. There are no good guys in that story. Hagar—vain, proud—brings it on. Sarah—cruel—sends her out. Abraham is a coward. Hagar is out in the desert with her son, and they run out of water. She sees her little boy rejected by his father and dying of thirst, and she lays him under the shade of a bush, and then she walks away because, as she says, "I can't bear to see my own son die." The angel of the Lord appears. If you read the text, you will see that when the angel speaks, the Lord speaks; and when the Lord speaks, the angel speaks. The angel of the Lord says, "Do not be afraid; God has heard the boy crying as he lies there. Lift the boy up and take him by the hand, for I will make him into a great nation" (see Genesis 21:17–18).

How can God do that? Hagar, Sarah, Abraham—they don't deserve God's blessing. They don't deserve the presence of God. How can the presence of God come into their lives with blessing? It is through the angel. Usually when I get to this point in a sermon, I say, "Ah, the angel points us to somebody." Motyer says:

> There is only one other in the Bible who is identical with and yet distinct from the Lord; one who without abandoning the full essence and prerogatives of deity or diminishing the divine holiness is able to accommodate himself to the company of sinners, and who while affirming the wrath of God is yet a supreme display of his outreaching mercy. The angel of the Lord can only be appreciated when understood as a pre-incarnate appearance of Jesus Christ. (Motyer, *Message of Exodus*, p. 51.)

Now you know why God can come near undeserving sinners: because years later there was another little boy, born to a poor woman, who lived a life of rejection and at the end of his life was abandoned by his father. He also was dying of thirst, and he cried out and God did not answer. Do you know why God did not answer? Though Hagar and Abraham and Sarah deserved abandonment and not blessing, on the cross Jesus Christ got the abandonment we deserve, so that we could get the blessing that he deserved. He cried out and nobody answered, so that when we cry out, even though we don't deserve to be answered, we will be answered.

Jesus is the angel, and therefore God can come near. God can come into your life, just as he came into Moses's life. He can come into your life and burn with his power and his beauty and his glory dwelling in you now. It is safe now. Why? Because Jesus Christ died on the cross.

5. John Calvin, *Calvin: Commentaries,* trans. and ed. Joseph Haroutunian (London: S.C.M. Press, 1958), pp. 68–69.

6. For the evidence for this assertion see Joel Marcus, *Mark 1–8: New Translation with Introduction and Comments,* Anchor Bible, vol. 27 (New York: Doubleday, 2000), pp. 332–40.

7. From Galatians 3:13, English Standard Version.

8. The Greek word in this verse usually translated "departure" is the Greek word *exodus.*

9. Ferguson, *Preaching Christ from the Old Testament,* p. 4.

10. Actually, marriage *is* an intercanonical theme, so seeing Christ in Judges 19–21 fits in with how we can read the Bible Christocentrically.

11. "Set his face" is the literal Greek expression. The Latin Vulgate and some other ancient versions add "like a flint," a term that means hard and unyielding. Most modern translations say something like "set out resolutely."

CHAPTER 4: PREACHING CHRIST TO THE CULTURE

1. My translation. See also both the translations of the English Standard Version and the New American Standard version.

2. Terry Eagleton, *Culture and the Death of God* (New Haven, CT: Yale University Press, 2014), p. 1.

3. See Peter Watson, *The Age of Atheists: How We Have Sought to Live Since the Death of God* (New York: Simon & Schuster, 2014); Sam Harris, *Waking Up: A Guide to Spirituality Without Religion* (New York: Simon & Schuster, 2014); Ronald Dworkin, *Religion Without God* (Cambridge, MA: Harvard University Press, 2013); and Alain de Botton, *Religion for*

Atheists: A Non-Believer's Guide to the Uses of Religion (New York: Vintage, 2013). All of these volumes are efforts to find inner peace, meaning, fulfillment community, and a sense of "fullness" and greatness that people have looked for traditionally in religion and belief in God.

4. Barna Group, "Barna Technology Study: Social Networking, Online Entertainment and Church Podcasts," May 26, 2008, www.barna.org/barna-update/media-watch/36-barna-technology-study-social-networking-online-entertainment-and-church-podcasts#.VELXX_l4o3g.

5. An example is Doug Pagitt's *Preaching Re-Imagined: The Role of the Sermon in Communities of Faith* (Grand Rapids, MI: Zondervan, 2005), which was written near the end of the debate. Pagitt criticizes not just preaching but public oratory in general, which he calls "speaching." His basic thesis is that the community, not the preacher, must determine truth, and oratory elevates one individual to an illegitimate place of authority. While this was put forth breathlessly as something radical, mainline homileticians such as Lucy Rose, in *Sharing the Word: Preaching in the Roundtable Church* (Louisville, KY: John Knox, 1997), and John McClure, in *The Roundtable Pulpit,* (Nashville, TN: Abingdon, 1995) had been saying the same thing. See also Leander E. Keck, who writes: "If something is worth communicating, don't spoil it by preaching it! Let it emerge in the give-and-take of the group; celebrate it by music, dance or drama. In preaching, people are as passive as chickens on a roost—and perhaps just as awake." Leander E. Keck, *The Bible in the Pulpit: The Renewal of Biblical Preaching* (Nashville, TN: Abingdon, 1978), p. 40. So in more mainline circles, the monologue sermon has been questioned for a generation. Nevertheless, Thomas G. Long, a prominent mainline professor of preaching, indicates that the dialogue or roundtable sermon is one of several temporary "experiments" that the church tries during times of anxiety over the effectiveness of preaching. (He lists them: "multi-media sermons, first-person sermons, musical sermons, dialogue sermons, sermons preached from bar stools . . .") Long argues that such experimentation does not lead to the wholesale jettisoning of the sermon form but serves

the purpose of helping people to think innovatively about preaching during the seasons of the "periodic pulpit melt-downs." Thomas G. Long, *Preaching from Memory to Hope* (Louisville, KY: John Knox Press, 2009), pp. xiv–xv.

Within more conservative circles, David C. Norrington's *To Preach or Not to Preach* concludes that "the regular sermon has no biblical basis, that it utilizes pagan methods hostile to the New Testament practice and that it appears to have had no part in early Christian growth." David C. Norrington, *To Preach or Not to Preach* (Milton Keynes, Exeter, UK: Paternoster Press, 1996; repr., Ekklesia Press, 2013), p. 95. Sermons, Norrington argues, are by definition abstract and generalizing—the preacher cannot know all that is going on in the lives of the listeners present. Sermons create passive believers who do not learn how to learn and internalize the biblical truth for themselves. One-way communication also means the preachers themselves do not learn, staying largely confirmed in their prejudices. Norrington believes that the regular sermon—the one-way weekly speech on the Bible from the pastor—is a nonbiblical practice that did not develop until the third or fourth century after Christ. He calls for an end to the sermon and the adoption of an interactive, communal reading of the Bible combined with the encouragement, counsel, and correction of the whole group (Norrington, *To Preach or Not to Preach,* p. 83). Norrington is generally seen to have failed to make his case that what he calls "regular preaching"—a monological oral presentation of Christian truth—is "unbiblical" and even "pagan." This is especially so given Hughes Old's historical research on the history of the sermon. Old points to the early church document the *Didache,* which assumes the existence of "a group of professional preachers who devote their lives to their ministry rather than lay preachers." Hughes Oliphant Old, *The Reading and Preaching of the Scriptures in the Worship of the Christian Church,* vol. 1, *The Biblical Period,* p. 256.

6. Andy Stanley and Lane Jones, *Communicating for a Change* (Eugene, OR: Multnomah, 2006), p. 89.

7. P. T. Forsyth, *Positive Preaching and the Modern Mind* (Milton Keynes, Exeter, UK: Paternoster Press Reprint, 1998), p. 73. As

an example, he writes that Athanasius "descended on the world, like the true preacher he was, rather than arose from it. . . . He compelled the world to accommodate itself to him." Ibid., p. 74.

8. Ibid., p. 2. It is interesting that in the same general era that Forsyth was lecturing and writing on preaching, Harry Emerson Fosdick and others in New York City were going in the opposite direction. Fosdick was an early liberal Protestant who advised preachers to focus on psychology, not the exposition of doctrine. He wrote, "Every sermon should have for its main business the solving of some problem—a vital, important problem, puzzling minds, burdening consciences, distracting lives—and any sermon which does tackle a real problem, throw even a little light on it, and help some individuals practically to find their way through it cannot be altogether uninteresting." Quoted in Thomas G. Long, *The Witness of Preaching*, 2nd ed. (Louisville, KY: John Knox Press, 2005), p. 30. Long's critique of the "sermon as counseling session" used by Fosdick and later by Norman Vincent Peale and many others in the mainline—and his account of how it fell out of fashion—is on pp. 30–37. See also Matthew Bowman, "Harry Emerson Fosdick and Baptism at Riverside," in *The Urban Pulpit: New York City and the Fate of Liberal Evangelicalism* (New York: Oxford University Press, 2014), p. 253.

9. Old shows that this expository method went directly against the cultural currents of the time. Classical oratory was dialectical. It began with a thesis about some important current issue, then divided the topic up, proposed and evaluated all the arguments on both sides, and made a case for how to solve it. Expository preaching let the text itself give the sermon its shape. It began with the text and moved out toward practical life, instead of the other way around. Old points to a sermon by Clement of Alexandria (c. 150—c. 215). After an introduction, Clement goes through a passage of Scripture verse by verse, explaining the meaning of the words and statements as he goes. Old remarks: "This to be sure was not a procedure he had learned from the classics of Greek oratory—the Greeks had nothing like the expository sermon to serve as a literary model." Old, *Reading and Preaching of the Scriptures*, vol. 1, *Biblical Period*, p. 299.

10. Forsyth, *Positive Preaching and the Modern Mind,* p. 73.

11. Luc Ferry, *A Brief History of Thought: A Philosophical Guide to Living* (New York: Harper, 2011), pp. 60–64.

12. Ibid.

13. I have written extensively about contextualization in *Center Church*, pp. 89–134. The brief next section of the chapter must be read in connection with that longer treatment.

14. Eckhard J. Schnabel, *Paul the Missionary: Realities, Strategies, and Methods* (Downers Grove, IL: IVP Academic, 2008). In Acts 13:13–43 Paul speaks to Jews and Gentile God fearers— those who accept the authority of the Bible. However, in Acts 14:6–16 he speaks to polytheistic peasants, in 17:16–34 to sophisticated Greek elites in Athens, and in Acts 26 to the multiethnic cultural elites of the Palestinian Roman colonies. For Schnabel's analysis of Paul's cultural adaptations and speeches in Acts, see pp. 155–208 and 334–53. "Exegetes and missiologists often use the term *contextualization* for this dimension of Paul's . . . speech" (p. 174).

15. So, when he tells Festus that his words are not "insane" but rather "rational," he uses the word *sophrosynes.* "The term has such nuances as . . . intellectually sound . . . without illusion . . . prudent." Gerhard Kittel, Gerhard Friedrich, and Geoffrey W. Bromiley, *Theological Dictionary of the New Testament* (Grand Rapids, MI: Wm. B. Eerdmans, 1985), p. 1150.

16. "Paul selects from the Old Testament and from Jewish traditions such motifs that could be immediately understood by Athenian philosophers, including terminological allusions and quotations." Ibid, p. 171. There are some who say that those who argue for contextualization put too much weight on Acts 17, but Paul's contextualizing work can be seen throughout the book of Acts. There are other biblical examples too. We have noted John's powerful use of the term *logos* in John 1. Also, the book of Deuteronomy can be shown to have been deliberately written in the form of a second-millennium Hittite suzerainty treaty, a literary form that would have been instantly recognizable to the ancient Near Eastern cultures of the time, which used it to set up covenant relationships between triumphant kings and vassal states. See

Meredith G. Kline, *The Treaty of the Great King* (Eugene, OR: Wipf and Stock, 2012).

17. Schnabel, *Paul the Missionary,* p. 171.

18. He agrees, for example, with the popular critique by the philosophers of man-made temples and sacrifices (Acts 17:24–25), and he also refers to humanity's search for God (Acts 17:27–28). Ibid., pp. 171–74.

19. Ibid., p. 171.

20. Ibid., p. 177.

21. Schnabel observes: "Paul uses the quotation from Aratus as an argument against the philosophers' rapprochement with the plurality and diversity of religious cults. If human beings have been created by the Creator God, it is preposterous that human beings would create images of a god and worship [them]." Ibid., pp. 179–80.

22. Keller, *Center Church,* pp. 124–26.

23. Paul "employs convictions, arguments and formulations that these intellectual Athenians were familiar with and that they would have acknowledged as valid." Schnabel, *Paul the Missionary,* p. 174. Nevertheless, in the end "Paul's response to the religious beliefs and practices of the Athenians was, ultimately, not accommodation but confrontation." Ibid., p. 82.

24. By learning and "using the intellectual, philosophical, and linguistic traditions of his audience" Paul was showing his listeners that he "takes them seriously as discussion partners." Ibid., p. 183. Philosopher Charles Taylor agrees: "The preaching of the Gospel, if it is to be other than an expression of the felt superiority of the preacher, demands . . . close and respectful attention to the life of the addressees . . . prior to the grace which the Gospel will bring." Charles Taylor, *A Secular Age* (Cambridge, MA: Harvard University Press, 2007), p. 95.

25. For more on contextualization, see David F. Wells, "The Nature and Function of Theology," in *The Use of the Bible in Theology: Evangelical Options,* ed. Robert K. Johnston (Louisville, KY: John Knox, 1985); Richard Lints, *The Fabric of Theology: A Prolegomenon to Evangelical Theology* (Grand Rapids, MI: Wm. B. Eerdmans, 1993), pp. 102–5; David K. Clark, "Evangelical Contextualization," in *To Know and Love God: Method for*

Theology (Wheaton, IL: Crossway, 2010), pp. 78–90; Bruce Riley Ashford, "The Gospel and Culture," in *Theology and Practice of Mission: God, the Church, and the Nations,* Bruce Ashford, ed. (Nashville, TN: B and H Academic, 2011), pp. 109–27.

All four writers—Wells, Clark, Lints, and Ashford— mention three approaches to contextualization: (1) the main-line/liberal view that sees all people as so culturally embedded that "praxis" and context have priority over Scripture (see Clark, "Evangelical Contextualization," p. 78); (2) the fundamentalist view, in which Christians understand themselves to be so free from cultural bias that they can read the truth straight out of the Scripture, and therefore they have no need of any process of contextualization; and (3) an evangelical approach, which acknowledges cultural bias in all people and the need for cultural translation and adaptation but which wants the Bible to remain normative over culture, not an equal "dialogue" partner with it. Despite the fact that evangelicals all generally try to work within framework (3), there are differences of approach.

David K. Clark critiques the writings of Wells and David Hesselgrave as a "code/decode" model that sees contextualization as only a method of communication transmission. (Some others closely aligned with Hesselgrave and Wells prefer to talk of translation and transmission rather than contextualization.) Clark believes this model is too confident that the Christian preacher can discern transcultural core principles that simply need to "change their clothing"—be put into new cultural forms and codes. Clark proposes instead a "dialogical model" in which the Christian preacher not only allows the Bible to critique the new culture but also allows the new culture to critique our previous reading of Scripture. For example, trying to reach a more communal culture might help American Christians see that their own understanding of Christianity was too individualistic and shaped by their culture, not by the Bible. Clark goes on to say that for this reason contextualization must be a much more searching process. It is not just something that we do from some perch, translating and reformulating without ourselves being examined and part of the process. Ibid., pp. 81–90. I agree with much of what Clark says, though I am not sure he differs as much from Hesselgrave and Wells as he thinks. In the end, evangelicals will differ in their practice, but there is a general agreement that some kind of process of contextualization is necessary.

26. I am indebted for this section to my son Michael Keller, a Ph.D. student at the Jonathan Edwards Center at Yale University, who supplied me the unpublished dissertation of Rachel M. Wheeler (see below) as well as transcripts of all Edwards's sermons from his Stockbridge years.

27. To read some of these sermons, see "To the Mohawks at the Treaty, August 16, 1751" and "He That Believeth Shall Be Saved," in *The Sermons of Jonathan Edwards: A Reader,* eds. Wilson Kimnach, Kenneth Minkema, and Douglas Sweeney (New Haven, CT: Yale University Press, 1999), pp. 105–20. See also "The Things That Belong to True Religion," "Heaven's Dragnet," "Death and Judgment," "Christ Is to the Heart Like a River to a Tree Planted by It," "God Is Infinitely Strong," "Warring with the Devil," and "Farewell Sermon to the Indians," in *The Works of Jonathan Edwards: Sermons and Discourses 1743–1758*, vol. 25, ed. Wilson Kimnach (New Haven, CT: Yale University Press, 2006), pp. 566–716.

28. Edwards's sermons to the Indians were briefer and compressed. Yet his simplicity was by no means simplistic. Edwards scholar Wilson Kimnach writes: "While brief, the Indian sermons are remarkably balanced in covering the nuances of Calvinistic theology." Kimnach, *Works of Jonathan Edwards,* vol. 25, p. 42. Nevertheless, the manner in which that theology was communicated changed significantly. This can be seen clearly in his first sermon to the Indians, "The Things That Belong to True Religion." Ibid., pp. 566–74. After reading his text, Acts 11:12–13, he does not begin with his usual textual exegesis, a detailed dividing and parsing of the verses. Instead he does something he had never done before— he begins with an extended story, the story of Cornelius, the first non-Jewish convert, and shows how his conversion fits into the history of redemption. The story is about a racial outsider, a "heathen warrior," who finds faith in Christ. The Jews had known the God of Israel, but Gentiles were polytheists

who had no such knowledge in their backgrounds—in all these ways Cornelius is like the Indians themselves.

Then Edwards presents the entirety of human history as the spreading out of the gospel—first from one family to a nation, then from the Hebrews to European Gentiles like Cornelius, who were slowly converted. He speaks about how his own English people had once worshipped idols in superstition, but they threw away those idols and became Christians. Now, Edwards argues, the gospel is spreading from the Europeans to the Indians, from the Old World to the New World. In this narrative Edwards identifies with the Indians—he is also part of a nation that once found Christianity "strange." But most of all this account puts the hearers themselves squarely in the middle of the great story of the world and of what God is doing in it. Edwards is not merely denouncing the Indians as superstitious pagans—he is showing how, as a people, they are part of God's plan. Here Edwards makes a remarkable move—he uses the gospel to do away with the racial "us" and "them" division.

A look at the rest of Edwards's sermons to the Indians shows numerous drastic changes that he made to his preaching in order to reach his new listeners. His sermons devote far less time to detailed biblical exegesis, and he also has fewer Scripture proofs in his doctrine and application sections. Ibid., p. 641. Instead, to emphasize the truth of the biblical doctrine Edwards relied more on "personal witness to the truth of the message . . . and an appeal to shared experience." Ibid., p. 641. Like Paul, he does not rely heavily on multiple Bible proofs with listeners who do not know the Bible, even though he always draws his teaching from the Scripture.

In addition, Edwards's traditional sermon outline changed. Previously each sermon invariably had included text (the exegesis of a biblical passage), doctrine (the distillation of the doctrinal implication of the text into a single sentence, and then the analysis of the aspects of the proposition), and application (the practical use of the doctrine in the lives of the hearers). However, "a hallmark of the Stockbridge Indian sermons is that . . . they have nothing labeled 'Doctrine,' but only . . . Observations." Wilson Kimnach, "Introduction: Edwards the

Preacher," in *Sermons by Jonathan Edwards on the Matthean Parables,* vol. 1, Kenneth P. Minkema, Adriaan C. Neele, and Bryan McCarthy, eds. (Eugene, OR: Cascade Books, 2012), p. 10n15. Rather than discoursing at length through analysis and division of subjects into parts, Edwards moved from an emphasis on analysis to synthesis. Kimnach, *Works of Jonathan Edwards,* vol. 25, p. 42. His sermons now consisted of concise packets of ideas. Ibid., p. 566.

In these sermons we see Edwards using not just narrative more heavily but also metaphor. "While his [homiletical] method did not involve over-simplification of essential concepts, or patronizing the Indians with a belittling gentleness, he often did adjust his diction and, most effectively, his imagery." Ibid., p. 676. Rebecca Wheeler writes that "at Stockbridge, he came to rely more heavily on metaphor and imagery. Drawing on the parables of the New Testament, Edwards preached of sowers of seed, of fishermen, of ground too dry for a seed to take, of trees fed by rivers that never ran dry, and of briars and thorns that impeded a traveler's way." Rebecca M. Wheeler, "Living upon Hope: Mahicans and Missionaries, 1730–1760" (Ph.D. diss., Yale University, 1999), p. 163. It was not merely that he used more images and metaphors, however. He also selected the ones he believed would resonate with the Indians.

His sermon "Warring with the Devil" was based on Luke 11:21–22: "When a strong man, fully armed, guards his own house . . ." Edwards depicts the "house" as the self or the soul, which may be under the power of Satan, who is shown to be a powerful warrior. Armed with the inordinate lusts of the human heart, he can take us captive. Sin is therefore imaged as the state of being in thrall of an armed enemy. But grace and salvation come through Christ in the form of a greater armed man, who can liberate us. There are several metaphors that the New Testament uses for the atonement, one of which is the "battlefield" metaphor (Hebrews 2:14–15; Colossians 1:15), Jesus' victory over Satan and evil. Wilson Kimnach, the foremost expert on Edwards's sermons, says that Edwards had seldom used the imagery of warfare in his preaching before, not even in wartime. The use of it here, however, was because "the Indian warrior culture provided his rhetorical opportunity." Kimnach, *Works of Jonathan Edwards,* vol. 25, p. 676.

One more adaptation by Edwards should be noted. Rebecca M. Wheeler, the scholar most conversant with Edwards's sermons and ministry to the Indians, writes: "The emphasis on the never-ending love of Christ [in these sermons] suggests a recognition that the pastor faced a congregation in need of love, comfort and solace." Wheeler, "Living upon Hope," p. 135. Kimnach also notices this change. Edwards's sermon "God Is Infinitely Strong" was an "awakening" sermon for the Indians, designed to call people to repentance and conversion. However, though it falls into this category, it is an awakening sermon "of the milder sort." Kimnach, *Works of Jonathan Edwards,* vol. 25, p. 642. Edwards was simply gentler with the Indians. Why? There are two reasons. Edwards saw the injustices that the Indians were suffering at the hands of English landowners. "Edwards proved a tireless advocate for the Indians . . . rectifying long-standing abuses." Kimnach, Minkema, and Sweeney, *Sermons of Jonathan Edwards,* p. xxxv. The European minister came to see how much of the Indians' suffering—alcoholism, poverty, diseases—had been largely imposed on them.

Kimnach and Wheeler also point out that Edwards's theological reflection on the Indians' state concluded that Indian non-Christians were less culpable than English non-Christians, because the English had been exposed to Christian truth and the gospel all their lives. Indian nonbelievers were simply not as blameworthy. Though still lost unless they believed in Christ, they had not had the same opportunity as Europeans to hear the story of the gospel. Wheeler writes: "Indian non-Christians were different from English non-Christians in that they were heathen, meaning they had no knowledge of Christ. . . . Despite the connotations of the term today, Edwards saw heathendom as the lesser of two evils, for heathens could not be blamed for their ignorance, but [English] sinners who had grown up with the gospel could be expected to know better." Wheeler, "Living upon Hope," pp. 178–79.

As a result of all of these factors, Edwards's preaching did not have the same note of severity that it had in other parts of

New England. He had compassion for their situation and provided stronger notes of consolation and comfort. To put it simply, he did not think that the forcefulness of a sermon such as "Sinners in the Hands of an Angry God" was as appropriate for the Indians.

Jonathan Edwards did not know the word "contextualization," but it is obvious that he was doing exactly what Paul was doing. If someone had asked him why he was adapting to a new culture, he likely would have insisted that he was only trying to bring the gospel to bear on people's hearts. He did not merely want to beat upon them and condemn them. He wanted to preach in such a way that it moved their hearts to see the truth of the gospel.

29. D. A. Carson has written: "[While] no truth which human beings may articulate can ever be articulated in a culture-transcending way . . . that does not mean that the truth thus articulated does not transcend culture." D. A. Carson, "Maintaining Scientific and Christian Truths in a Postmodern World," *Science & Christian Belief* 14, no. 2 (October 2002): 107–22, www.scienceandchristianbelief.org/articles/carson.php. Also see D. A. Carson, "The Role of Exegesis in Systematic Theology," in *Doing Theology in Today's World: Essays in Honor of Kenneth S. Kantzer*, John D. Woodbridge and Thomas Edward McComiskey, eds. (Grand Rapids, MI: Zondervan, 1991), pp. 48–56; and D. A. Carson, "A Sketch of the Factors Determining Current Hermeneutical Debates in Cross-Cultural Contexts," in D. A. Carson, ed., *Biblical Interpretation and the Church: The Problem of Contextualization* (Eugene, OR: Wipf and Stock, 2002), pp.11–29.

30. Robert Murray M'Cheyne, *Sermons of Robert Murray M'Cheyne* (Edinburgh, Scotland: Banner of Truth Trust, 1961), p. 43.

31. For more on how to preach about justice and mercy, see Timothy Keller, *Generous Justice: How Grace Makes Us Just* (New York: Dutton, 2010).

32. David Foster Wallace, commencement address at Kenyon College, May 21, 2005, available at http://moreintelligentlife.com/story/david-foster-wallace-in-his-own-words. See also a printed version in Dave Eggers, *The Best*

Nonrequired Reading 2006, 1st ed. (New York: Mariner Books, 2006), pp. 355–64.

33. One Scripture text that makes almost exactly Martin Luther King Jr.'s point is Daniel 6:22, where Daniel says that he has done no wrong, though he broke the law of the land (of the Medes and the Persians), because he has not broken God's law.

34. Martin Luther King Jr., "Letter from Birmingham Jail," August 1963, www.uscrossier.org/pullias/wp-content/uploads/2012/06/king.pdf.

35. Another reinforcing cultural reference to point to is W. H. Auden, who had turned away from faith but then early in World War II came to realize exactly what Martin Luther King Jr. later said about God's law as a basis for judging human action. Auden had abandoned faith in God and turned to the secular idea of self-creation of identity and value, rather than any belief in a moral order to the universe. This left him no way to condemn the rising Fascism in Italy and Spain and the Nazis themselves, who were all defending their actions by drawing on the same sources of self-expressivism that he was. I tell Auden's story in *Encounters with Jesus: Unexpected Answers to Life's Biggest Questions* (New York: Dutton, 2013), pp. 13–16. See also Charles Taylor, "The Slide to Subjectivism," in *The Malaise of Modernity* (Ontario, Canada: Anansi Books, 1991), pp. 55–69. Taylor does not mention Auden, but he sketches the roots of Fascism and the fascination with violence as they came from the self-expressivism of the Romantic movement.

36. "Beethoven . . . turned out pieces of breath-taking rightness. Rightness—that's the word! When you get the feeling that whatever note succeeds the last is the only possible note that can rightly happen at that instant, in that context, then chances are you're listening to Beethoven. Melodies, fugues, rhythms—leave them to the Chaikovskys and Hindemiths and Ravels. Our boy has the real goods, the stuff from Heaven, the power to make you feel at the finish: Something is right in the world. There is something that checks throughout, that follows its own law consistently: something we can trust, that will never let us down." Leonard Bernstein, *The Joy of Music* (New York: Simon & Schuster, 2004), p. 105.

37. Thomas Nagel, *The Last Word* (New York: Oxford University Press: 1997), p. 130.

38. Andrew Delbanco, *The Death of Satan: How Americans Have Lost the Sense of Evil* (New York: Farrar, Straus, and Giroux, 1995), p. 3.

39. Ibid., pp. 190–92.

40. Quoted in Stuart Babbage, *The Mark of Cain: Studies in Literature and Theology* (Grand Rapids. MI: Wm. B. Eerdmans, 1966), p. 17.

41. All the while, consider the great danger of misplaced motivation in this area. So-called cultural references—the use of quotes from films, popular music, newspapers, Web sites, social media outlets, journals, and books—can be made mostly to gain personal credibility for the speaker. You may do it to seem sophisticated or erudite or hip. You may hope that people will accept you as "one of them" because you are so au courant or simply accessible and normal. If that is the response you get from people (or worse, what you actually want or need from them), then you must admit and change your motives. With that as your motivation you will choose cultural references to draw attention to yourself rather than to make visible and challenge the beliefs of secular culture as well as lay bare your listeners' own hearts. That should be the only goal.

42. A great example is the Catholic writer Flannery O'Connor: "I don't think you should write something as long as a novel around anything that is not of the gravest concern to you and everybody else, and for me this is always the conflict between an attraction for the Holy and the disbelief in it that we breathe in with the air of our times. It's hard to believe always but more so in the world we live in now. There are some of us who have to pay for our faith every step of the way and who have to work out dramatically what it would be like without it and if being without it would be ultimately possible or not." Quoted in James K. A. Smith, *How (Not) to Be Secular* (Grand Rapids, MI: Wm. B. Eerdmans, 2014), pp. 10–11.

43. Karen H. Jobes, *1 Peter,* Baker Exegetical Commentary on the New Testament (Grand Rapids, MI: Baker, 2005), p. 231.

44. See more exposition and examples of challenging and confronting the culture in Timothy Keller, *Center Church: Doing Balanced, Gospel-Centered Ministry in Your City*, pp. 124–28. Some of the examples here are taken from this section of *Center Church* as well as from Timothy Keller, *The Reason for God: Belief in an Age of Skepticism* (New York: Dutton, 2008).

45. More of the passage: "This [natural] world running on chance and death, careening blindly from nowhere to nowhere, somehow produced wonderful us. I came from the world, I crawled out of a sea of amino acids, and now I must whirl around and shake my fist at that sea and cry Shame! . . . Either this world, my mother, is a monster, or I am a freak. . . . There is not a person in the world that behaves as badly as praying mantises. But wait, you say, there is no right or wrong in nature; right and wrong is a human concept! Precisely! We are moral creatures in an amoral world. . . . Or consider the alternative. . . . It is only human feeling that is freakishly amiss. . . . All right then—it is our emotions that are amiss. We are freaks, the world is fine, and let us all go have lobotomies to restore us to a natural state. We can leave . . . lobotomized, go back to the creek, and live on its banks as untroubled as any muskrat or reed. You first." Annie Dillard, *Pilgrim at Tinker Creek* (New York: Harper Perennial Modern Classics, 2007), pp. 178–79.

46. Volf's point of contact is our desperate modern desire for nonviolent peacemaking between enemies. His point of contradiction counterintuitively builds on that. He concludes: "It takes the quiet of a suburban home for the birth of the thesis that human nonviolence is a result of a God who refuses to judge." A belief in a God of judgment and vengeance is actually a major resource for nonviolence! These quotes are taken from Miroslav Volf, *Exclusion & Embrace: A Theological Exploration of Identity, Otherness, and Reconciliation* (Nashville, TN: Abingdon, 1996), pp. 303–4. C. S. Lewis makes a very different argument to people who are skeptical of the idea of a God of wrath and judgment. In a passage in *The Problem of Pain*, Lewis argues that when we love someone, we get angry if anything comes in to hurt or mar him or her. If a father loves a daughter, and he sees her ruining her

own life, he gets angry not in spite of his great love for her but because of it. The point of contact with secular people is comfort with the concept of a loving God. But Lewis moves from contact to contradiction by saying, "If you believe in a loving God, you will *have* to believe in a God of wrath against sin." (I cite this example in *Center Church,* p. 126.)

47. Taylor, *Malaise of Modernity,* p. 72. Italics are mine.
48. Taylor, *Secular Age,* pp. 103–9, p. 594–617.
49. See Donald B. Kraybill, et al., *Amish Grace: How Forgiveness Transcended Tragedy* (San Francisco: Jossey-Bass, 2007).
50. Robert Bellah, et al., *Habits of the Heart: Individualism and Commitment in American Life, with New Preface* (Berkeley: University of California Press, 2007).

CHAPTER 5: PREACHING AND THE (LATE) MODERN MIND

1. P. T. Forsyth, *Positive Preaching and the Modern Mind* (Exeter, UK: Paternoster Press, repr. 1998), pp. 20–21.
2. Ibid, p. 30. Forsyth offers much helpful counsel about how to preach to the modern mind. He says that modern people will not agree to cede God authority over their lives through the application of mere guilt, pressure, or force. They will lay down their arms and surrender only if their hearts are convicted and melted. How can that be done? We must show people that "[God] is not an other, but he is my other." This is because we were created to know and serve him; therefore his power is "congenial power," which fits our nature and need. They must see the "homonomy of his authority . . . its kinship with [their] soul[s]." Also, we must prove to them that if God is not our authority, something else will be. "If within us we find nothing over us we succumb to what is around us." Forsyth strikes an unmistakably Augustinian note: If we don't acknowledge God as our meaning in life, it "gives externals their enslaving power over us." They become our "Overlords." If we live for career or family or politics, then these things master us. We will not be able to live without them. We will overwork to achieve them and be uncontrollably frightened or bitter if anything prevents us from having them. Ibid., pp. 29–30.

3. While all of P. T. Forsyth is well worth reading, I believe his doctrine of the Scripture and of divine revelation left him less able to confront the "modern mind" than he believed. On the one hand he says, "The ideal ministry must be a Bibliocracy." Ibid., p. 46. He argues that in our ministry to the modern mind "not only do we adhere to texts" but we also must offer "expository preaching—for a long text and the elucidation of a passage. The public soon grows weary of topical preaching alone, or newspaper, in which the week's events supply the text." Ibid., p. 5. He criticizes those who let contemporary issues set the agenda and who then bring in the Bible, seen as significant only to the degree it helps us think about our pet issues. On the contrary, Forsyth argues that the preacher to the modern mind should teach the Bible so fully and skillfully that he comes to see it as "the one manual of eternal life, the one page that glows as all life grows dark, and the one book whose wealth rebukes us more the older we grow because we knew and loved it so late." Ibid., p. 24. Despite these powerful appeals, he also writes, "I do not believe in verbal inspiration. I am with the critics, in principle." Yet he adds, strikingly, "but the true minister ought to find the words and phrases of the Bible so full of spiritual good and felicity that he has some difficulty in not believing in verbal inspiration." Ibid., p. 24. He seems to be saying that while modern historical criticism makes it impossible for him to hold that the Bible is the plenary, infallible revelation of God, the preacher ought to preach as if it is anyway. This contradiction, I believe, would eventually take its toll on a preacher. For a balanced summary, evaluation, and critique of Forsyth's thought, see Samuel J. Mikolaski, "P. T. Forsyth," in *Creative Minds in Contemporary Theology,* ed. Philip E. Hughes, 2nd ed. (Grand Rapids, MI: Wm. B. Eerdmans, 1969), pp. 307–40.
4. *Planned Parenthood v. Casey,* 505 U.S. 833, 851 (1992).
5. Charles Mathewes and Joshua Yates, "The 'Drive to Reform' and Its Discontents," in Carlos D. Colorado and Justin D. Klassen, *Aspiring to Fullness in a Secular Age: Essays on Religion and Theology in the Work of Charles Taylor* (Notre Dame, IN: University of Notre Dame Press, 2014), pp. 156 and 159.

6. C. S. Lewis, *The Abolition of Man* (London: Fount Paperbacks, 1978), p. 46.

7. Just one example is Charles Taylor, whose work is the basis for much of the rest of this chapter. He puts the word "postmodern" in quotes, calls it "trendy," and sees it as an extreme and therefore temporary, untenable intensification of modern individualism. See Charles Taylor, *A Secular Age*, pp. 716–17. The three books by Taylor that lie behind the rest of this chapter include *Sources of the Self: The Making of the Modern Identity* (Cambridge, UK: Cambridge University Press, 1989); *A Secular Age;* and *The Malaise of Modernity.*

8. Mark Lilla, "Getting Religion," *New York Times Magazine,* September 18, 2005.

9. Taylor's arguments against "subtraction story" accounts of secularity permeate the entire book. Taylor introduces the concept of the "subtraction" story on p. 22 of *A Secular Age*. He sums it up as: "human beings having lost or sloughed off, or liberated themselves from certain earlier confining horizons, or illusions, or limitations in knowledge." The rise of science seemed to make God-explanations untenable (e.g., the theory of evolution) or unnecessary and obsolete (e.g., using medical science, rather than prayer, to cure illness). Once science merely subtracted the superstition of belief in God and the supernatural, then (it is believed) we saw what was there all along—the value and equality of human beings and human life, the power of the self to reason and order society, and so on. Terry Eagleton, from a Marxist perspective, concurs with Taylor in rejecting the idea that secularity just happened once people woke up to the scientific facts.

10. Mark Lilla, "The Hidden Lesson of Montaigne," in *New York Review of Books* 58, no. 5 (March 24, 2011), quoted in James K. A. Smith, *How (Not) to Be Secular*, p. 1.

11. Terry Eagleton, *Culture and the Death of God*, pp. 33–34.

12. See also Alasdair MacIntyre, *After Virtue: A Study in Moral Theory,* 3rd ed. (Notre Dame, IN: Notre Dame, 2007); Alasdair MacIntyre, *Whose Justice? Which Rationality?* (Notre Dame, IN: Notre Dame, 1989); and the more recent Thomas Pfau, *Minding the Modern: Human Agency, Intellectual Traditions, and Responsible Knowledge* (Notre Dame, IN: Notre

Dame, 2013). Terry Eagleton too rejects the idea that secularity has no history of construction, that it is simply "the facts." See Eagleton, *Culture and the Death of God,* chapter 1, "The Limits of Enlightenment," pp. 1–44.

13. On this term see Taylor, *Secular Age,* p. 427.

14. An example of this is the "Ten Non-Commandments" put together by two atheist authors who wanted to lay out the ideals on which secular people can build their lives. From Lex Bayer and John Figdor, *Atheist Mind, Humanist Heart* (New York: Rowman and Littlefield Publishers, 2014); listed in Daniel Burke, "Behold Atheists' New Ten Commandments," CNN .com, December 20, 2014, www.cnn.com/2014/12/19/living/atheist-10-commandments/index.html?hpt=hp_t4. More than half of them are, ironically, ethical principles that have grown out of the world's great religions, including Christianity: "Be mindful of the consequences of all your actions and recognize that you must take responsibility for them. . . . Treat others as you would want them to treat you, and can reasonably expect them to want to be treated. Think about their perspective . . . We have the responsibility to consider others, including future generations. . . . Leave the world a better place than you found it." See "Appendix: Illustrations of the Tao," in C. S. Lewis, *Abolition of Man,* pp. 49–59. Atheist philosopher John Gray has recently argued that these prescriptions only make sense if there is a God. "The source of these values is not science. In fact, as the most widely-read atheist thinker of all time argued, these quintessential liberal values have their origins in monotheism." John Gray, "What Scares the New Atheists," *Guardian,* March 3, 2015, www.theguardian.com/world/2015/mar/03/what -scares-the-new-atheists. The other "non-commandments" arise more directly out of late modernity's baseline cultural narratives and are treated later in this chapter, for example: "Every person has the right to control of their body," "God is not necessary to be a good person or to live a full and meaningful life," and "There is no one right way to live."

15. Alan Ehrenhalt, *The Lost City: The Forgotten Virtues of Community in America* (New York: Basic Books, 1995), p. 2, quoted in Taylor, *Secular Age,* p. 475.

16. Taylor, *A Secular Age,* p. 475.

17. Ibid., pp. 275–80.

18. Ibid., p. 278.

19. See the chapters "The Immanent Frame" and "Cross Pressures" in Taylor, *Secular Age,* pp. 539–617. For a summary of Nietzsche's critique, see Gray, "What Scares the New Atheists."

20. See Alvin Plantinga, "Deep Concord: Christian Theism and the Deep Roots of Science," in *Where the Conflict Really Lies* (New York: Oxford University Press, 2011), pp. 265–306; and C. John Sommerville, "Science Gets Strange," in *The Decline of the Secular University* (New York: Oxford University Press, 2006), pp. 75–84. See also Diogenes Allen, *Christian Belief in a Postmodern World* (Louisville, KY: John Knox, 1989).

21. C. S. Lewis, *Surprised by Joy: The Shape of My Early Life* (New York: Harcourt and Brace, 1955), pp. 207–8.

22. Taylor, *Secular Age,* pp. 582–98.

23. Robert N. Bellah, et al., *Habits of the Heart: Individualism and Commitment in American Life,* 2nd ed. (Oakland, CA: University of California Press, 2007).

24. These hierarchies were originally justified as reflecting the cosmic order. Taylor writes, "Modern freedom came about through the discrediting of such orders." Taylor, *Malaise of Modernity,* p. 3.

25. For example, see Krister Stendahl, "The Apostle Paul and the Introspective Conscience of the West," *Harvard Theological Review* 56, no. 3 (July 1963): 205.

26. "Let It Go," by Robert Lopez and Kristen Anderson-Lopez, was sung in the Disney movie *Frozen* and won the 2013 Oscar for Best Original Song. It is both interesting and ironic to compare the sung speech of the character Elsa in *Frozen* with that of Martin Luther before the Holy Roman Emperor. Both say, "Here I stand." But Luther meant he was free from fear and from other authorities because he was bound by the Word of God and its norms. Elsa speaks for the contemporary culture by saying she can be free only if there are no boundaries at all.

27. "A crucial feature [of secularity] is the sense that all these answers are fragile, or uncertain; that a moment may come, where we no longer feel that our chosen path is compelling,

or cannot justify it to ourselves or others." Taylor, *Secular Age,* p. 308.

28. Gail Sheehy, *Passages: Predictable Crises of Adult Life* (New York: Bantam Books, 1976), pp. 364 and 513, quoted in Taylor, *Malaise of Modernity,* p. 44.

29. Taylor, *Malaise of Modernity,* p. 44.

30. Ibid., p. 47.

31. See Alain de Botton, *Status Anxiety.* This is de Botton's point. An atheist philosopher, he argues that modern identity, with its emphasis on achievement through competition, creates far more anxiety than traditional identities.

32. Taylor, *Secular Age,* pp. 67–73. First, the doctrine of justification by faith alone changed the older sacred/profane distinction—the idea that ordinary life out in the world was profane and defiling and only work inside the church was sacred and higher and ennobling. The Protestant reformers believed that the two-tiered structure of the medieval church not only led to superstition and idolatry and spiritual elitism but also led to the denigration of ordinary human life—of working, farming, eating, and building a family. The medieval view was that these things were "lower" and distracted from "higher" spiritual pursuits. Taylor observes that this elitism and denigration of ordinary life and work was much the fruit of Greek mind-body dualism rather than a biblical understanding of sin and grace. The Protestant reformers freed people from the belief that deprivation of material pleasures was inherently helpful in achieving salvation. Luther and Calvin did away with the sacred/profane distinction or, as Taylor says, "the sacred is suddenly broadened: for the saved, God is sanctifying us everywhere, hence also in ordinary life, our work, in marriage, and so on." Ibid., p. 79. Second, justification by faith meant a new emphasis on individual action. It was now not enough to simply be part of the church you were born into or merely perform minimal duties. You must repent and believe, and that can be done only personally, as an individual actor. The Catholic view was that salvation came by being joined to the visible church. In that sense you were saved literally through being part of a community, through being baptized as an infant and incorporated into

the church, not directly through individual action. Salvation by faith alone meant that salvation came prior to membership in a visible church. That was profoundly "individuating." This also weakened the idea that you relate to God through your group, class, family, or community—through being a good member of your class. Taylor rightly adds that making the Bible the only authority—rather than the church—also undermined the older sociality. It led to the belief that individuals can go directly to the Bible and God without the church.

33. Taylor, *Secular Age,* p. 484.
34. Ibid.
35. Smith, *Lost in Transition: The Dark Side of Emerging Adulthood* (New York: Oxford University Press, 2011), chapter 5, pp. 195–225.
36. Taylor, *Secular Age,* p. 484.
37. David Friend and the editors of *Life, The Meaning of Life: Reflections in Words and Pictures on Why We Are Here* (New York: Little, Brown, 1991) p. 33.
38. Thomas Nagel, *What Does It All Mean? A Very Short Introduction to Philosophy* (New York: Oxford University Press, 1987), p. 95–96.
39. Ferry is cited in Taylor, *Secular Age,* p. 308.
40. See Timothy Keller and Kathy Keller, *The Meaning of Marriage: Facing the Complexities of Commitment with the Wisdom of God* (New York: Riverhead, 2013), pp.1–46. In these pages we explore in some detail why the cultural narratives of freedom and identity do not fit with the realities of relationships or fulfill our aspirations for marriage.
41. D. A. Carson, *The Gospel According to John,* Pillar New Testament Commentary (Grand Rapids, MI: Wm. B. Eerdmans, 1991), p. 350.
42. For more on how to preach this theme, see "Christianity Is a Straitjacket" in Keller, *Reason for God,* pp. 35–50.
43. Taylor, *A Secular Age,* p. 371.
44. Ibid., p. 581. "Once human beings took their norms, their goods, their standards of ultimate value from an authority outside of themselves: from God, or the gods, or the nature of Being or the cosmos. But then they came to see that these

higher authorities were their own fictions, and they realized that they had to establish their norms and values for themselves, on their own authority. . . . They dictate the ultimate values by which they live." Ibid., p. 580.

45. Ibid., p. 588.

46. Charles Taylor, "A Catholic Modernity?" in *Dilemmas and Connections: Selected Essays* (Cambridge, MA: Belknap Press, 2014), p. 182.

47. Ibid.

48. "Before the reality of human shortcomings, philanthropy . . . can gradually come to be invested with contempt, hatred, aggression. The action is broken off or worse, continues but is invested with new feelings, becoming progressively more coercive and inhumane. The history of despotic socialism is replete with this tragic turn . . . [as are] a host of 'helping' institutions from orphanages to . . . schools for aboriginals." Ibid., p. 183.

49. Ibid., p. 184.

50. Ibid., p. 185.

51. Greg Epstein, *Good Without God: What a Billion Nonreligious People Do Believe* (New York: William Morrow, 2010); and Lex Bayer and John Figdor, *Atheist Mind, Humanist Heart: Rewriting the Ten Commandments for the Twenty-First Century* (New York: Rowman & Littlefield, 2014).

52. Mari Ruti, *The Call of Character: Living a Life Worth Living* (New York: Columbia University Press, 2014), p. 36.

53. Taylor, *Malaise of Modernity,* p. 18.

54. Taylor, "Conditions of an Unforced Consensus on Human Rights," *Dilemmas and Connections,* p. 123.

55. Ibid.

56. See Timothy Keller, *Generous Justice: How God's Grace Makes Us Just* (New York: Riverhead, 2012). See especially chapter 7, "Doing Justice in the Public Square," for ideas on how to talk to secular friends who agree on the importance of social justice but who cannot root their convictions in any moral sources outside themselves.

57. See Richard W. Wills, *Martin Luther King, Jr., and the Image of God* (New York: Oxford University Press, 2011).

58. I give extensive treatment to this thesis in *Generous Justice*.

59. Alasdair MacIntyre, *After Virtue*, 3rd ed. (Notre Dame, IN: Notre Dame, 2007) can also be of help here. MacIntyre famously argues that science cannot possibly determine how we should live because we cannot discern whether behavior in a human being is good or bad unless we know our purpose—what we are here for. Science cannot discern such a thing, and therefore empirical reason is useless to help us know the best way for society to function or for justice to be done.

CHAPTER 6: PREACHING CHRIST TO THE HEART

1. Gordon Wenham, *Genesis 1–15*, vol. 1, Word Biblical Commentary (Waco, TX: Word Books, 1987), p. 144.

2. Donald Hagner, *Matthew 1–13*, vol. 33A, Word Biblical Commentary (Nashville, TN: Thomas Nelson, 1993), p. 158.

3. D. A. Carson, *The Expositor's Bible Commentary: Matthew, Chapters 1–12* (Grand Rapids, MI: Zondervan, 1995), p. 177.

4. Two recent books that make this case are by James K. A. Smith: *Desiring the Kingdom: Worship, Worldview, and Cultural Formation* (Grand Rapids, MI: Baker Academic, 2009); and *Imagining the Kingdom: How Worship Works* (Grand Rapids, MI: Baker Academic, 2013). Smith builds on Augustine's idea that what makes us what we are is the order of our loves, and therefore what changes us is changing not what we think but what we love. Smith rightly critiques an approach to ministry that is too rationalistic and focused on information transfer and the transmission of right doctrine and beliefs. His response is that we change not by changing what we think as much as by changing what we worship—what we love and fill our imaginations with. He gives much more attention, however, to the liturgy and the shape of worship services, and little to preaching. I believe preaching can carry much of the weight of the ministry task of reshaping the heart. True to Smith's critique, however, there is a relative dearth of evangelical books on preaching to the heart, in comparison with how to exegete and explain a biblical text. Some exceptions are Sinclair Ferguson, "Preaching to the Heart," in *Feed My*

Sheep: A Passionate Plea for Preaching (Grand Rapids, MI: Soli Deo Gloria, 2002), pp. 190–217; Samuel T. Logan, "The Phenomenology of Preaching," in *The Preacher and Preaching* (Phillipsburg, NJ: Presbyterian and Reformed, 1986), pp. 129–60; and Josh Moody and Robin Weekes, *Burning Hearts: Preaching to the Affections* (Ross-shire, Scotland: Christian Focus, 2014). I would add that "preaching to the heart" not only is quite biblical but also is an important way to adapt to our secular age, in which inherited religion will be on the decline. People will be coming to church not because they ought to, because it is an entailment of being part of a social body or community, but only if they choose with their hearts to do so.

5. Two great places to get a short, readable explanation of Edwards on the affections are "Editors' Introduction," in John E. Smith, Harry S. Stout, Kenneth P. Minkema, *A Jonathan Edwards Reader* (New Haven, CT: Yale, 1995); and Sam Logan's article on preaching and the affections, "The Phenomenology of Preaching" in *The Preacher and Preaching: Reviving the Art in the Twentieth Century,* Samuel T. Logan, ed. (Phillipsburg, NJ: Presbyterian and Reformed, 1986). The summary in this section follows closely *Edwards Reader,* pp. xix–xx.

6. No wonder Edwards, in one of his few theological reflections on preaching itself, says, "The main benefit obtained by preaching is by impression made upon the mind at the time, and not by an effect that arises afterwards by a remembrance of what was delivered. And though an after-remembrance of what was heard in a sermon is oftentimes very profitable; yet, for the most part, that remembrance is from an impression the words made on the heart at the time; and the memory profits, as it renews and increases that impression." Jonathan Edwards, "Some Thoughts Concerning the Present Revival of Religion in New England," in *The Great Awakening,* ed. C. C. Goen, vol. 1., Works of Jonathan Edwards (New Haven, CT: Yale, 1972), p. 397.

7. See Jonathan Edwards, "A Divine and Supernatural Light," in *Jonathan Edwards Reader,* pp. 111–14; and Jonathan Edwards, "The Mind," in *Jonathan Edwards Reader,* pp. 22–28.

8. Edwards, "Divine and Supernatural Light," p. 112.

9. Wilson H. Kimnach, "Jonathan Edwards's Pursuit of Reality," in *Jonathan Edwards and the American Experience,* ed. Nathan O. Hatch and Harry S. Stout (New York: Oxford University Press, 1988), p. 105. Edwards's use of "don't" rather than "doesn't" reflects the vernacular of the time.

10. Ibid.

11. For more on subtexts and other matters regarding "preaching affectionately," see chapter 7.

12. See Timothy Keller, *Prayer: Experiencing Awe and Intimacy with God* (New York: Dutton, 2014).

13. Wilson H. Kimnach, Kenneth P. Minkema, and Douglas A. Sweeney, "Editors' Introduction," in *The Sermons of Jonathan Edwards: A Reader* (New Haven, CT: Yale University Press, 1999), p. xxi.

14. Ibid., p. xviii.

15. Ibid., p. xix.

16. Kimnach, Minkema, and Sweeney, *The Sermons of Jonathan Edwards,* p. 56.

17. Thomas G. Long, *The Witness of Preaching,* 2nd ed. (Louisville, KY: John Knox, 2005), p. 295.

18. See Robert A. Harris, "A Handbook of Rhetorical Devices," VirtualSalt.com, January 19, 2013, www.virtualsalt.com/rhetoric.htm.

19. Important safety tip: If the person or persons you are visualizing are actually going to be in the audience that hears the sermon you are preparing, be sure not to use details that would make it appear that you are using the pulpit to publicly rebuke an individual. That is an unbiblical thing to do! (Matthew 18 and 5 tell us to go to a person privately if we have something against them.) You want your sermon to apply to large numbers of people, not just one. Use the thought of individuals to stimulate specific applications, but don't write them out in such a way as to cause the audience to play a guessing game about the parties you are referring to.

20. Here are the different kinds of people you may be speaking to. Does the text speak to any of them?

- Conscious unbeliever: Is aware he is not a Christian.

  - Immoral pagan: Is living a blatantly immoral/illegal lifestyle.
  - Intellectual pagan: Claims the faith is untenable or unreasonable.
  - Imitative pagan: Is fashionably skeptical, but not profound.
  - Genuine thinker: Has serious, well-conceived objections.
  - Religious non-Christian: Belongs to an organized religion, cult, or denomination with seriously mistaken doctrine.

- Nonchurched nominal Christian: Has belief in basic Christian doctrines, but with no or remote church connection.

- Churched nominal Christian: Participates in church but is not regenerated.

  - Semiactive moralist: Is respectably moral but his religion is without assurance and is all a matter of duty.
  - Active self-righteous: Is very committed and involved in the church, with assurance of salvation based on good works.

- Awakened: Is stirred and convicted over his sin but without gospel peace yet.

  - Curious: Is stirred up mainly in an intellectual way, full of questions and diligent in study.
  - Convicted with false peace: Without understanding the gospel, has been told that by walking an aisle, praying a prayer, or doing something, he is now right with God.
  - Comfortless: Is extremely aware of sins but not accepting or understanding of the gospel of grace.

- Apostate: Was once active in the church but has repudiated the faith without regrets.

- New Believer: Is recently converted.

  - Doubtful: Has many fears and hesitancies about his new faith.
  - Eager: Is beginning with joy and confidence and a zeal to learn and serve.
  - Overzealous: Has become somewhat proud and judgmental of others and is overconfident of his own abilities.

- Mature/growing: Passes through nearly all of the basic conditions named below but progresses through them because he responds quickly to pastoral treatment or knows how to treat himself.

- Afflicted: Lives under a burden or trouble that saps spiritual strength. (Generally we call a person afflicted who has not brought the trouble on himself.)

  - Physically afflicted: Is experiencing bodily decay.

    - the sick
    - the elderly
    - the disabled

  - Dying
  - Bereaved: Has lost a loved one or experienced some other major loss (e.g., a home through a fire)
  - Lonely
  - Persecuted/abused
  - Poor/economic troubles
  - Desertion: Is spiritually dry through the action of God, who removes a sense of his nearness despite the use of the means of grace.

- Tempted: Is struggling with a sin or sins that are remaining attractive and strong.

  - Overtaken: Is tempted largely in the realm of the thoughts and desires.
  - Taken over: Has had a sin become addictive behavior.

- Immature: Is a spiritual baby who should be growing but is not.

  - Undisciplined: Is lazy in using the means of grace and gifts for ministry.
  - Self-satisfied: Has had pride choke his growth, is complacent, and has perhaps become cynical and scornful of many other Christians.
  - Unbalanced: Has had either the intellectual, the emotional, or the volitional aspect of his faith become overemphasized.
  - Devotee of eccentric doctrine: Has become absorbed in a distorted teaching that hinders spiritual growth.

- Depressed: Is not only experiencing negative feelings but also shirking Christian duties and being disobedient. If a person is a new believer, or tempted or afflicted or immature, and does not get proper treatment, he will become spiritually depressed. Besides these conditions, the following problems can lead to depression:

  - Anxious: Is depressed through worry or fear handled improperly.
  - Weary: Has become listless and dry through overwork.
  - Angry: Is depressed through bitterness or uncontrolled anger handled improperly.
  - Introspective: Dwells on failures and feelings and lacks assurance.

- Guilty: Has a wounded conscience and has not reached repentance.

- Backslid: Has gone beyond depression to a withdrawal from fellowship with God and with the church.

  - Tender: Is still easily convicted of his sins and susceptible to calls for repentance.
  - Hardening: Has become cynical, scornful, and difficult to convict.

21. See the appendix for more on the gospel-logic moves "Here's what you must do," then "Here's why you can't do it," then "Here's the one who did it for you," and finally "Here's how faith in him enables you to do it too." Following this logic in a sermon means that often you bring in practical application in more than one place.

CHAPTER 7: PREACHING AND THE SPIRIT

1. D. M. Lloyd-Jones, *Preaching and Preachers,* 40th anniversary ed. (Grand Rapids, MI: Zondervan, 2011), p.68.
2. On Colossians see Peter T. O'Brien, *Colossians–Philemon,* vol. 44, *Word Biblical Commentary* (Waco, TX: Word Books, 1982); Douglas J. Moo, *The Letters to the Colossians and to Philemon,* Pillar New Testament Commentary (Grand Rapids, MI: Wm. B. Eerdmans, 2008); and Andrew T. Lincoln, "The Letter to the Colossians: Introduction, Commentary, and Reflections," in *The New Interpreter's Bible,* vol. 11 (Nashville, TN: Abingdon Press, 2000), pp. 553–669. For the parallel 1 Corinthians 1:20–2:5, see Anthony C. Thiselton, *The First Epistle to the Corinthians: A Commentary on the Greek Text,* The New International Greek Testament Commentary (Grand Rapids, MI: Wm. B. Eerdmans, 2000); Roy E. Ciampa and Brian S. Rosner, *The First Letter to the Corinthians,* Pillar New Testament Commentary (Grand Rapids, MI: Wm. B. Eerdmans, 2010); and Gordon D. Fee, *The First Epistle to the Corinthians,* The New International

Commentary on the New Testament (Grand Rapids, MI: Wm. B. Eerdmans, 1987).

3. Lincoln, "Letter to the Colossians," p. 616.
4. Moo, *Letters to the Colossians*, p. 161.
5. Thiselton, *First Epistle to the Corinthians*, p. 222.
6. Jonathan Edwards, "Sermon 2: Love More Excellent Than Extraordinary Gifts of the Spirit," in *Charity and Its Fruits*, Kyle Strobel, ed. (Wheaton, IL: Crossway, 2012), pp.62, 66–67.
7. Jonathan Edwards, "The Excellency of Jesus Christ," in *The Sermons of Jonathan Edwards: A Reader*, Kimnach, Minkema, Sweeney, eds., pp. 161–96.
8. Sir Thomas Malory, *Le Morte d'Arthur* (1485), Book XXI, chapter xiii.
9. C. S. Lewis, "The Necessity of Chivalry," in *Present Concerns* (London: Fount, 1986), p. 13.
10. See Derek Thomas's list of subtexts (though he doesn't call them that) in his essay "Expository Preaching" in *Feed My Sheep: A Passionate Plea for Preaching* (Grand Rapids, MI: Soli Deo Publications, 2002), pp. 80–83. They are described hilariously, and there is much overlap with what I am saying in this section.
11. Charles Kraft, *Communication Theory for Christian Witness* (Nashville, TN: Abingdon, 1983), p. 78.

Appendix: Writing an Expository Message

1. Good books on expository preaching include the following. I've put them in chronological order. William Perkins, *The Art of Prophesying*; Alan M. Stibbs, *Understanding God's Word* (Chicago: InterVarsity Press, 1950), *Obeying God's Word* (Chicago: InterVarsity Press, 1955), and *Expounding God's Word* (Chicago: InterVarsity Press, 1960) (these three short volumes together constitute a course on expository preaching); D. M. Lloyd-Jones, *Preaching and Preachers* (1971; 40th anniv. ed., Grand Rapids, MI: Zondervan, 2011); Haddon Robinson, *Biblical Preaching* (Grand Rapids, MI: Baker, 1980); John R. W. Stott, *Between Two Worlds: The Challenge of Preaching Today* (Grand Rapids, MI: Wm. B. Eerdmans, 1982); J. I. Packer, "Why Preach?" Samuel T. Logan, "The Phenomenology of Preaching," Edmund P.

Clowney, "Preaching Christ from All of Scripture," Sinclair Ferguson, "Exegesis," Glen C. Knecht, "Sermons Structure and Flow," and John F. Bettler, "Application," all in *The Preacher and Preaching: Reviving the Art in the Twentieth Century,* Samuel T. Logan, ed (Phillipsburg, NJ: P+R Publishing, 2011); Bryan Chapell, *Christ-Centered Preaching: Redeeming the Expository Sermon* (Grand Rapids, MI: Baker Academic, 1994); Peter Adam, *Speaking God's Words: A Practical Theology of Preaching;* William Philip and Dick Lucas, *The Unashamed Workman: Instructions on Biblical Preaching,* Preaching Workshops on Video Series 1 (London: Proclamation Trust, 2001); William Philip, ed., *The Practical Preacher: Practical Wisdom for the Pastor-Teacher* (Ross-shire, Scotland: Christian Focus, 2002); David Murray, *How Sermons Work* (Welwyn Garden City, UK: Evangelical Press, 2011); Mark Dever and Greg Gilbert, *Preach: Theology Meets Practice* (Nashville, TN: Broadman and Holman, 2012); Gary Millar and Phil Campbell, *Saving Eutychus: How to Preach God's Word and Keep People Awake* (Sydney, Australia: Matthias Media, 2013); Alec Motyer, *Preaching? Simple Teaching on Simply Preaching* (Fearn, Tain, Ross-shire, UK: Christian Focus, 2013); David Helm, *Expositional Preaching: How We Speak God's Word Today* (Wheaton, IL: Crossway, 2014).

2. These four steps are synthesized from Motyer, *Preaching?;* Helm, *Expositional Preaching;* Robinson, *Biblical Preaching;* Chapell, *Christ-Centered Preaching;* Millar and Campbell, *Saving Eutychus;* Stott, *Between Two Worlds;* Logan, *Preacher and Preaching;* Stibbs *Expounding God's Word;* Dever and Gilbert, *Preach;* and Thomas G. Long, *The Witness of Preaching,* 2nd ed. There are considerable individual differences among these books. Some propose writing a "thesis statement" for the sermon and others do not. Most have more numerous steps and all have more explicit instructions. However, these four basic instructions, and roughly in this order, are made by all of the writers in one form or another.

3. I am not here giving advice on the selection of texts for preaching (except for what is in this note). A "preaching text" or "preaching portion" is a section of Scripture selected to be read and preached upon. A preaching text is too short if it can't be

explained without constant reference to the verses nearby. If that happens, then those verses should have been read and considered as part of the preaching portion. A preaching text is too long if (a) there's simply too much to cover, and (b) there are multiple "big ideas" in the preaching portion. Here the selection of a central idea helps with the determination of how many verses to read and treat. If you are preaching about forgiveness, then select the verses that sustain the discussion of forgiveness and don't go beyond to where other major topics eclipse the subject of forgiveness. For a good overview on how to select a text, see David Murray, "Selection: What Is a Text" and "Variation: Varying the Sermons," in *How Sermons Work*, pp. 21–33 and 59–69. Murray counsels to look for preaching texts that have complete ideas and major truths (that run through the whole Bible) and that are brief (enough to cover in one preaching), clear (enough to not require the preacher to go all over the Bible to elucidate it), varied (so that you don't keep a congregation locked in one book, genre, or topic for months), and spiritually suitable (for the occasion and the people's needs and capacities) (pp. 31–32).

4. For this step in sermon preparation I especially recommend Sinclair Ferguson, "Exegesis," in Logan, *Preacher and Preaching*.

5. If you are adept, translate it yourself from Greek or Hebrew and then study the text you've produced. This is very desirable, because it gets you quickly to see the Greek or Hebrew terms that are often left out or have nuances that the English rendering can't convey. However, even if you can do this, you must also study the English translation from which you will be reading and preaching.

6. Some people do the running commentary on a computer screen by cutting and pasting the whole Bible text and then writing their own commentary in another color, such as red, beneath each verse. Others write the text out longhand on one half of a notebook page (writing longhand is proven to help you learn and retain in a way that typing does not) and putting their comments parallel on the other side of the page.

7. Perhaps the best online reference tool is www.BibleStudy Tools.com. The best tools for purchase are Logos Bible Software and BibleWorks.

8. The unparalleled resource here is Leland Ryken, et al., *Dictionary of Biblical Imagery* (Downers Grove, IL: InterVarsity Press, 1998). The user of this volume will find it remarkable how many of these images point to Christ.

9. The best resource for this is G. K. Beale and D. A. Carson, eds., *Commentary on the New Testament Use of the Old Testament* (Grand Rapids, MI: Baker Academic, 2007). This book is unique. Each New Testament book has an article by a scholar who not only treats exhaustively every quotation by the New Testament author of the Old Testament but also points out all the allusions to the Old Testament, even if not direct citations or quotes. The book can be used in both directions. If you are preaching on a New Testament text, you will get help seeing the Old Testament background, but if you are preaching on an Old Testament text, you can locate your text in the Scripture index in the back of the volume and find the New Testament author who refers to it. This is an excellent way to discern truly intercanonical themes that run through the length of the whole Bible and inevitably find their fulfillment and climax in Christ and his salvation.

10. Motyer, *Preaching?*, pp. 61–62.

11. Robinson, *Biblical Preaching*, pp. 31–50.

12. Millar and Campbell, *Saving Eutychus*, p. 64.

13. Ferguson, "Exegesis," in S. Logan, *Preacher and Preaching*, p. 197.

14. Stibbs, *Expounding God's Word*. He writes: "The would-be expository preacher . . . must . . . seek to discern what is—for the occasion of ministry which he has in mind—the main thrust or obvious message from God in the passage at which he is working. Some passages are very fertile. They are capable of a number of selective treatments according to the points in them chosen for emphasis and according to the corresponding particular aim and application which the preacher may have in view. What is important is that the preacher should decide on one definite subject or emphasis for each particular occasion of ministry, and should then use from the material and ideas which he has acquired by his working at the text only those which are obviously related to his subject.

In a sermon, as distinct from a running commentary, reference to points irrelevant to the chosen subject must be ruthlessly omitted [in order to achieve] brevity and coherence, but also a significant development and drive [toward] his intended aim and his proposed closing application," pp. 40–41.

15. David Jackman, "From Text to Sermon," in *The Practical Preacher: Practical Wisdom for the Pastor-Teacher,* William Philip, ed., p. 66.

16. There are others who give the same advice as Jackman—namely, that every sermon should be informed by both what the text says and the needs and capacities of the listeners. Nineteenth-century theologian Robert Dabney says, "Rhetorical unity requires these two things. The speaker must, first, have one main subject of discourse, to which he adheres with supreme reference throughout. But this is not enough. He must, second, propose to himself one definite impression on the hearer's soul, to the making of which everything in the sermon is bent. . . . Oration . . . concludes by saying to the hearer, 'Do this,' that its terminus is in a volition, and that its aim is to pass through the understanding into the motives of the soul. Unity of discourse requires, then, not only singleness of a dominant subject, but also singleness of practical impression. To secure the former, see to it that the whole discussion may admit of reduction to a single proposition. To secure the latter, let the preacher hold before him, through the whole preparation of the sermon, the one practical effect intended to be produced upon the hearer's will." Robert Dabney, "Cardinal Requisites of the Sermon," in *Sacred Rhetoric; or, a Course of Lectures on Preaching*, p. 109. The facsimile reprint is entitled *Evangelical Eloquence: A Course of Lectures on Preaching.* Much more recently, and at the other end of the theological spectrum, Thomas G. Long says we should look for both the *focus* and the *function* of a text. These are roughly similar to Dabney's "subject" and "practical impression." Long, *Witness of Preaching,* pp. 99–116.

17. I have adapted and combined Stibbs's material like this:

At a wedding: Stibbs would especially focus on verse 2: Jesus was invited to the marriage. The main point or topic: Jesus should be invited into your married life. The outline: (1) The difference Jesus' presence made—he did not "kill joy." (2) What to do with problems in the home or marriage. Do what Mary did: Bring them to Jesus. Do what he directs in his Word. (3) Yet he pointed to a greater joy than wine. His own marriage and spousal love for you. (4) You need to trust him the way Mary did. (5) As this wedding turned out to be a sign to the entire world about the glory of Jesus, so your marriage can be a witness to Jesus, pointing others to him.

At a prayer meeting: Stibbs would focus on verse 3: Mary going to Jesus with a need ("They have no more wine"). The main point or topic: The important features of prayer. The outline: (1) Go to Jesus with your needs; but also go to Jesus with your friends' needs. (2) Acknowledge his power, expecting him to do what you cannot; but also acknowledge his wisdom, as Mary did (in verse 5), trusting him even when his timing and actions are hard to understand. (3) Jesus had a prayer turned down. "Let this cup pass from me." Jesus can answer your prayers, despite our sins, because he died on the cross. The wine points to his blood. (4) Now be ready to act in obedience to his Word.

At an address to Christian workers: Stibbs would focus on verse 5: "Do whatever he tells you." The main point or topic: To show what it takes to be useful in Christ's service. The outline: (1) Mary and the servants were used by Jesus to give miraculous help to the bride and groom. (2) The requisites: Concern for the need of others. Going to Christ in believing prayer. Readiness to do what he asks even if it doesn't fit in with our wisdom. Readiness to make the venture of faith, counting on God. (3) The results: The Lord's power is manifested. We become coworkers with him. We often get credit for what Jesus has done (the "master of the banquet" praises the bridegroom). (4) And this is a picture of Jesus' salvation. We get credit for what he has done. His righteousness is imputed to us. This is our ultimate strength.

Preaching to a local congregation (with non-Christians present): Stibbs would focus on verse 11. We should see in this text the remarkable person of Jesus. The incident is the "opening" of his ministry and therefore a brief but complete look at who he is. The main point or topic: Truths to which the wine bears witness. The outline: (1) The old wine. Ultimately anything we rely on for joy in life will run out. No matter how hard we try to build a great life, something comes in and ruins it. Our efforts are never enough. (2) The new wine tells us of Christ's person. He has power over the created order because he is the Creator come to earth. He can make all things new. (3) The new wine tells us of Christ's work: (a) He comes to bring blessing to us, not judgment. Contrast God's judgment on Egypt (Exodus 7:17–21). There God turned water into blood so they couldn't drink. Now Jesus turns water to wine so they can drink. (b) He provides this joyful thing—this wine—through his death. (In verse 4, as always, "hour" refers to the hour of his death in the gospel of John.) The water pots stood for purification, and so his blood cleanses us and forgives our sin. (c) Before Jesus can give us the cup of blessing, he will have to take the cup of divine wrath. (4) Jesus' strange statement shows that, sitting in the midst of this party, this joy, he is anticipating his coming sorrow. But if we believe in Jesus, then we can sit in the midst of a world of sorrow, anticipating our coming joy. We will eventually sit with him at the great wedding feast of the Lamb.

18. Motyer, *Preaching?*, pp. 64–65.
19. Ibid.
20. The New International Version translates *hilasmos*— "propitiation"—as "atoning sacrifice." This masks the meaning of this crucial biblical word, which denotes the turning away of God's wrath.
21. The earliest Christian preaching was more influenced by the rabbinical practice of giving commentary on that week's

reading from the Torah than by the Greek and Roman tradition of rhetoric, in which one proposition was announced, divided, defended, and promoted.

But in the medieval era preachers began to divide and arrange their material into an outline that reflected classical rhetorical *dispositio*—the more formal arrangement of material. Contemporary people might be surprised to learn it was the medieval monastics—particularly the Dominicans and Franciscans of the twelfth century—who introduced something now taken for granted today. "The preaching orders," Hughes Old writes, "began to discover the importance of the sermon outline." Hughes Oliphant Old, *The Reading and Preaching of the Scriptures in the Worship of the Christian Church: Vol. 3, The Medieval Church*, p. xvii.

The reasons for this are complex. One reason was many of the monastics were preaching out in public spaces, not just in worship services, and they sought ways to rivet the attention of the listeners. Also, medieval theology had developed into a highly systematic form consisting of loci or topics unfolded through many subpoints, divisions, and counterpoints. The sermon outline—in which one's subject is announced, divided into its parts, and then unfolded—was thus a natural outgrowth of the Scholastic method of doing theology, which was itself indebted to classical learning and rhetoric. In any case, as Old says, "nothing could be more medieval than a three-point sermon outline." Ibid.

22. Greek and Roman classical oratory sought to discover the most compelling way of making oral presentations. One crucial aspect of effective oratory (often called one of the "five canons") was *dispositio* or "arrangement." It referred to the structure and organization of an address. The consensus (put forth by Cicero and Quintilian) was that the speech should have the following divisions:

Exordium. The introduction. The goal is to rivet attention and arouse interest in your subject so the listener is motivated to give you a hearing.

Narratio. The presentation of the heart of your subject. This may be a single proposition or it may be a somewhat longer presentation of a set of facts (essentially a "case") followed by a summary *propositio.*

Partitio. The division of your subject into its constituent issues to be addressed in the rest of the speech.

Confirmatio. The part of the address in which you confirm your proposition by proving and supporting each issue or constituent part of the case.

Refutatio. The part of the address in which you weaken the opposing view(s) by answering each counterargument or objection to your position.

Peroratio. In conclusion, in which you summarize your point, restating it clearly and forcefully in order to arouse sympathy and call for action.

Philipp Melanchthon, a colleague of Martin Luther, was a leading scholar of the humanities. He, along with others such as Agricola and Erasmus, worked to recover and adapt the classical rhetorical methods of Aristotle, Cicero, Seneca, and Quintilian for the church of the day. Melanchthon's efforts came together especially in his *Institutiones Rhetoricae* ("Elements of Rhetoric,"1521), which laid out a new synthesis of ancient oratory for the use of Christian preachers. (This important work was translated into English as *The Art or Crafte of Rhetoryke* in 1532. A facsimile of this edition was published by EEBO Editions/ProQuest on July 13, 2010.)

He called the preacher to begin with a single doctrinal theme or topic shown to be drawn from the biblical text. Once the preacher shows through exegesis how the proposition was biblically grounded, he should then proceed systematically to, second, define its key terms, distinguishing it from alternatives and then, third, to identify its different aspects or causes. Melanchthon advised using Aristotle's four causes—the material "what," the formal or "how," the efficient or "who," and the final or "why." Finally, the preacher should apply the doctrine's meaning to the listeners. Scott Manetsch, *Calvin's Company of Pastors* (New York: Oxford University Press, 2013), p. 157. Melanchthon's approach then looked something like this:

Exegetical introduction. *This section uses* exegesis to draw out a single doctrinal proposition from the text, e.g., from Romans 3:10–20, "Our good works cannot save us—we need a Savior."

Who? *The agents.* What is the efficient cause? In other words, whom is the text referring to who lives like this? Everyone: "There is no one righteous, not even one" (verse 10). This includes all people without exception. Jew and Gentile. Religious and nonreligious.

What? *Description.* What is the (material) reason that our good works cannot save us? In other words, of what do our deeds consist? What are they like? They are mixed with evil deeds. Even religious people have deceitful, malicious tongues, etc., and seek not peace but rather strife (verses 13–17).

How? *Underlying elements.* What is the (formal) reason that our good works cannot save us? In other words, what about the good deeds themselves make them inadequate? It is our motives—"no one . . . seeks God" (verse 11) and "there is no fear of God before their eyes" (verse 18). Even when formally doing good things, we are not seeking God in them.

Why? What is the final or ultimate reason that our good works cannot save us? It is the holiness of God. "No one will be declared righteous in God's sight" (verse 20).

Under each heading a case is to be made, usually through verses taken from elsewhere in the Bible. But other illustrations and arguments can be used.

Application. What does this mean for us? It means we need a Savior. It means we should give up trying to put together a saving righteousness of our own. It means we should repent of both our overt sins and of trying to save ourselves through inadequate "good deeds."

Melanchthon's approach was a modification of the conventions of classical *dispositio* or subject arrangement. It had an *exordium* or introduction, which drew the theme from the Scripture. It then did forms of *narratio, partitio,* and *confirmatio,* breaking the topic down into points by which it was clarified, examined in depth, and defended. Finally came the "peroration," in which the theme was driven home with exhortation and appeal. This approach was immensely popular among the new generation of Protestant preachers, especially with the English Puritans. They began with one very short text—often just one verse—which was studied briefly in order to draw out the "doctrine"—a proposition. The proposition was then broken into a number of inferences and aspects—both points and subpoints—and each one proved from the Bible. Finally each of the inferences was given a number of practical applications. Hughes Old claims that this form was "not so much expository as scholastic or thematic." Old, *Reading and Preaching of the Scriptures: Vol. 4, The Age of Reformation,* p. 284. It followed medieval Scholasticism and classical rhetoric, though the arguments used were almost strictly citations from other parts of the Bible. This was not the patristic model that the reformers used, in which multiple doctrinal and practical points were drawn out of a passage of Scripture and treated in series. Instead the Puritans modified and maintained the medieval scholastic sermon form, drawing out one point and theme, breaking it into many parts, and analyzing each exhaustively. Ibid., p. 327. So, as Old concludes, this usually meant that, despite presenting themselves as expository preachers, Puritans who spent multiple sermons on a single verse were actually doing topical-thematic preaching, catechetical preaching—whatever their intentions. And historically and ultimately it led to "the gradual development of thematic preaching" rather than ex-position. Ibid.

23. For this step in sermon preparation I particularly recommend Glen C. Knecht, "Sermons Structure and Flow," in Logan, *Preacher and Preaching.*

24. Motyer, *Preaching?*, pp. 79–80.

25. Over the past forty years there has been a major reaction against the traditional sermon outline in mainline Protestant-ism. Thomas G. Long, professor of preaching at Emory University, does a good job of charting out both the rise and current fall of the "narrative preaching" movement within the white, mainline Protestant churches of the past generation. This movement rebelled mightily against the traditional sermon outline, which was based on a central proposition that was explained and defended. Long says that one of the reasons that mainline preachers and theologians pushed back on sermon outlines was their skepticism about the very idea of propositional revelation, what they scornfully called the "box of ideas" view of the Bible. They rejected the traditional understanding of a biblical passage as "a repository of theological ideas, or truths" from which the preacher could "pluck out the main theological nugget." Thomas G. Long, *The Witness of Preaching,* 2nd ed. (Louisville, KY: John Knox, 2005), p. 101. They opposed the rationalistic, neat, highly structured sermon outline.

While this critique was largely based on a nonevangelical understanding of biblical revelation, some of the arguments hit home. One was that the highly structured sermon outline did not fit narrative portions of the Bible. "No one who reads a rousing novel or sees a powerful play or views a provocative movie would be tempted to squeeze those rich experiences into only one main idea." Ibid., p. 101. To put it another way, does anyone think that a single "nutshell" proposition is any substitute for a movie? For example, instead of actually watching the movie *All Quiet on the Western Front,* why not just put it in a nutshell: "War is terrible and accomplishes nothing." Would that proposition convey its meaning as well as the 138-minute movie? Particularly the very last scene, where the main character reaches out to gently touch a butterfly but exposes himself to a sniper and is shot and killed? Of course not. The narrative conveys far more meaning than can be boiled down into a simple verbal statement.

Long points to Fred Craddock's landmark 1971 book *As One Without Authority* as a key volume in the mainline pushback against the traditional sermon outline. The volume called for "a general revolt against propositional preaching." Ibid., p. 103. Instead, Craddock urged that sermons not be marked by "deduction"—in which a thesis is announced and then explained and supported. Instead he wanted "induction"—the gradual unfolding of a story narrative or of a metaphor. He wanted image-rich, nondiscursive preaching, anything but "a thesis in three points." Ibid. Long says that this became a watershed, and Craddock's proposal swept the mainline churches. It was influenced by the "new hermeneutic" of the time that saw interpretation as an existential event or encounter. One of the most influential of Craddock's followers was Eugene Lowry, who insisted that the Bible was largely "nonpropositional" and that trying to break a passage into principles or truths "distorts or even reforms the experiential meaning of the gospel." Ibid., p. 104. While Craddock himself did expect that the preacher should eventually get to "*the point* the [biblical] author sought to make" [Fred Craddock, *As One Without Authority* (Nashville, TN: Abingdon, 1971), p. 100], many others rejected even that level of "rationality." Many mainline homileticians insisted that the preacher should be essentially narrating and allowing listeners to draw their own conclusions as they encountered the text in their unique way.

Long admits that, as exciting and liberating as this sounds when first presented, much of this was "confusing to preachers and students," and he concludes that it is wrong to insist, as Lowry does, that the impact of a text is not related to its actual ideas and propositional content. Long, *Witness of Preaching*, p. 107. Long quotes Lowry as saying, "Perhaps you went to church and were overwhelmed in the singing of 'Amazing Grace'—and not at all because of the particularities of the propositional content of the third stanza." Lowry is right that a hymn's impact on the heart can't be reduced to merely the content in the lyrics. But while the power of a hymn is more than its content, it can't be less. Long argues that it goes much too far to say that the experience of singing the hymn has nothing to do with the propositional content. He slyly asks if we think that singing "Mary Had a Little Lamb" in church would have the same effect on the singers. "What a text *says* clearly governs what it *does*," concludes Long. Ibid., p. 107.

What did mainline preachers offer in place of the sermon outline? Long discusses several mainline church homileticians of the past generation and traces out how each of them tried to replace the traditional sermon outline. Fred Craddock and Eugene Lowry proposed that the sermon should be preached as an answer to a question or problem. Craddock usually made the problem the actual meaning of the text, while Lowry preferred some personal "felt need" problem in the listeners' lives. In either case the question is answered or the problem solved in a series of "moves" that are perceptible but not announced as headings, topics, or points. Another prominent mainline preacher, David Buttrick, provided detailed analysis of what each of these "moves" should look like. Buttrick believed no move should take more than four minutes (arguing that people will not have the attention span for more) and that a sermon should be twenty minutes long, with no more than five or six "moves." He also gave directions for each move, urging that it be clearly demarcated with single opening and summary sentences. Long, *Witness of Preaching*, pp. 131–34. Long describes how the "narrative preaching" movement is now in disarray or eclipse. See Thomas G. Long, "A Likely Story: The Perils and Power of Narrative in Preaching," in *Preaching from Memory to Hope* (Louisville, KY: John Knox Press, 2009), pp. 1–26.

What can we learn from this episode in the church? The mainline writers do not really escape the need for an outline. "Moves" are still points in an outline that must be thought out and that give structure to the address. What the mainline thinkers agree on, however (and it comes out in the term "moves"), is that the sermon shouldn't be a recitation of facts nor simply one side in a debate. It should engage not just listeners' minds but also their hearts. It should take the listeners somewhere. This idea—despite the many missteps and mistakes of the narrative preaching movement—is a keeper.

26. Eugene L. Lowry, *The Homiletical Plot, Expanded Edition: The Sermon as Narrative Art Form* (Louisville, KY: John Knox Press, 2000).

27. This has been culled from a number of sources, but look especially at N. T. Wright, *The New Testament and the People of God* (Minneapolis, MN: Fortress Press, 1992), pp. 47–81.

28. This is similar to Bryan Chapell's "Fallen Condition Focus" in *Christ-Centered Preaching*, pp. 40–44. Chapell is far more concerned with finding what the text itself says is the sin-induced problem and then preaching on the solution in Christ. Lowry is more willing to choose the problem first and then find a text that helps us discuss it.

29. Lowry, *Homiletical Plot*, pp. 44–47.

30. Ibid., pp. 65–68 and 100–103. I am referring to J. R. R. Tolkien's famous essay, "On Fairy-Stories," in *Tree and Leaf* (New York: HarperCollins, 2001), pp. 1–82. The consolation . . . the joy of the happy ending . . . the sudden joyous 'turn' . . . this joy which . . . stories can produce supremely well, is not essentially 'escapist' nor 'fugitive.' . . . It is a sudden and miraculous grace: never to be counted on to recur. It does not deny the existence of *dyscatastrophe*, of sorrow and failure. Indeed, the possibility of these is necessary to the joy of deliverance. Rather, it denies (in the face of much evidence, if you will) universal final defeat, and thus is *evangelium*, giving a fleeting glimpse of Joy, Joy beyond the walls of the world, poignant as grief. It is the mark of a good story, of the higher or more complete kind, that however wild its events, however fantastic or terrible the adventures, it can give . . . when the 'turn' comes, a catch of the breath, a beat and lifting of the heart, near to (or indeed accompanied by) tears, as keen as that given by any form of literary art, and having a peculiar quality. In . . . the 'turn' . . . we get a piercing glimpse of joy, and heart's desire, that for a moment passes outside the frame, rends indeed the very web of story, and lets a gleam come through." Tolkien, "On Fairy-Stories," pp. 68–69. Later Tolkien argues that

REDEEMER

The Redeemer imprint is dedicated to books that address pressing spiritual and social issues of the day in a way that speaks to both the core Christian audience and to seekers and skeptics alike. The mission for the Redeemer imprint is to bring the power of the Christian gospel to every part of life. The name comes from Redeemer Presbyterian Church in New York City, which Tim Keller started in 1989 with his wife, Kathy, and their three sons. Redeemer has begun a movement of contextualized urban ministry, thoughtful preaching, and church planting across America and throughout major world cities.

the ultimate story—the gospel—is the essence of all other stories with the joy-giving happy ending. "This 'joy' . . . merits more consideration. The peculiar quality of the 'joy' in a successful Fantasy can . . . be explained as a sudden glimpse of an underlying . . . Reality. . . . The Gospels contain . . . a story of a larger kind which embraces all the essence of fairy-stories. They contain . . . the greatest and most complete conceivable eucatastrophe. But *this* story has entered history and the primary world. . . . The Birth of Christ is the eucatastrophe of Man's history. The Resurrection is the eucatastrophe of the story of the Incarnation. This story ends in joy. . . . There is no tale ever told that men would rather find was true, and none which so many skeptical men have accepted as true on its own merits. For the Art of *it* has the supremely convincing tone of Primary Art, that is, of Creation. To reject it leads either to sadness or to wrath. . . . [T]*his* story is supreme; and it is true. Art has been verified. God is Lord, of angels, and of men—and of elves. Legend and History have met and fused." Tolkien, "On Fairy-Stories," pp. 71–73.

31. Lowry, in the 2000 expanded edition of his book, says there should be four phases of the sermon's narrative plot: Conflict, Complication (getting down to the heart reasons for the intractable nature of the problem), Good News, and Unfolding. In his view there should be a fourth movement in the sermon, after revealing Christ as the "hero" or solution to the problem. The fourth phase proposes how the listeners should live in the future on the basis of this particular exhibition of the nature and power of the gospel. In other words, this is the "application" phase.

32. English Standard Version translation.